"At the end of a long faithfulness in the end of one careful study after another, K finest arguments for the full support of women in all levels of ministry in the local church . . . Running through the whole book is a graciousness of disagreement propped by a firmness of conviction. This book will be on my desk every time I think about church leadership."

—SCOT MCKNIGHT, Northern Seminary, Lisle, Illinois

"As a 'soft-complementarian,' I heartily endorse Kevin Giles' masterful work, *What the Bible Actually Teaches on Women*. As an academic who has written and taught on gender for almost twenty-five years, I found this to be one of the best and most enriching books I've read on the subject . . . This book evidences a lifetime of extensive biblical study and real world pastoral ministry. I am very grateful this book is now available to the body of Christ."

—STEVE TRACY, Professor of Theology and Ethics, Phoenix Seminary

"*What the Bible Actually Teaches on Women*, is nothing short of an egalitarian thesis hammered on the church's door . . . Giles exposes the theological abuses of Christian patriarchy while critiquing its heinous impact on human life globally . . . Few books are more comprehensive in tracing the river of destruction fueled by 'male headship' presented as God's ideal. This book is essential reading for ministry students and Christians concerned for the church's influence in our world today."

—MIMI HADDAD, president, CBE International

"Through careful analysis of the Bible and tradition, Kevin Giles compellingly and convincingly . . . demonstrates that those who argue for the continued subordination of women to men are distorting the biblical witness with dire consequences, not only for Trinitarian doctrine but for women's rights and their very humanity . . . I highly recommend this book as the definitive study guide for understanding the theological basis for the equality of women and men."

—PAUL D. MOLNAR, St. John's University, Queens, New York

"In . . . *What the Bible Actually Teaches on Women*, Kevin Giles upholds the clear teaching of Scripture that God has created, redeemed, and Spirit-gifted equally both men and women. This truth has breathed the fresh air of empowerment into women in the majority world culture where, instead of mutuality in relationships, women are condemned to subordination, depriving them of God-given leadership roles in church, family, and society."

—RICHARD HOWELL, General Secretary, Asia Evangelical Alliance

"This book has a strong advocacy tone because it consistently argues that the Bible teaches the equality of the sexes in contrast to those who maintain the subordination of women as the creation ideal . . . This book marks the high point of a life of careful scholarship and is a rich resource for academics, pastors, and lay members of the global church. The reader cannot but gain a new confidence in the relevance of the biblical story for our world."

 —CHARLES RINGMA, Asian Theological Seminary, Manila

"Kevin Giles has given himself to this issue for decades now, and it shows. He is intimately familiar with all the standard arguments, and, as a result, his deconstruction of the 'complementarian' case is simply devastating. He pursues weak arguments relentlessly in this book, showing all the contradictions, prevarications, and biblical errors of those who profess 'male headship' . . . After this book, they will have little or no ability to pretend that their persistence has any basis in the Bible."

 —STEPHEN R. HOLMES, University of St Andrews

"Kevin Giles' . . . speaks against other positions to awaken! He takes up a wider theology, the widest, in this volume. Not unlike Athanasius, he isn't content with proof-texting for in-house evangelical consumption, but sets the question of how we women and our brothers, husbands, and male friends in ministry, are to minister together."

 —RUTH NEWMARCH, Associate Minister at St Thomas Anglican Church, Burwood, Victoria, Australia

"Kevin's latest book, *What the Bible Actually Teaches on Women,* is the culmination of his forty years of work on this question. It is a comprehensive study that convincingly outlines what in fact the Bible says on women, and covers issues I have not seen covered elsewhere. I think his arguments are compelling. I hope the book will be widely read."

 —PHILIP FREIER, Archbishop of the Diocese of Melbourne

"There are few writers more qualified than Kevin Giles to provide us with perspective on the always controversial issue of women and their roles in Christian families and the church . . . He helpfully critiques and deconstructs the recent and perennial arguments for a so-called complementarian point of view on women and their roles. As it turns out, and as Giles shows, both Jesus and Paul took more radical views than their patriarchal peers on women and their roles, and we are still trying to catch up with the implications."

 —BEN WITHERINGTON, III, Asbury Theological Seminary

"Kevin Giles has used thorough biblical scholarship, especially of the New Testament, and knowledge of historical parallels, to frame one of the most effective critiques of the 'complementarian' view. This book is must reading for everyone concerned with understanding the Christian view of women at a more profound level."

—MILLARD ERICKSON, Western Seminary, Portland, Oregon

"Kevin Giles offers a robust and systematic examination of what the Bible says about women, in particular, their fitness to serve in all levels of Christian ministry. It is a book that will annoy some, and excite others, but no one should ignore it."

—MICHAEL F. BIRD, Ridley College, Melbourne, Australia

"I am enormously grateful to Kevin Giles for distilling the wisdom of a lifetime in this outstanding book. Set in the context of contemporary theological debate and social history, he undertakes a masterful analysis of Christian teaching on gender and human relationships. His profound and penetrating exegesis of the biblical text unearths truths often missed, misunderstood, or glossed over in so much literature on the subject . . . Whatever your current thinking, you will find Kevin Giles offers stimulating and refreshing new insights, and draws you again to a warming vision of Christ's redemptive love which permeates his work."

—ELAINE STORKEY, Newnham College, Cambridge University

What the Bible Actually Teaches on Women

What the Bible Actually Teaches on Women

KEVIN GILES

CASCADE *Books* · Eugene, Oregon

WHAT THE BIBLE ACTUALLY TEACHES ON WOMEN

Cascade Books
An Imprint of Wipf and Stock Publishers
199 W. 8th Ave., Suite 3
Eugene, OR 97401

www.wipfandstock.com

PAPERBACK ISBN: 978-1-5326-3368-3
HARDCOVER ISBN: 978-1-5326-3370-6
EBOOK ISBN: 978-1-5326-3369-0

Cataloguing-in-Publication data:

Names: Giles, Kevin |
Title: What the Bible actually teaches on women / by Kevin Giles
Description: Eugene, OR : Cascade Books, 2018 | Includes bibliographical references and index.
Identifiers: ISBN 978-1-5326-3368-3 (paperback) | ISBN 978-1-5326-3370-6 (hardcover) | ISBN 978-1-5326-3369-0 (ebook)
Subjects: LCSH: Women in Christianity. | Women in the Bible. | Women's rights—Religious aspects—Christianity. | Women—Biblical teaching.
Classification: LCC BS680.W7 G39 2018 (print) | LCC BS680.W7 (ebook)

Manufactured in the U.S.A.

Contents

Preface

THIS IS ALMOST CERTAINLY my last book. I am in very good health and more informed than I have ever been, but in my late seventies it is time to give up writing on my great passion, the health and well-being of the church in our age. I hope you enjoy reading this book, and find it both helpful and informative. I have certainly enjoyed writing it. In it I give my current thinking on *what the Bible actually teaches on women* after more than forty years of studying and debating this question. I was among the evangelical pioneers who in the early 1970s sought a way to interpret the Bible so that it was seen to affirm the substantial, not just the spiritual, equality of the sexes. In 1977, when the intramural evangelical debate on what the Bible taught on the man-woman relationship was just beginning, I published my first book, *Women and Their Ministry: A Case for Equal Ministries in the Church Today*. Since that time I have published extensively on this issue. Without boasting, I can say I have been one of the most prolific contributors to this debate. I understand this debate comprehensively. I have read, and in most cases own, all the major books by complementarians, and I have published reviews of several of the most important books by them.[1]

What has brought me most notoriety has been my ongoing opposition to the so-called "Trinity argument." When evangelicals in opposition to the substantial equality of the two differentiated sexes found their "biblical" arguments for the permanent subordination of women left many of the best informed evangelical theologians unconvinced, they began appealing to the doctrine of the Trinity. They argued that just as the Father rules over the Son, so men rule over women. "Headship" belongs

---

1. Giles, "Biblical Teaching"; Giles, "Book Review: Grudem and Piper"; Giles, "Book Review: Wayne Grudem's *Evangelical Feminism*"; Giles, "Critique of the Novel," parts 1 and 2; Giles, "Dear Professor *Köstenberger*."

to God the Father and to men, and they quoted 1 Cor 11:3 as proof that these two ideas are intrinsically connected.[2] In 2016 those making this argument found they had to capitulate. I had convinced them that this argument introduced the Arian heresy in new wording.[3]

These many years of involvement in this debate are not my only qualifications to write this book. I was a pastor for forty years—and still am, but not leading a church anymore. I have witnessed the very positive contribution of women in a *leadership team* of a church and how negative it can be for women to be excluded from leadership. I hope you noticed the word "team." The mono-ministry model where one person is in charge of each church is not found in the New Testament, and is not prescribed by anything said in the New Testament. The idea that one person, specifically a man, should be in charge of each church, who does most of the preaching and presides at Holy Communion, was invented by men for men in the early centuries of Christian history. It is thus not at all surprising that this model of ministry does not work well for most men in the twenty first century and very poorly for most women, especially married women with children. A far better model is found in the New Testament, a model where in every church there is collective leadership; what we would call today a "team" of leaders.[4] In every team men and women should minister side by side as we see them doing in the New Testament. The church is made up of men and women, God gives the Spirit to men and women in equal measure and the church needs the contribution of men and women, complementing each other. A man or woman can be the leader of such a team, because for Paul all ministry/leadership in the church is predicated on Spirit-gifting, not gender. What my long involvement in church ministry has shown me is that such teams are transformational for congregational life, and they allow women to flourish in church leadership. I thus write not as an academic theologian with no or very limited experience of congregational life, a theoretician. I write as a practitioner of over forty years who has seen that the inclusion of women in church leadership is good news for the church.

Before moving on I need to warn my readers that the ordination of women hardly gets a mention in this book. This book is almost entirely a

2. Before June 2016 this was almost universally held complementarian teaching. For a classic affirmation of this argument see Burk, "Why the Trinity Must Inform."

3. I tell this story in my 2017 book, *Rise and Fall of the Complementarian.*

4. I argue this in my book, *Patterns of Ministry.* Köstenberger and Köstenberger, *God's Design,* 194, agree as long as all the leaders are men.

critique of biblical arguments used in support of the permanent subordination of women, the reason why complementarians reject the ordination
of women as church leaders. My primary concern is for the 50 percent
of the human race who complementarians argue God has subordinated
to men, not the far less than 1 percent of Christian women who are or
would like to be ordained, as important as they are.

I am also qualified to write on the husband-wife relationship because I have been happily married for fifty years. I know how a good
marriage works. My wife, Lynley, and I have had to work at how to make
our marriage good for us both when each of us is strong-minded and
relatively able, while having four children and significant jobs. Lynley is
a marriage counsellor and educator who at one time led a large team
involved in this work. Since her "retirement," she still has people ringing
her every week, wanting to see her, most forty or more years younger
than she is. For Lynley and me, the idea of "the casting vote" made by
me to settle disputes makes no sense at all. We have often not agreed
at first on important matters, and yet by praying about the issue, giving each other time to think through what we disagree on, and a bit of
compromise usually by both of us, we have come to a common mind, and
then each of us has owned fully the decision. In her counselling work,
mostly with Christian couples, Lynley has found that assertions of male
"headship" are a big problem in many modern Christian marriages. She
never tackles this matter by rational argument or by debating on what the
Bible says. She has discovered this never works. She simply explores with
couples how they could make their marriage work better by sharing decision making, and genuinely listening to one another. When men discover
everything can be better when they treat their wife as an adult, they are
invariably open to change. If they do change, and become like virtually all
happily married couples today, including the majority of complementarian ones,[5] they discover that a fully equal marriage works wonderfully
and makes for marital happiness. They may leave the counselling room
with the man still believing in his mind that he is the head of their home,
but in practice he has opted for a relationship where the responsibilities,
decision making, and the rewards of the marriage are shared equally.

This brings me to another reason why I am qualified to write and
why I write. In my long pastoral ministry I learned something I would not
have believed while at seminary. Some Christian men who attend church

5. So Russell Moore, "After Patriarchy, What?" Moore is a dogmatic
complementarian.

most weeks, sometimes active as church office bearers, some clergy, can be abusive husbands.[6] It seems needy men who are inclined to be controlling hear headship teaching to be giving them the right to insist that they are obeyed. Every one of the abusive husbands I have met said to me, "My wife should do as I tell her. This is what the Bible teaches."[7] The experts on this matter tell us about 1 in 4 women in their lifetime experience some form of partner abuse. The more I heard women tell me of their abuse the more I questioned if in fact the rule of the man over the woman is the God-given ideal and what Jesus endorsed. In practice, it seems male headship all too often has malevolent consequences for women.

Raising this painful-to-face fact of abuse in Christian marriages leads me to mention what we have seen in the developing world. After Lynley and I "retired," we have always travelled together. Once free of full time pastoring and counselling we have gone overseas once or twice a year, in most cases for me to take up lecturing engagements. Lynley then often gets invited to run a seminar for couples on topics such as "making good marriages better" or "how to face the stresses of marriage when in full-time ministry." In these travels, especially in Southeast Asia, India, the Middle East, Turkey, and Africa, we have seen first-hand the awful consequences of teaching the subordination of women. We have met women who have been sold into prostitution, married as children and damaged for life in the birth of their first child, beaten regularly by their husband, expected to do all the heavy work while their husband watches them. And in some countries they know that if they leave their husband their family will almost certainly kill them and go unpunished. This is why the subordination of women has become for us far more than an interesting debate about what the Bible teaches on the man-woman relationship, or about the ordination of women. It is about the wellbeing of half of the human race. It is a cry for justice for all women.

I have yet another qualification: I think God has given to me the gift of discernment (1 Cor 12:10)—the ability to judge what is of God and what is not. For this reason, I can tell the difference between an appeal to the Bible that reflects what the Bible says and an appeal to the Bible that reflects the agenda and beliefs of the one who makes this appeal; an argument that captures the mind of Christ and an argument that does not, and in everyday terms, the ability to tell the difference between a

6. In chapter 8, I come back to wife abuse in Christian marriages and deal with it more fully.

7. On this see Lim, "She Left an Abusive Marriage."

good argument and a bad argument. In no debate is discernment more needed. When power is involved men think up clever arguments that sound plausible but upon scrutiny are without substance and without validity. In what follows, I will be critically evaluating the arguments made by complementarians for male headship and female subordination and arguing that they are all special pleading, like the appeals to the Bible made by evangelical and Reformed theologians in support of slavery and apartheid.

Finally, I add that I have been a scholarly student of the Bible for nearly sixty years and hold an earned doctorate in New Testament studies.

I think I am well-qualified to write this book.

WHY I WRITE

From the day, some forty years ago, that I clearly saw the permanent subordination of women is not taught in the Bible I have felt compelled to oppose this idea. I have believed that God has called me to speak up in opposition to this teaching, no matter what the cost. I have accepted this calling because:

1. It upsets me deeply to see the Bible being used, as it has often been historically,[8] to uphold social ordering that is man-made and can be changed by men. This is always an appeal to the Bible by those in power to justify their power over others. I believe the Bible, and the Gospel in particular, is a liberating message. It sets people free; it lifts up the lowly. Complementarian teaching does not do this.

2. It is unpardonable to dogmatically assert that what I say the Bible says is what God says, when other believing theologians holding firmly to the authority of Scripture are of another opinion. The undeniable truth is that the complementarian interpretation of the Bible is at best only one possible interpretation of the Bible. And if it is only one possible interpretation, it is not a sufficient basis to subordinate half of the human race.

3. The complementarian case is one big put down of women by powerful men. The world is not flat and women, as we have learned in the last forty years, are not a subordinate class. They make very good leaders and when given equal opportunity in education on average

---

8. The rule of kings and aristocrats, slavery, apartheid, etc.

do better than men. Teaching that God has set women under men demeans women and can have awful consequences for them. In the Third World, it has awful outcomes for women, as I will document, and in the modern Western world it marginalizes women in the life of the church, demeans them, diminishes their opportunity for happiness in their marriages, and makes them vulnerable to intimate partner abuse.

4. It is necessary to oppose falsehoods. Most of what complementarians say about egalitarian evangelicals is simply not true. The charges they make have no factual basis, and they offer none. Evangelical egalitarians do not deny the authority of Scripture, they affirm it. Evangelical egalitarians do not deny male-female differentiation, they affirm it. Evangelical egalitarians do not come to Scripture with secular feminist presuppositions that rule their interpretative work;[9] they seek first of all to give the historical meaning of Scripture. They are not "evangelical feminists," in a pejorative sense; they are fellow evangelicals who call themselves "evangelical egalitarians."

I think these are very good reasons for me to write this book.

THANKS

In the writing of a book the author is usually indebted to a number of people. I thank first, of all my friends, Denise Cooper-Clarke, Warren Thomas, and Neville Carr who read the manuscript in draft looking for awkward or convoluted sentences and missing punctuation. They found lots of both. Richard Hess, professor of Old Testament at Denver Seminary, who read my chapter on Gen 1–3 and the addendum on man and woman in the fallen world of the Old Testament and made a number of helpful suggestions. Aimee Byrd, Paul Collyer, and Mimi Haddad who read and commented on chapter 2, discussing the cultural changes of the post 1960s period. Professor Ben Witherington, who has written the

---

9. The first two accusations are so common they need no documentation. On the hermeneutical charge that is frequently made in complementarian literature and by the Köstenbergers, see their *God's Design*, 321–53. This argument is too silly for words. Are the Köstenbergers arguing that egalitarian scholars of the calibre of Gordon Fee, Howard Marshall, Lynn Cohick, Craig Keener, Linda Belleville, Ben Witherington, Philip Payne, Richard Bauckham, and Cynthia Westfall, just to name a few, twist the Scriptures to get them to say what they want them to say?

definitive study on Jesus and women,[10] read the chapter on this topic and passed it. My friend, the master of linguistic and textual study, Philip Payne, read the two chapters on Paul and four related addenda, and critically commented on them. He did not agree with me on all matters. I would also like to thank the staff of Cascade Books who worked on the manuscript helpfully and graciously. Then I must thanks those who agreed to read the manuscript and make a commendation. This can be a time-consuming task. Finally, I thank my wife, Lynley, for not complaining when I went off to my study to be alone for hours on end. We did still have time for a lunch out each week and a few coffees.

FINALLY A WORD TO READERS WHO WANT TO USE THIS BOOK AS A DISCUSSION STARTER

If you would like to use this book in a study circle or home group as a discussion starter and wish to leave after each study feeling stimulated, enriched, and looking forward to the next discussion, you will need to be gentle and kind to one another, allowing others to have opinions different to your own. Few matters can arouse so much heat and hurt as discussing the status and ministry of women. Some have been taught that the Bible does subordinate women to men, and they cannot get out of their mind what their teachers have told them several much-quoted texts mean. Others may think that to question what they have been told the Bible teaches is to question the Bible itself (to deny biblical authority). For others the relationship between the sexes is a deeply personal issue. They hear comments on equality as a denial that God has made us men and women, two differentiated sexes. For them, to deny male "headship" is to deny male-female distinctions. In one group I was leading, discussing what the Bible says on marriage, a man suddenly went red in the face and blurted out in a high voice, "What would happen in my marriage if I treated my wife as an equal?" He had a good question, but to help him see other possibilities, grace and tact were needed. In such situations it is important not to go on the attack.

In the following studies you are considering what the Bible *actually* says. Always think about the historical and cultural context in which the passage is set. This context is very different to what we know in the twenty-first century.

10. Witherington, *Women in the Ministry.*

A practical suggestion: Study groups run so much better if times are set and kept. If the commencement time is 8 p.m., expect people to be on time and start, say, by 10 minutes past, after everyone has had time to say hello to others. If a cuppa is served first, then start sharp at 20 minutes past. Also set and keep a time to close the discussion at the end. Many groups find setting a given time for each question also helps—say a maximum of ten minutes on any question.

I include no questions at the end of this preface. The questions at the end of the next chapter take up issues raised in this preface and in that chapter.

1

Complementarian Theology

IN THIS BOOK I am writing in opposition to "complementarian theology" as it has been developed and refined over the last fifty years. Complementarian theology is a human construct generated to provide a way to read the Bible so that it consistently speaks of the creation-given subordination of women and its counterpart, "the headship" of men, in a way acceptable to the modern ear. For those who embrace this theology this reading of the Bible seems compelling. I now outline how the Bible is interpreted by those who have put on this pair of spectacles.

In God's good creation before the fall, the woman was subordinated to the man; the woman's punishment for her sin, namely that the man would rule over her (Gen 3:16) introduced nothing new, just the possibility that in a fallen world this rule might be harsh. Deborah, the judge and prophet, was not an authoritative leader like the male judges and prophets; men and women could be prophets and prophesy, but prophecy is not an authoritative ministry like teaching. Jesus had female disciples, he always affirmed women and spoke respectfully to them but he said or did nothing that called into question the principle of male headship. Indeed, in choosing twelve *male* apostles he affirmed this principle. Paul on his part explicitly spoke of the man as head over the woman in 1 Cor 11:3 and later in this chapter said the covering of the woman's head symbolized her subjection to male authority (v. 10). Her subordination is also indicated in that Paul says she was made "from" man (v. 8) and "for" man (v. 9). In

1

Eph 5:22–24, Paul exhorts wives to be subordinate/submissive to their husbands because the husband is the head of the wife. In 1 Cor 14:34 and 1 Tim 2:12 the apostle tells women to be silent in church; the Timothy text specifically prohibits women from teaching in church and exercising the authority rightly exercised by male pastors. This prohibition is unambiguous and predicated on weighty theology, "the order of creation." Adam was created first and this indicates that he was put in charge in the Garden of Eden (1 Tim 2:13). Eve breached Adam's headship by acting independently of him in speaking with the Serpent and eating of the forbidden tree (1 Tim 2:14). In doing so she committed the sin of "role reversal." The apostolic parallel exhortations to wives and slaves to be subordinate or obedient are to be contrasted, not compared. The exhortations to wives are grounded in the order of creation and are thus trans-temporal and transcultural; the ones to slaves are not and are thus time-bound. Junia was not an apostle like any of the men called apostles, and the women Paul commends for their ministry were all subject to male leadership. Yes, in Gal 3:28 Paul speaks of the equality of the sexes in salvation but this does not negate male-female role differentiation. This biblical case for the subordination of women is ultimately grounded in the life of God in eternity as 1 Cor 11:3 indicates. Just as the Father is "head over" the Son, so is the man "head over" the woman. The primary premise is that in creation God gave to men and women differing "roles." These "roles" define what it means to be a man or a woman. Evangelical egalitarians should not be listened to; preferably ignored. They have embraced secular feminist ideas by denying male-female differentiation and they reject the plain teaching of Scripture on the male-female relationship, thereby denying the authority of Scripture.

There are innumerable books that spell out the complementarian position that I have just outlined, all saying much the same thing, some better written than others. Not wishing to cover and footnote all these books I decided to make one book, *God's Design for Man and Woman: A Biblical-Theological Survey* by Andreas and Margaret Köstenberger, my primary account of the complementarian position and the one I will usually quote. I selected their book because they give the most informed and best-argued presentation of the complementarian case as it stood in 2014 when they wrote. Andreas Köstenberger is a professional New Testament scholar, a first class linguist, and a much published author. He is the most competent and able of the complementarian theologians. Margaret, his gifted wife, who co-authors the book, is a specialist on contemporary feminism.[1] At the front of their book, eighteen respected evangelical leaders enthusiastically commend it, agreeing that it is the best account of the complementarian position to be published so far. Russell Moore, in his commendation, speaks of "the brilliant and respected Andreas and Margaret Köstenberger." I have set myself as an old retired pastor a challenging task in debating with the "brilliant" and well-informed Köstenbergers. Andreas knows my work well. I have taken him to task in print before,[2] and we have corresponded many times, but he never mentions me or my writings in *God's Design*. He ignores my work and our previous debates.

In an addendum to follow I outline where I agree with the Köstenbergers and where I have concerns about their work.

THE ALTERNATIVE POSITIONS ARE ALTERNATIVE THEOLOGIES

To understand the Köstenbergers' and my books it must be recognized that we are both writing *theology*.[3] Here I note they subtitle their book, *A Biblical-Theological Survey*. Our alternative positions can be briefly and succinctly stated, but each is grounded on the exegesis of a limited number of texts integrated into a holistic framework. We do not differ simply on our interpretation of a few texts. Theology is not the same as exegesis or biblical theology. Exegesis has as its goal to give the historical meaning of texts in their literary context, and biblical theology has as its goal to give the historical meaning of what is said in the Bible or parts of the Bible in a holistic way. The Köstenbergers and I agree perfectly on this.[4] Theology, in contrast, seeks to address the contemporary world of

1. See her book, *Jesus and the Feminists*. For a devastating review of it by the New Testament scholar, Aida B. Spencer, see her "Book Review," 26–29. She calls *Jesus and the Feminists* "a very simple book" (26). What she means is that the book gives a simple answer to every complex question in regard to what the Bible says on the man-woman relationship.

2. Giles, "Critique of the Novel," part 1 and 2; and Giles, "Dear Professor Köstenberger."

3. In my book, *Eternal Generation of the Son*, 38–62, I have a chapter on "Doing evangelical theology" and I update and summarize this in my more recent book, *Rise and Fall*, 67–80.

4. Köstenberger and Köstenberger, *God's Design*, 18–19, 320, 331.

the theologian. The theologians' charter is to tell the church of their age what should be believed.

I think at this point I need to highlight how close the Köstenbergers and I are on what we are doing and the challenges of doing this. We both predicate our work on the exegesis of the texts that speak on the man-woman relationship; we both seek to find coherence in the diverse comments in Scripture on this matter, and we both draw inferences as to how what is said in Scripture applies to the church today. In other words, we are both writing theology. Like me, they admit that what is said on women in Scripture is "complex";[5] like me, they recognize their task is "to connect the dots in a way that is both coherent and consistent";[6] and like me they believe "not everything [said] in the Bible has equal weight."[7]

From this point on we go in diametrically opposed ways. For them, the coherent theme of what is said in Scripture on the man-women relationship is revealed in Gen 2. God has given leadership to men. The Old Testament, Jesus, Paul, and the other apostles all affirm this principle. This is what Christians should believe today.[8] On this basis complementarians teach that *God is pleased when women accept their creation-prescribed subordinate "role" in the home, the church, and the world.*

In stark contrast, for me, the coherent theme of what is said in Scripture is revealed in Gen 1 and 2, which teach the same truth in different ways. Man and woman before the fall have the same status, dignity, and leadership abilities, although one is man and one woman. The rule of the man over the woman is entirely a consequence of the fall. From Gen 4 onwards, the whole biblical story is set in this fallen world where men seek to rule over women but God keeps raising up women leaders to remind his people this is not the creation ideal. Jesus emphatically affirms the creation-given substantial equality of the two sexes. On this basis, I and all egalitarian evangelicals believe that *God is pleased when we recognize and affirm that men and women are of the same status, dignity, and leadership potential and are therefore accorded equality in the home, the church, and the world.*

5. Köstenberger and Köstenberger, *God's Design*, 257.

6. Köstenberger and Köstenberger, *God's Design*, 262.

7. Köstenberger and Köstenberger, *God's Design*, 332.

8. Köstenberger and Köstenberger, *God's Design*, 18–19, 262–63, 337-38.

OUR CHALLENGE

The challenge this book puts before the reader is to decide which of these two competing and opposing *theologies* of the sexes reflects the mind of God; which one most accurately reflects what Scripture is teaching? Which is right and which is wrong? There is no middle ground between believing that men and women are substantially and essentially equal in dignity, status, and leadership potential and that women are permanently subordinated to men. There are criteria for making such judgments about theological positions. I outline them.

1. *Good theology accurately captures what the Scriptures say on the important texts that speak to the issue in question.* In what follows you will need to judge who seems to most accurately reflect what Scripture is actually saying in the disputed texts: Gen 1–3; 1 Cor 11:3–16; 14:34–35; Gal 3:28; and 1 Tim 2:11–14. Who gets Jesus right? Who gets Paul's understanding of ministry/leadership in the church right? And who best explains the significance of Deborah, the ruler of Israel, and Junia, the woman apostle?

2. *Good theology explains how what is said in various texts can be read to speak with one voice on the question in discussion.* Who, in the Köstenbergers words, connects "the dots in a way that is both coherent and consistent"?[9]

3. *Good theology draws inferences that follow the trajectories Scripture itself implies.* Theologians must make inferences, deductions. They have to answer questions that arise after the canon is closed; questions in some cases the Scriptures do not anticipate. The Köstenbergers make innumerable inferences, following other complementarians. For example, they argue that because men are generally the leaders in biblical times this *implies* God prescribes male leadership. Surely it *implies* a fallen world where men have at least until recent times ruled over women? Another example: the Köstenbergers *infer* that because Jesus chose twelve male apostles he prescribed male leadership. This inference does not resonate with what Jesus said and did. He affirmed the substantial equality of the sexes. Egalitarian theology, in contrast, consistently follows the trajectory set by what Gen 1:27–28 explicitly teaches and what Jesus affirms and implies, namely that gender equality is the God-given ideal.

9. Köstenberger and Köstenberger, *God's Design*, 262.

4. *Good theology clarifies issues. What is being articulated is not in doubt.* Complementarian theology fails badly on this. It majors on euphemistic turns of phrase[10] and it uses words to obfuscate what is being said. Two examples of this are seen in the pervasive use of the word "role" to speak of fixed power relations and the self-designation "complementarian." We all should believe the sexes are complementary. Why not name the position the "hierarchical" view of the sexes?

5. *Good theology is truthful.* What is said is factual. The Köstenbergers and all complementarians argue that evangelical egalitarians reject the authority of Scripture, embrace cultural relativity, and deny male-female differentiation, arguing for "undifferentiated equality."[11] All of this is just not true.[12] They also tend to ignore counter evidence or alternative evidence, or misrepresent it. I will give numerous examples of this as we proceed.

6. *Good theology has good outcomes.* In the case of any theology of the sexes the test is whether it encourages men to treat women as they themselves would like to be treated (Matt 7:12). Is it good news for women? Complementarian theology fails this test. It fails because we men would not like to be told God has made us the subordinate sex, and because teaching the subordination of women often has dire consequences for them, especially in the developing world. It is this practical test that judged mistaken the impressive "biblical theologies" devised by evangelical and Reformed theologians in support of slavery in the nineteenth century and of apartheid in the twentieth century.[13]

---

10. A classic example of this is seen in Köstenberger and Köstenberger, *God's Design*, 23, point number 3. Other good examples are seen in the Köstenberger's "exegesis" of 1 Tim 2:14 (p. 211) and 1 Tim 2:15 (pp. 212–16). What they say on these two texts has virtually no relationship with what is said by Paul.

11. Köstenberger and Köstenberger, *God's Design*, 24, 39, 162, 196, 349, etc.

12. This affirmation, to be accurate, needs some qualification. To say human beings are made man or woman is like saying God has made human beings with two eyes, two arms, and two legs. It is possible to be born with one of any of these, or to lose one in life's journey. We live in a fallen world where variation is to be expected. When it comes to physical and psychological sex differences in human beings, sexual and psycho-sexual differentiation can be blurred or confused, as we see in people with intersex and transgender issues.

13. I tell this story in some detail in chapter 7.

7. *Good theology usually reflects what is called "the tradition,"* meaning what has been theologically concluded in the past. Theological traditions can be strong or weak or anything in-between. The weightiest theological traditions are found in the creeds and the confessions of the church, which codify what Christians collectively have agreed is the teaching of Scripture. In regard to what the Bible teaches on the man-woman relationship, no creed or confession says anything on this. All we have is a tradition that exactly reflects the cultural norms of past times. Theologians before the 1960s uniformly spoke of men as "superior" and women as "inferior," and they were often explicitly misogynistic. They taught that women are more susceptible to sin and deception.[14] Both complementarian and evangelical egalitarian theologians today reject such ideas, agreeing that they do not capture the teaching of Scripture. Breaking with this tradition is not a problem, especially for evangelical theologians who agree that Scripture must always stand over all other authorities. In this debate, what needs to be acknowledged is that the past cannot offer guidance for the present. Since the 1960s, theologians have been seeking to answer an *entirely new question*: what should Christians believe about women in a culture that has emphatically endorsed the full equality of women for the first time in human history? On this entirely new question we must turn to the Bible and listen afresh to what it is actually saying about men and women.

8. *Good theology makes sense of the world in which we live.* Again complementarian theology fails this criterion. The reality today is that the best of marriages are profoundly equal and women are leading in every sphere of life and doing it well. Most people, most Christians, and most evangelicals in the Western world are pleased to see women liberated and flourishing. The idea that women are a subordinate class makes no sense in the modern Western world. What is more, most Christians and most evangelicals believe that affirming the substantial or essential equality of the sexes captures the mind of Christ. It is a commendable idea to be fully embraced. The world is a better place when the equality of the sexes is emphasized. In one of their better moments the Köstenbergers recognize this fact. They say,

14. I document all this in my book, *The Trinity and Subordinationism*, 145–55; and I will return to the historical understanding of women several times in what follows.

> There is no question that feminism—a movement concerned
> with the advancement of women's rights and with the achieve-
> ment of women's complete parity with men in society, the home
> and the church—has had many positive results since its incep-
> tion almost two centuries ago. Women's status and experience
> in the Western world, in particular, have been altered for the
> better in many ways. . . . In this way, justice has been served,
> and many women have been lifted from second-class status to
> genuine equality with men.[15]

A contemporary theology that opposes the substantial equality of
the sexes is not good theology. It is bound to be rejected. Most Christians,
including all Roman Catholics[16] and all evangelical egalitarians, now oppose theologies that subordinate women to men, believing that they are
mistaken and damage the church.

MAKING A CRITICAL RESPONSE

Because arguing that women are the subordinate sex makes absolutely no
sense in today's world we must question the validity of complementarian
theology. The world is not flat; it is round. Women are not the subordinate sex; they make excellent leaders. Seeking to refute complementarian theology is not an easy task. It is a well-thought-out and well-honed
theological construct. What is more, most of the men who hold to this
theology and propagate it want it to be true. Sometimes it seems that for
many of them no other doctrine is more important. We men would like
to believe God has put us in charge. This theology convinces many evangelicals because it seems to be grounded firmly on what Scripture says.
When the case is put as I outlined it at the beginning of this chapter—by
appeal to all strands of the biblical revelation and in particular to texts
that speak of the man as the head of the woman, commanding women to
be silent and forbidding them to teach or exercise authority in church—
most Christians have no answer and many feel compelled to accept the
complementarian position, even if most do not consistently apply it.

What must be done to refute complementarian theology is to return
to Scripture and critically examine each one of the many building blocks
that create this seemingly impressive theological construct. When this

---

15. Köstenberger and Köstenberger, *God's Design*, 294–95.

16. I will come back to Roman Catholic teaching on the sexes several times in what
follows. See Pope John-Paul II binding encyclical, *Mulieris Dignitatum*.

is done we find every single one of the building blocks, the texts quoted, cannot bear the weight asked of them. This is the approach I will take in this book. What I will show is that not one of the texts or ideas to which appeal is made can stand scrutiny. Woman are not subordinated to the man in God's good creation before the fall; the rule of the man over the woman is a consequence of the fall (Gen 3:16), it is a reflection of sin; Deborah is a powerful national leader raised up by God; to prophesy means to speak the word of the Lord in the power of the Spirit—and often it involves teaching; Jesus was opposed to the idea that women in creation are subordinated to men; in choosing twelve men to be apostles, Jesus did not make male leadership an abiding principle; Paul endorses as a general rule the leadership of women and their teaching ministry; Junia was almost certainly a woman apostle; in Eph 5:21–33 Paul subverts patriarchy not endorses it; 1 Cor 11:3–16 certainly differentiates the sexes, but does not subordinate women to men—they can both lead the church in prayer and prophecy; 1 Cor 14:34–35 does not forbid women to teach/preach in church, does not ground the subordination of women in the creation order, it seems to forbid only women asking disruptive questions and what is more, the text is very likely not from the pen of Paul; 1 Tim 2:11–12 forbids a woman from teaching a man (in a house church setting) in a dominating way; there is no appeal to a supposed hierarchical ordering of the sexes in creation, or for that matter in any other passage in the Bible; the creeds and confessions of the church rule that the Bible does not eternally hierarchically order the divine persons, and the constant appeal to creation-given differing gender "roles" for men and women cannot be justified or pardoned. It has no biblical basis and deliberately obfuscates what is being argued.

These assertions will be backed up by detailed argument and appeal to the best of scholarship in later chapters. Some of this scholarly support for what I have just said comes from many very highly respected, erudite evangelical scholars. At least seven presidents of the Evangelical Theological Society support most or all of these assertions, including the current president, the scholarly Professor Craig Keener.[17] It certainly does not help the complementarian cause for their leaders to summarily dismiss this scholarship, ignore counter scholarly opinion, refuse open and honest debate with informed evangelical egalitarians, and to say all our critics do not accept the authority of Scripture. This last assertion is

---

17. Later I will give a long list of evangelical scholars who reject complementarian "exegesis" and list the mentioned presidents of the ETS.

just not true. For their complementarian theology to succeed, each or even most of its building blocks must be able to stand examination and criticism. They cannot.

Before we begin to carefully examine each part of the complementarian theological construct, I next speak of two very relevant matters for this book, one in each of the following chapters. First I tell of how in 2017 and 2018 complementarian theology came under tremendous pressure and criticism, something completely unexpected. This makes this book very timely. Second, I tell the story of how and why the traditional way of understanding the relationship of the sexes collapsed and was rejected by most people, most Christians, and a very significant percentage of evangelicals in the post-1960s period.

ADDENDUM: ANDREAS J. KÖSTENBERGER AND MARGARET E. KÖSTENBERGER, *GOD'S DESIGN FOR MAN AND WOMAN: A BIBLICAL-THEOLOGICAL SURVEY*

This is a very important book. It is written to a large extent by Andreas Köstenberger,[18] a first-class New Testament scholar, assisted by his able wife who wrote her doctorate on Jesus and modern feminism.[19] It comes after forty years of intense debate on the man-woman relationship and sets out accurately and fully the complementarian position as it stands at this time. On the first two pages, eighteen well-known complementarians, including Al Mohler, Wayne Grudem, Mary Cassian, Russell D. Moore, Owen Strachan, James Packer, and D. A. Carson give the book glowing commendations.

Because of the theological weight of this book, I decided to make it my debating counterpart. I will quote and discuss what the Köstenbergers say on specific issues in every chapter following, but at this point I'll outline what we agree on and where I think the Köstenbergers' arguments are untenable.

18. I make this conclusion on the following observations. Many, if not most of the exegetical conclusions reached, Andreas has argued elsewhere. In all the more theological and biblical sections of the book, Andreas's style is evident and most importantly, only a fully informed, academically equipped biblical scholar of Andreas's stature could write most of this material. In Margaret's book, *Jesus and the Feminists,* her discussion of the Gospels is at a more popular level.

19. Published as Köstenberger, *Jesus and the Feminists.*

I sent this addendum to the Köstenbergers for their critical appraisal and comment and I offered to send the whole book for them to read before I sent it to the publisher. I want at all costs to avoid misquoting them or misrepresenting their views. They made no reply.

On many matters, the Köstenbergers and I are on the same track. We are both pro-family people, happily married with families, involved in Christian ministry, believing God has created the human race male and female. On male-female differentiation we are both emphatic. God has given the two sexes different bodies and different chromosomes and the results of this are far-reaching.

The Köstenbergers and I are also of one mind on the authority of Scripture—the Bible should be our ultimate authority in matters of faith and conduct, not culture or human experience. We agree that the secular values of our world are corrosive of the evangelical faith. All three of us deny that we are "fundamentalist" of the pre-1960 kind.[20] They illustrate this fact when they say, "Not everything in the Bible has equal weight."[21] (Jesus taught this; Matt 19:1–9; 23:23; etc.). Importantly, we are also agreed that exegesis and biblical theology have as their goal to give the historical meaning of what the Bible says. When exegetes attempt to apply the historical meaning of a text to the present, they become preachers and theologians.

What convinced me that their book was the best complementarian book to interact with was that the Köstenbergers and I were in 100 percent agreement on how the Bible should be studied in any quest to determine what it actually says about the man-woman relationship. We agree that we should begin where the Bible begins, with Gen 1–3. In the New Testament we should begin with Jesus' teaching and then move to Acts and the apostolic writings.[22] Most other complementarian books adopt more of a "proof text" methodology. We also agree on the nature and focus of exegesis and biblical theology. Both are historical, descriptive disciplines.[23] In the critical and scholarly study of Scripture we are seeking to hear first of all what the biblical writers were saying in their own cultural and historical context. We also agree that application is not an easy task with gender passages, because the lot of women in the ancient

20. Köstenberger and Köstenberger, God's Design, 345.
21. Köstenberger and Köstenberger, God's Design, 332.
22. Köstenberger and Köstenberger, God's Design, 17–18, 80–81.
23. Köstenberger and Köstenberger, God's Design, 19, 321, 325–28.

world was so profoundly different to what it is today.[24] Application, in any case, is not the responsibility of the exegete. I say again, this is the responsibility primarily of the theologian.

We also agree completely, especially in the case of the emotive issue of the male-female relationship, on the great danger of falling into circular reasoning in coming to the Bible. They explain what this involves. "This is what I've *always* believed, so that is what I want the Bible to *say*, and lo and behold, that is what the Bible is actually *saying*."[25] The question before us is which one of us is most guilty of this error?

NOW TO MY CONCERNS

Honest Debating

I believe the first rule for honestly debating someone is to articulate accurately their views. The Köstenbergers do not do this. Evangelical egalitarians are not liberals who cannot accept what the Bible says because they set culture over Scripture. We also believe the Scriptures have ultimate and final authority in matters of faith and practice. True, we egalitarians accept that the change in culture on women has led us to see things in Scripture others in past times did not see but so too do the Köstenbergers.[26] We agree that culture *per se* is not necessarily counter-Christian in all its aspects;[27] sometimes cultural change can be for the good of all.[28] It is good when a change in culture opens the eyes of the theologians to what has not been seen in Scripture before, as has often happened.

The Köstenbergers repeated charge is that egalitarian evangelicals teach "undifferentiated gender equality,"[29] and that in Christ all male-female "distinctions have been abolished."[30] This is not true. I do not believe this and I have never met an egalitarian evangelical who denies creation-given male-female differentiation. If these accusations are true, some reference to those who teach these things should to be given. None

---

24. Köstenberger and Köstenberger, *God's Design*, 262–66, 323–24.

25. Köstenberger and Köstenberger, *God's Design*, 325.

26. Köstenberger and Köstenberger, *God's Design*, 263, 283–85.

27. Köstenberger and Köstenberger, *God's Design*, 263.

28. Köstenberger and Köstenberger, *God's Design*, 187–89.

29. Köstenberger and Köstenberger, *God's Design*, 162, 165, 195, 311, etc.

30. Köstenberger and Köstenberger, *God's Design*, 165.

is given because no informed evangelical egalitarian denies male-female differentiation.[31] What evangelical egalitarians deny is that male leadership and its counterpart, the permanent subordination of women, is the creation-given ideal. The Köstenbergers know this is the issue; why I ask can they not come clean on this?

There are numerous other examples where the Köstenbergers misrepresent or distort the views of evangelical egalitarians. Almost invariably what they say evangelical egalitarians believe is not true. If you want to know what evangelical egalitarians believe you need to read books by evangelical egalitarians.

Obfuscating Language

A second rule for any honest debate is that we clearly and unambiguously say what we believe in opposition to our debating opponents. The Köstenbergers and other complementarians do not do this. They deliberately obfuscate what they are actually arguing.[32] You need a code book to understand what is being said. Nowhere is this more obvious than in the incessant use of the word "role" by the Köstenbergers and other complementarians. This word is not found in any of the most common modern English translations of the Bible. It was first used in the theater in the late nineteenth century, and then in sociological texts in the twentieth century. It only came into common usage in the 1960s when people started talking about how male-female roles were changing. In everyday usage the term refers to characteristic behavior that can change. In complementarian speak it is a code word for fixed power differences allocated on the basis of gender. What defines a man is that he has been given by God the leadership "role," and the woman the subordinate "role." This can never change.

Without ever telling their readers that they are using the word "role" in a way no dictionary defines it, complementarians say that the primary

31. I repeat an earlier footnote because this affirmation, to be accurate, needs some qualification. To say human beings are made man or woman is like saying God has made human beings with two eyes, two arms, and two legs. It is possible to be born with one of any of these, or to lose one in life's journey. We live in a fallen world where variation is to be expected. When it comes to physical and psychological sex differences in human beings, sexual and psycho-sexual differentiation can be blurred or confused, as we see in people with intersex and transgender issues.

32. See more on this, Giles, "Genesis of Confusion."

issue in contention is "God-given male-female role distinctions,"[33] or "distinct and nonreversible male-female roles."[34] These gender-allocated roles, they argue, give to men and women their "identity."[35] Again we must ask why the Köstenbergers are not open and honest with their debating opponents. The primary issue in contention is not who does the housework, shopping, child care, gardening, or household repairs, as the use of the word "role" would suggest to anyone not a complementarian. What fundamentally divides the two sides in this debate is that one side makes the permanent subordination of women the creation ideal; the other side makes the essential equality of the sexes the creation ideal. Again I ask, why can't the Köstenbergers say this in plain English?

Ignoring Counter Evidence and Opinion

In my view what is most objectionable about *God's Design* is that it purports to be a scholarly work, yet counter-evidence and opinion are ignored. If you were not informed, you would know that what is said so emphatically is a minority or discredited opinion.

The most egregious example of this is the Köstenbergers' treatment of Gen 1–3. They interpret these chapters to be teaching that in God's good creation before the fall, the man was set over the woman, and thus for all time in all places men are to lead. This "interpretation" of these chapters is rejected by virtually all modern Old Testament scholars who are not complementarians[36] and has been denied by Pope John II, facts conveniently ignored.[37]

Similarly, in discussing 1 Cor 14:33b–36, they virtually ignore the massive amount of textual evidence that Philip Payne has amassed calling

33. Köstenberger and Köstenberger, *God's Design*, 196. See also 14, 15, 18, 74, 160, 161, 163, 182, 269, etc.

34. Köstenberger and Köstenberger, *God's Design*, 182.

35. Köstenberger and Köstenberger, *God's Design*, 19, 160, etc.

36. The numerous modern commentators and theologians who write in opposition of their interpretation of Gen 1–3 are not mentioned. The reader is led to infer that their *interpretation* is Gen 1–3 is what the Bible is actually saying, and there is no serious and weighty alternative. True they do say in a footnote in *God's Design* (26n3) that in the nineteenth century, Elizabeth Cady Stanton denied the pre-fall subordination of women but they make much of her liberal view of the Bible.

37. John Paul II, *Mulieris Dignitatum*. I will say more on this in the next chapter.

into question the Pauline authorship of this passage.[38] It is summarily dismissed in a very brief footnote.

Payne is a first-class New Testament scholar, textual critic, and linguist. His PhD is from Cambridge. He has written the definitive study on the key texts in contention in his over-500-page book.[39] Much of his work is in direct opposition to what Andreas has published over the years. The Köstenbergers basically ignore all that he says. He gets a brief mention in three footnotes. Professor Linda Belleville is another formidable critic of Andreas's work.[40] Her work is entirely ignored. I am not the scholar that Philip Payne or Linda Belleville are, but I have extensively debated with Andreas and he knows my work well.[41] I have taken him to task on his use of the word "role," his ignoring of the fact that Paul can exhort both women and slaves to be subordinate or obey, and on other matters. I get no mention.

Another example: in this intramural evangelical debate over the status and ministry of women, the meaning of the Greek words *kephalē*/head and *authentein* in 1 Tim 2:12 have been among the most contested issues. The complementarians have argued that *kephalē*/head when used metaphorically always means "head-over"/"authority over," never "source," and *authentein* speaks positively of the authority male pastors exercise that is forbidden to women.[42] The Köstenbergers imply in both cases that this is the assured conclusion of the best of scholars. It is not. On both matters the complementarians have lost the argument. To ignore this fact or dismiss summarily counter evidence is inexcusable.

Facts and Inferences

The Köstenbergers consistently conflate what the Bible says with what they *infer* it teaches. It is a fact that the significant leaders in the Old Testament, the priests, the kings, and the written prophets, are men. Jesus

---

38. Payne, *Man and Woman*, 217–70, and more recently with added evidence, Payne, "Vaticanus Distigme-Obelos Symbols."

39. Payne, *Man and Woman*.

40. Belleville, "Teaching and Usurping Authority," 205–23.

41. Giles, "Critique of the Novel," parts 1 and 2; and Giles, "Dear Professor Köstenberger."

42. When we come to discuss these terms, I will document the evidence for my assertions.

was also a man,[43] and he appointed twelve male apostles, and the majority of the leaders in "the Pauline circle" of coworkers were men. This observation cannot and should not be disputed. On the basis of these *facts*, the Köstenbergers *infer* the principle: the leadership of men is the God-given ideal.

The Bible is a historical record and as such by its very nature reflects the world of the writers. In the ancient world and right up to modern times men gave leadership. In all the nations around Israel and throughout the Roman Empire, men exercised authority in the public domain. The fact that leaders in the Bible were male simply *reflects* a traditional culture.

That the Köstenbergers' *inference* is incorrect is indicated by the exceptions. God raises up Deborah, a married woman, as a ruler of Israel and as a prophet, and there are many other women prophets who speak for God. In the "Pauline circle," three of Paul's "coworkers" are women (Rom 16:3, Phil 4:3), and one woman is an apostle (Rom 16:7)—and apostles are "first in the church" (1 Cor 12:28).[44]

The Köstenbergers point out correctly that Paul asks women to cover their heads when they pray and prophesy in church (1 Cor 11:5). From this fact they *infer* the principle that men are to be the leaders in the church because head-covering symbolizes "submission to authority."[45] They offer no documentation or evidence for this *inference*. In contrast, Cynthia Long Westfall who masterfully documents the evidence *infers* that head-covering for a woman indicates her marital status and honor.[46]

The Problem of Prophecy

The Köstenbergers and I agree that both in the Old and in the New Testament age women could be raised up by God as prophets and that they prophesied.[47] This is a fact and as such a very inconvenient truth for them and all complementarians for a number of reasons. First, for centuries

---

43. Köstenberger and Köstenberger, *God's Design*, 83.

44. These assertions will all be documented in due course.

45. Köstenberger and Köstenberger, *God's Design*, 173, 178.

46. Westfall, *Paul and Gender*, 27.

47. I have written extensively on prophecy and prophesying. See Giles, "Prophecy, Prophets, False Prophets"; and Giles, *Patterns*, chap. 8, 149–73.

theologians have agreed that prophecy is a form of preaching/teaching.[48] Second, Paul says prophecy is of "second" importance in the church, after the ministry of the apostle and before the teacher (1 Cor 12:28). For him, it is a very important ministry because it builds up/edifies God's people (1 Cor 14:1–6). Third, the ministries of teaching and prophecy overlap. Prophets often taught.[49] These facts raise huge problems for complementarians. They have to explain how what is said about women prophets and prophesying can be reconciled with their *interpretation* of 1 Tim 2:11–14, namely, that it forbids women to teach/preach or exercise authority in the church and makes this a binding universal principle grounded in the creation order.

The Köstenbergers follow other complementarian apologists by arguing that prophecy is a non-authoritative ministry to be contrasted with teaching.[50] They say, "The primary thesis of this book is that the authoritative function of prophecy does not rest in an institutionalized office but in the utterance as the word of God itself."[51] This sounds like an impressive argument, but once you realize that there were no clearly defined institutionalized offices, definitely not a defined office of the teacher,[52] in the apostolic age this argument fails. The teacher and teaching have no inherent authority; what is authoritative, like prophecy, is "the utterance as the word of God itself." What is said in teaching as in prophecy must be evaluated. It seems to me that the Köstenbergers are seeking to give an understanding of prophecy that the Bible resists, to further their own agenda. The Bible is unambiguous: God raises up prophets to speak in his name. Part of their work is to teach God's people what God demands.

---

48. Giles, *Patterns*, 150, and n. 4 and 5.

49. Giles, *Patterns*, 161–63, 185.

50. Köstenberger and Köstenberger, *God' Design*, 57, 65–66, 160.

51. Köstenberger and Köstenberger, *God' Design*, 142, n. 16.

52. I pay a lot of attention to this issue in my book, *Patterns of Ministry*. I accept that incipient forms of institutional leadership appear in the apostolic age. We see this in that those who prophesied and taught could be called prophets and teachers, and house-church leaders could be called overseers/bishops, and that older, respected men in each city or location (Acts 14:23; Titus 1:5) could be identified as elders—always collectively. This is not an institutional administrative office, limited to those called pastors, of which the Köstenbergers speak.

Hermeneutical Error

Andreas tells us that one of his specialities is the art and science of hermeneutics. He says he has recently coauthored a book on this.[53] I agree with virtually everything he says in his appendix on this matter[54] and specifically on interpreting gender passages,[55] except for his nasty comments about, and gross misrepresentation of, the views of evangelical egalitarians. No informed evangelical egalitarian is guilty of the hermeneutical sins of which he accuses them. One of their sins, he says, is to give unlikely meanings to Greek words.[56] This is exactly what Andreas does with the key words *kephalē* and *authentein*.

However, where Andreas gets it most wrong is with his own hermeneutical rule that the so-called "two horizons" must be distinguished and kept separate. The first "horizon" is the biblical text, which must be interpreted in its own literary and historical context, strenuously avoiding imposing our modern day theology, concerns or beliefs (especially on gender relations) onto the text. The second "horizon" is the contemporary world. Here the goal is to make the right application of what is said in Scripture. Keeping strictly to this rule, Andreas says, "safeguards the authority of Scripture."[57] I agree. The problem is that all too often the Köstenbergers read their gender agenda into the text. What they tell us is what they believe and teach, not what the Bible teaches. I give here just one example, their most egregious and the most problematic for their whole book. They assume that in the first century there were churches much like today, large gatherings of believers, with "institutionalized office" bearers[58] who exercised "real authority to which others are called to submit,"[59] and who each week preached a sermon. This understanding of the church and church-leadership they read into the New Testament and then seek to apply to the church today to exclude women. In this process they prove what they already believe. The New Testament is made to say what they presuppose about the church and its leadership. The historical truth is that the first Christians met in homes in relatively small

53. Köstenberger and Köstenberger, *God' Design*, 321.
54. Köstenberger and Köstenberger, *God' Design*, 321–34.
55. Köstenberger and Köstenberger, *God' Design*, 335–53.
56. Köstenberger and Köstenberger, *God' Design*, 350.
57. Köstenberger and Köstenberger, *God' Design*, 337.
58. Köstenberger and Köstenberger, *God' Design*, 57, 65, 122, 142, n. 16.
59. Köstenberger and Köstenberger, *God' Design*, 189.

numbers, where everyone was free to minister and teach (Rom 15:4; Eph 5:19; Col 3:16; cf. Eph 4:35; Col 3:1). Women led in prayer and prophecy (1 Cor 11:5). There were no "institutionalized office" bearers.[60] *Church gatherings and church leadership in the apostolic age and today are to be contrasted, not compared.*

Authority as Power-Over

Upholding the authority of men over women is the primary concern of the Köstenbergers. They argue consistently that "authority is sovereignly assigned to man by God," and women should submit to this.[61] Authority is given to men in creation before the fall and is an abiding principle.[62] In the New Testament, Jesus "placed authority into men's hands."[63] Paul is of the same opinion. He taught that "because Adam was created first, creation order indicates that authority rests with Adam" and thus all men.[64] For the biblical writers, they say, male leaders "have real authority to which others are called to submit."[65] This is the authority rightly exercised by husbands and pastors.

There is no ambiguity, God has given to husbands "power over" their wives, pastors over their congregation, and ideally men over women in society.[66] The one problem with this claim is that it directly contradicts the teaching of Jesus. On six occasions, he said those who would lead in his community are to be servants, not rulers (Matt 20:26–28; 23:11; Mark 9:35; 10:43–45; Luke 9:48; 22:24–27), and once he demonstrated what this involved (John 13:4–20). Jesus contrasted his understanding of leadership with that of the world. In his community a leader is "one who serves" (Luke 22:25–26), not one who has power over others. It seems to me what the Köstenbergers and most if not all complementarians do is endorse the leadership style of this world that Jesus rejects. Admittedly, the Köstenbergers speak of "servant leadership," but it is not the servant

60. All this reflects the scholarly consensus. I spell out all these facts and reference them in my chapter on Paul. For more on all this, see my book, *Patterns of Ministry*.

61. Köstenberger and Köstenberger, *God' Design*, 187.

62. Köstenberger and Köstenberger, *God' Design*, 23, 27, 37, 45, etc.

63. Köstenberger and Köstenberger, *God' Design*, 91–92.

64. Köstenberger and Köstenberger, *God' Design*, 211.

65. Köstenberger and Köstenberger, *God' Design*, 188.

66. Köstenberger and Köstenberger, *God' Design*, 283–85.

leadership of which Jesus speaks. They say, "Servant leadership is biblical, but not leadership that is drained of all notions of authority."[67] And then they add, Christian leaders "have real authority to which others are called to submit."[68] Their case is that God has given to men authority, in the sense of "power over," and denied this to women.

I leave my discussion of *God's Design* at this point. I hope I have convinced you that what the Köstenbergers say needs to be carefully and critically assessed. My conclusion is that their arguments are all too often circular. They appeal to the Bible to prove what they already believe, to prove that in plain English God has *permanently subordinated women to men.*

---

67. Köstenberger and Köstenberger, *God' Design*, 188.
68. Köstenberger and Köstenberger, *God' Design*, 189.

2

Complementarianism in Crisis

SINCE THE LATE 1960s, evangelical and Reformed Christians have been bitterly divided over *what the Bible actually teaches* about the man-woman relationship. On one side stand those who since 1990 have designated themselves "complementarians"; on the other, "evangelical egalitarians." Each insists they are teaching what the Bible teaches. There has been a huge amount written by both sides, saying much the same thing time and again. We need a breakthrough, which is now possible for the first time. For about twenty years, from the mid-1960s to the late 1980s, there was a healthy and open debate in which both sides argued about the most likely interpretation of the few disputed texts. Respectful, though sometimes heated, public debates in these two decades on what the Bible taught on the status and ministry of women were common in the USA, England, Canada, and Australia. I took part in several of these debates in Australia in print and in public forums.

In 1987, with the publication of the Danvers Statement,[1] which enunciates what is now called the "complementarian" position, the debate came to an abrupt halt because the authors of the Danvers Statement claimed that what they were teaching was what the Bible teaches. Those who taught otherwise were accused of rejecting what the Bible taught; of denying biblical authority. Following the publication of the Danvers Statement came the definitive study in 1991 setting out the complementarian

1. "Danvers Statement."

position, *Recovering Biblical Manhood and Womanhood: A Response to Biblical Feminism.*[2] This book likewise asserted that the subordination of women is what the Bible teaches and those who argued otherwise were rejecting the plain teaching of Scripture. From then on, in the minds of complementarians, evangelicals who argued that the Bible affirms the creation ideal of the substantive equality of the sexes were twisting the Scriptures to further their feminist agenda and denying biblical authority. This was the end of any debate and dialogue on what the Bible actually says on the man-woman relationship between complementarians and evangelical egalitarians.

I write hoping that this open and respectful debate that kept both sides in fellowship until 1987 can recommence and below I outline why complementarians may at this time be willing to engage again with egalitarians to consider what the Bible actually teaches on women.

IN 2016 A SEISMIC SHIFT BEGAN

In the later part of 2016 the complementarians were shaken to their core when some of their own publicly and forcefully attacked the leaders of the complementarian party for teaching heresy, by claiming the Bible hierarchically ordered the Father, Son, and Spirit and made this the ground for the hierarchical ordering of the sexes.[3] In the face of this onslaught, the leaders of the complementarian party had to recant on this issue.[4] This was a huge defeat because they had argued that 1 Cor 11:3 clearly taught just this. What this means is that not only did they have to admit that eternally hierarchically ordering the divine persons led to the Arian heresy, but also that their interpretation of this text had been wrong. What they had claimed was the undeniable and plain interpretation of 1 Cor 11:3 was mistaken. On this verse the egalitarians had been right all along. This was an earth-shaking admission. In this verse, Paul does not hierarchically order in authority either the Father and the Son or man and woman.

2. Grudem and Piper, *Recovering Biblical Manhood.* See my review in Giles, "Book Review: Grudem and Piper," 276–81.

3. Before June 2016 this was almost universally held complementarian teaching. For a classic affirmation of this argument see Burk, "Why the Trinity Must Inform." On what happened in June 2016 see my book, *Rise and Fall.*

4. I tell this story in Giles, *Rise and Fall.*

What initiated this defeat was the blast of a cannon fired by the complementarian Reformed theologian Dr. Liam Goligher, senior pastor of the historic Tenth Presbyterian Church in Philadelphia. On June 2, 2016, on the Alliance of Confessing Evangelicals podcast, *The Mortification of Spin*, he wrote these words:

> I am an unashamed biblical complementarian. The original use of that word took its cue from the biblical teaching about the differences yet complementarity of human beings made in the image of God, while not running away from the challenges of applying biblical exhortations for wives to submit to their own husbands in the Lord or the prohibition on ordination for women in the church. . . . But this new teaching is not limiting itself to that agenda. It now presumes to tell women what they can or cannot say to their husbands, and how many inches longer their hair should be than their husbands! They, like the Pharisees of old are going beyond Scripture and heaping up burdens to place on believers' backs, and their arguments are slowly descending into farce.[5]

In support of Goligher, Carl Trueman, professor of church history at Westminster Theological Seminary, Philadelphia, added,

> Complementarianism as currently constructed would seem to be now in crisis. But this is a crisis of its own making—the direct result of the incorrect historical and theological arguments upon which the foremost advocates of the movement have chosen to build their case and which cannot actually bear the weight being placed upon them.[6]

> All Liam Goligher and I did was pull on a rope. The next thing we knew, the whole ceiling came crashing down around us. If that tells you anything at all, it is surely something about how well the [complementarian] ceiling was constructed in the first place.[7]

All this was totally unexpected and startling. On June 16, 2016, Caleb Lindgren in an online edition of *Christianity Today* gave an account of this conflict under the heading, "Gender and the Trinity: From Proxy

5. Goligher, "Is It Okay to Teach Complementarianism?"
6. Trueman, "Fahrenheit 381."
7. Trueman, "Motivated by Feminism?"

War to Civil War."[8] This article let the whole evangelical world know of this bitter conflict within complementarianism. At this point the blogosphere exploded. More than 150 posts on complementarianism appeared in five weeks. As the heading of Lindgren's article makes clear, the attack on the leaders of the complementarian movement was precipitated when informed theologians recognized that to teach the eternal subordination of the Son led to the Arian error; but as my quotes make plain, this resulted in much sharp criticism of complementarian teaching on women.

For the rest of 2016 the assault on complementarian teaching by complementarians continued. Writing from an English context, the Reformed theologian and blogger Andrew Wilson agrees with Trueman. He said, "Complementarianism as it is now constructed is in crisis," needing to be corrected. He then added,

> I think robust challenges to faulty formulations of doctrine will, in the end, produce health rather than decay. Admittedly there is a certain type of complementarian argument that, in all likelihood, will be either gradually jettisoned, or refined and nuanced until it can no longer be recognized as the same thing. [9]

Later he asked, when does complementarianism teaching "slide into sheer silliness?"[10]

Particularly telling are the criticisms of Aimee Byrd, who with Carl Trueman and Todd Pruitt, hosts The Alliance of Confessing Evangelicals podcast *The Mortification of Spin*. She writes under the name, "Housewife Theologian." She is of Reformed theological conviction and believes only men should pastor churches. She says,

> Some of the teachings that have been coming from CBMW [The Council of Biblical Manhood and Womanhood, the flagship of the complementarian movement] are very troubling, [and I find them] dangerous to the church, to men, women, and children, and there doesn't seem to be many willing to ask questions or challenge the propaganda.[11]

---

8. Trueman, "Motivated by Feminism?"

9. Wilson, "Complementarianism in Crisis."

10. "When complementarianism 'slides into sheer silliness.'"

11. Byrd, "Sanctified Testosterone."

She particularly took objection to a complementarian, Jason Allen's designation of the complementarian position as "sanctified testosterone."[12] She thinks it is testosterone lacking in sanctification!

In another blog she says,

> Women have been betrayed by the packaging and mass selling of hyper-authoritative teaching under the guise of complementarity. Men who know better are just helping to perpetuate it. And women who know better are also silent.
>
> While there has been helpful teaching that has come from CBMW, other teaching reduces women to ontologically subordinate roles. And some husbands have even used this kind of teaching to fuel abuse in their relationships.[13]

I could add many similar critiques of complementarian teaching by complementarians, but I am sure you can see from what I have said that complementarianism is in crisis.

GROWING OPPOSITION AND PRESSURE

After forty years of debate and division, the number of informed evangelicals with a high view of the Bible who have become convinced egalitarians continues to grow. Complementarians have not been able to convince other informed evangelicals that what they teach is what the Bible teaches. Those who think complementarianism does not reflect what the Bible actually teaches on women are among the most able evangelical theologians on the world scene. The following were all once complementarians who have changed their minds: F. F. Bruce, Leon Morris, Millard Erickson, Kenneth Kanzer, Elaine Storkey, N. T. Wright, I. Howard Marshall, Gordon Fee, Gilbert Bilezikian, Myron Augsburger, Richard Bauckham, Philip Payne, Walter Kaiser, Ben Witherington, Mimi Haddad, Stanley Gundry, Kenneth Bailey, Aida Besancon Spencer, Walter Leifield, Joel Green, Cynthia Long Westfall, Ray Bakke, Alan F. Johnson, Ronald Sider, Miriam Adney, Roger Nicole, Craig Keener, Cornelius Plantinga, John Stackhouse, David Hamilton, Ron Pierce, John Phelan, Michael Bird, Roberta Hestenes, (President) Jimmy and Rosalynn Carter, Stuart and Jill Briscoe, and Paul and Kay Rader.[14] This list

12. Byrd, "Sanctified Testosterone."
13. Byrd, "Silence of Our Friends."
14. For the testimony of many of these people and others see, Johnson, *How I*

is representative not exhaustive. What should be carefully noted is that no fewer than seven of these people have been elected as the president of the Evangelical Theological Society, a society that can only be joined if a declaration of belief in the inerrancy of Scripture is signed annually. (Roger Nicole, Kenneth Kantzer, Walter Kaiser, Stanley Gundry, Alan F. Johnson, Millard Erickson, and in 2018 Craig Keener.)

I stand in this group. For more than fifteen years I adamantly believed that in creation before the fall God set the man over the woman and thus male leadership is an abiding principle. I was converted at twenty-one and was told that this is what the Bible taught, which delighted me as a young man (I thought to myself, "Now I know why Christianity is called "good news"). I was of this opinion until age thirty-five when I changed my mind. My second "conversion" came when I began to study in depth what the Bible actually said on the man-woman relationship in preparation for a lecture my bishop asked me to give on women in the Bible. One of the most important "conversions" to the belief that the Bible teaches the "essential equality" of the sexes is unquestionably that of Pope John Paul II, who not only changed his mind but also changed the mind of the whole Catholic Church on women.[15]

THE COMPLEMENTARIAN "BIBLICAL CASE" HAS NOW COLLAPSED

Another huge challenge for complementarians at this time is that they have lost almost every exegetical battle they have fought in recent years. Most commentators now reject that Gen 1–3 subordinates woman before the fall. Most studies agree that Jesus affirmed the essential or substantive equality of the two sexes. Most theologies of Paul conclude that he had a charismatic theology of ministry in which leadership in the church was given by the Spirit and that gender was inconsequential, and that Junia was a woman apostle. On the much disputed words *kephalē*/head and *authentein* the jury has given its verdict; *kephalē*/head can mean either "head-over" or "source," and *authentein* refers to a form of objectionable authority. 1 Cor 14:33b–36, one of the key complementarian "proof

---

Changed My Mind About Women.

15. Glendon, "Pope's New Feminism." See also Pope John Paul's binding encyclical, *Mulieris Dignitatum.* I will say more on this in the chapter Gen 1–3 following.

texts," has been shown to be almost certainly not from the pen of Paul.[16]
In Ephesians, Paul is not endorsing patriarchy but seeking to subvert it
and he gives a distinctive understanding of Christian marriage where the
husband gives himself for his wife, like Christ did for the church. The
exhortations to women and slaves to be subordinate or obedient are of
exactly the same nature, practical advice to those living in a culture that
took the subordination of women and slavery for granted. The ones addresses to wives are *not* grounded in a supposed pre-fall subordination
of women.

In the Köstenberger's book, *God's Design,* the exegetical, linguistic,
and textual defeats just mentioned are ignored.

APPLYING COMPLEMENTARIAN TEACHING IN OUR CONTEMPORARY WORLD IS NOT POSSIBLE

In the affluent West we all live in a profoundly egalitarian culture. It is
assumed that women can do most things men can do, and some things
even better. They make excellent leaders. Virtually all Christians, including evangelical ones, have come to the conclusion that the liberation
of women is a good thing. Most Christian men are pleased to see their
wives and daughters getting the best education, doing well in the work
place, leading in all spheres of life, and enjoying profoundly equal marriages. A theological position that is not believed and practiced is hugely
problematic.

The most rewarding marriages today are egalitarian. The "headship"
of the husband in the historic sense of the man making all the major decisions and being the "bread-winner" is no longer a viable option. "Happy
marriages" are profoundly equal. The most unexpected voice admitting
this comes from the uncompromising complementarian Russell Moore,
who when he wrote was the dean of the School of Theology and senior
vice president for academic administration at Southern Baptist Seminary. Quoting scientific sociological studies, he says, most evangelical
couples who claim to be complementarians are "pragmatically egalitarian," and often the wife gives the lead.[17] In these homes the idea of male
headship, he says, "has been reorganised along expressive lines, emptying
the concept of all its authoritative content."[18] This means "*complemen-*

---

16. All these assertions will be argued and documented as we proceed.

17. Moore, "After Patriarchy," 571. See also on Moore's views, Carter, "Debatable."

18. Moore, "After Patriarchy," 573.

tarian Christianity is collapsing around us."[19] What most couples have discovered, says Moore, is that "familial harmony, relational happiness and emotional health"[20] are the reward of profoundly equal marriages. Why he thinks imposing old style "patriarchy" is the answer to this crisis for complementarians escapes me.

In our churches women are exercising significant leadership in all but the most doctrinaire complementarian churches. They have been appointed as office bearers and pastors. Excluding women from church leadership and from preaching is becoming ever more difficult. Indeed, this issue now divides complementarians. Many argue that male "headship" does not exclude women from preaching/teaching; only from being the senior pastor, and some do not think it excludes this either. Wayne Grudem, the *de facto* leader of the complementarian movement, calls these people "one point" complementarians and says many evangelicals are of this persuasion.[21] These complementarians, he explains, teach that the husband should be the head of the home but they do *not* think this principle excludes women from church leadership or preaching. In the Sydney Anglican Diocese this issue splits the complementarian majority. A succession of Archbishops since the 1970s, all complementarians, have issued licences for women to preach. They have been "one point" men. They have been bitterly opposed by other Sydney complementarians who are "two point" people. They argue the headship of the man must be upheld in the home and the church and this excludes women from leading a church and from preaching.

Finally, we have the problem for complementarians that they cannot consistently apply their headship doctrine in the world outside of the home and the church. The prerogative of men to lead in society, once assumed, has been rejected. Women are now heads of state, prime ministers, judges, managing directors, generals in the armed forces, and ship's captains. Most Christians accept this without dissent, and those with daughters often hope that they will become community leaders. This is a huge problem for complementarians. They characteristically deal with this by saying nothing about how their doctrine of male headship applies in the world, but it must apply in the world according to their own theology. The foundational premise of their theology is that the man was appointed to lead in creation before the fall. It is the creation-given ideal

19. Moore, "After Patriarchy," 572. Italics added.
20. Moore, "After Patriarchy," 570.
21. Grudem, *Evangelical Feminism*, 520.

and therefore must apply in all of God's creation. If this is the case, and no informed complementarian will deny this, then men should lead in the home, the church, and the state. Theologically, complementarianism is a "three point" doctrine. Here we need to remember that until modern times everyone, including all Christians, believed God had appointed men to lead in the home, the church, and the state.[22] On this matter complementarians need to be honest. They need to admit that in today's world it is impossible to apply their doctrine of male headship outside the home and the church. They know this is the case and so they try in every way they can to ignore this insurmountable problem for their creation-based theology of female subordination.

A theological position that cannot be consistently applied in practice and is ignored or rejected by most Christians, including evangelical ones, is precariously placed. There are only three options for those who today teach that men should be in leadership in the home, the church, and wherever possible in society: they can seek to apply their doctrine consistently and honestly, selectively apply what they can and ignore the inconsistencies of their practice, or abandon it. All evangelical egalitarians have done the latter because they have concluded that the Bible does not make male headship the creation ideal. Rather, the man's rule over the woman reflects the fallen order.

I quote the complementarian theologian Russell Moore one more time. He says, "Egalitarians are winning the evangelical gender debate . . . because in some sense, we are all egalitarians now."[23]

THE ABUSE OF WOMEN

In 2017, another issue shook the complementarian world to its foundations. Complementarians were confronted publicly by the fact that headship teaching can encourage needy, controlling men, of which there is a significant percentage in every church and among the clergy, to be abusive of their wives. And worse, it was the common experience of abused women that when they looked to their conservative evangelical pastor for help they all too often were not believed or were advised to accept the leadership of their husband and his abusive behavior. This problem in evangelical circles had been bubbling along for some years

22. I document this fact in Giles, *Trinity and Subordinationism*, 146–48.
23. Moore, "After Patriarchy," 576.

before 2017, but was always suppressed or denied by complementarians. This was something they did not want discussed and definitely would not acknowledge as a big problem. However, after the Harvey Weinstein scandal, which broke in October 2017, the issue boiled over for evangelicals. The kettle started whistling a shrill call that could not be ignored. On the hashtags #metoo and #churchtoo[24] large numbers of evangelical women came out and spoke of their abuse in their home by men who justified their behavior by insisting that their wives should obey them, quoting headship teaching in support, and of the failure of evangelical pastors to help them. Later in December 2017, 140 leading evangelical women from diverse and political backgrounds began an online petition, #silenceisnotspiritual where those who felt the issue of abuse of women in evangelical churches needed to be addressed and things need to change could sign their names.[25] When I signed the petition early in January 2018, 6,000 Christian leaders had signed.

The two spoken and unspoken questions in all these posts were, does complementarian teaching encourage needy and controlling men to abuse their wives, and second, does complementarian teaching lead complementarian men to condone the abuse of wives?

Next followed the Paige Patterson scandal.[26] In the latter part of the twentieth century, and the early part of the twenty-first century, Patterson was one of the, if not the, most powerful and influential leader of the Southern Baptist denomination, the largest Protestant denomination in the USA. He was a key player in the conservative victory over the moderates in Southern Baptist seminaries and is a leading complementarian. He helped draft the 1987 Danvers Statement.

Early in 2018, a transcript of a recording of an address he gave in 2000 was published. In this he tells a battered wife with two black eyes to stay with her husband "even if he gets a little more violent," pray for him, and at home "be as submissive in every way you can and elevate him." At first, he refused to modify his words or recant them but later under huge pressure he made some ameliorating comments. This pressure came from very large numbers of Baptist women, who in an open letter to the trustees of Southwestern Baptist Theological Seminary, of

24. Gleeson, "#ChurchToo."

25. Shellnut, "Women Speak Up."

26. There are many accounts of this sad story on the internet. I list just a few. Shellnut, "Divorce After Abuse"; Shellnut, "Paige Patterson Fired"; Boorstein and Pulliam, "Women Led"; Moss, "Paige Patterson's Views."

which Patterson was the president, called on them to censure Patterson. Their initial response was to ask him to resign but when it came out he had behaved improperly to women in other ways and lied to the trustees he was dismissed on May 30, 2018.

The charges were the following:[27]

- He counseled an evangelical woman to stay with her abusive husband and taught that abuse was not a reason for divorce.

- He publicly objectified a teenage girl by commenting on her good looks and criticizing the appearance of many female theological students.

- In 2003 he pressured a young Southeastern college student (where he was then president), named Megan Lively, not to report an incident of sexual assault to the police.

- In 2015, this time as president of Southwestern, when another young female student reported that she had been raped, he insisted on speaking to the girl alone so that he, in his own words, "could break her down."

- And finally, he lied to the trustees of Southwestern about these matters.

Again, evangelical Christians, many of them complementarians, cried out, "If this is how complementarianism works out in practice, can it be what the Bible teaches?"

Possibly no one put this question more forcibly and painfully than Beth Moore, the best-known Southern Baptist. In 2010, *Christianity Today* called her "the most popular Bible teacher in America." She has 863,000 Twitter followers, far in excess of any male evangelical leader.[28] As a Southern Baptist she is of course not ordained and mainly speaks to women. She has long upheld complementarian teaching. However, in the wake of the "me too" movement and the Paige Patterson scandal she broke ranks and wrote on May 3, 2018, "A Letter to My Brothers" [of complementarian conviction].[29] In this she says "she learned early to show constant pronounced deference—not just proper respect" to evangelical male leaders, accept frequent unjustified criticism from them, and

27. See in particular, Pulliam Bailey, "Southern Baptist Seminary."
28. McAlister, "How Beth Moore Is Helping."
29. Moore, "Letter to My Brothers."

to be ignored and talked down to by these men. But in late 2016 when
it emerged that key evangelical leaders' views of women "smacked of
misogyny, objectification and astonishing disesteem," she spoke up. She
says,

> I came face to face with one of the most demoralizing realiza-
> tions of my adult life: Scripture was not the reason for this colos-
> sal disregard and disrespect of women among these many men.
> It was only an excuse. Sin was the reason. Ungodliness.

At this point in time, she came to accept and acknowledge that
"many women have experienced horrific abuses within the power structures of our [evangelical] world," and male evangelical leaders have been
silent. She says these same evangelical leaders "who are quick to teach
submission are often slow to point out that women were also among the
followers of Christ (Luke 8), that the first recorded word out of his resurrected mouth was 'woman' (John 20:15) and that same woman was
the first evangelist." These men love to turn to the Household codes in
their sermons, where wives are told to be submissive, but are "slow to
also point out the numerous women with whom the Apostle Paul served
and for whom he possessed obvious esteem." What is now demanded, she
concludes, is a "round table discussion" where these issues can be faced
and addressed honestly and openly.

Not unexpectedly, many read her words as a rejection and con-
demnation of complementarianism. Beth Allison Barr, for one, read it
as a "recanting" of complementarianism, even though Moore does not
explicitly say this. She does, however, Barr notes, apologize for "being
part of the problem" created by complementarian teaching that demeans
women, and of her "cowardly" deference to its teachers, and she reminds
her readers of the frequent affirmations of women and their leadership in
Scripture that complementarian theologians ignore or downplay.

Melanie McAlister, writing in the *Washington Post* on June 22, 2018,
in reference to Beth Moore's letter says, "The SBC leaders are well aware
that they are [now] facing a continuing crisis over how women are treated [in their churches and seminaries]. Women such as Beth Moore have
started to challenge men's abuse of power."[30] She then asks, could this be
the beginning of the end of the complementarian ideology? What is so
paradoxical in this whole story is that one of the most influential leaders of the complementarian movement, Paige Patterson, who had starkly

30. McAlister, "How Beth Moore Is Helping."

argued for the permanent subordination of women for over fifty years was undone by women who would not be silenced. The women he had told to "be as submissive in every way, be silent in church, and respect the leadership of the men set over them," said to him, "It's now time for you to step down and be silent."

In Australia, these revelations have shaken the powerful and evangelistically motivated Sydney Anglican Diocese to its core. In 2017, first one clergy wife of a Moore College trained clergyman bravely came forward to say he had been repeatedly violent to her and as a result she had left the marriage in fear of her life. Then other clergy wives stepped forward and said the same and soon after women married to lay leaders stood up to say the same.[31] In the annual Synod of 2017, Archbishop Glen Davies, a dogmatic complementarian, had no other option; he had to make an apology to the hundreds of women who had been abused in the diocese and were not listened to. The Synod then passed a resolution making an apology to all the women involved for how they had been treated.[32]

This public airing of the abuse of women in evangelical homes and of the reluctance of so many evangelical and Reformed clergy to support them in this situation is a huge problem for complementarians. No longer can they deny that headship teaching can have awful consequences for women. Worse still is that these public revelations of what happens in too many evangelical homes discredits the Gospel and makes Christianity seem like bad news for women.

CRISIS BUT NOT CAPITULATION

Complementarians may be in crisis, but they are not going to throw in the towel on women any time soon. Ostensibly this debate is over what the Bible actually teaches on the man-woman relationship but in reality it is all about power, about who is to lead in the church and the home. Those holding power never give it up willingly. Later we will illustrate this point in the case of slavery and apartheid, both of which were at one time supported strongly by evangelical and Reformed theologians by appeal to the Scriptures.

31. One graphic account is given by Young, "Abuse Inside Christian Marriages."

32. Gleeson, "Anglican Diocese of Sydney"; Gleeson, "Sydney Anglican Church"; "Australian Churches Risk."

It is because complementarian theology is in crisis that this book is needed. For the first time in some thirty years, evangelical egalitarians have a chance to be heard.

3

Why the Debate About the Equality of the Sexes Has Occurred at This Time in History

FROM EARLIEST TIMES, MEN have ruled over women. There are two main reasons for this. Men on average are stronger than women and thus can assert their authority over them. And second, men do not have babies and do not need to breast feed them. They thus have freedoms and control over their own lives that women as wives and mothers do not have. In other words, men are advantaged by nature. Men also have been advantaged by education. Where education has been available, men have monopolized it. They have been the educated leaders, mathematicians, philosophers, artists, and musicians. From what is the reality, the belief followed that this is how things should be. Men are to rule over women and they make the best leaders. This belief was then codified and legitimated in religious texts. All the sacred texts of the great religions of the world in one way or another give God's imprimatur to male rule. Virtually all Christians until the 1960s believed that the Bible taught that the man should rule over the woman, not just that it reflected a patriarchal culture.

The right of men to rule over women began to be questioned in the nineteenth century but little progress was made. Few women gained an education or could support themselves, and if they were married they were either pregnant or nursing a baby for most of their life. In the 1960s a number of forces coalesced to make radical change possible. These things inaugurated one of the most profound and far-reaching social revolutions in the history of the world, women's liberation.

I outline what happened.

When men in their millions went off to fight in the Second World War, women in their millions were called on to do their jobs. Women learned trades, staffed factories, drove trucks, flew airplanes, worked as accountants, and managed businesses of all kinds. Then the men returned and the women were sent back to be homemakers and have children. Initially there was little discussion or unhappiness about this. However, by the 1960s many of these women began to recall how fulfilling their work experiences had been for them and what they had achieved before they were "sent home." What is more by the 1960s women were completing high school and going on to university or college in growing numbers, only to find that they were expected to get married, have children, and run the home for the rest of their lives. They realized they were capable of much more.

For centuries men's greater physical strength gave them an advantage in the labor market. The majority of jobs were open only to men because of their physical demands. However, by the 1960s brains were becoming more important than brawn. This change accelerated with increasing use of computers. When brains are more important than brawn, many of the most rewarding jobs become available to women. Today when more women than men are graduating from colleges and universities, women percentage-wise are advantaged in the job market.

In this post-war period as women began moving in greater numbers into the work force, the new labor-saving devices were coming onto the market. Washing machines, vacuum cleaners, fridges, electric mixers, and stoves cut down on the time and effort needed for household chores. Even ironing became less time consuming as clothing that needed little or no ironing became common. Women even began to find relief from all the housework because in many homes men began to do a little of the work around the home. In the 1960s, my dad was very proud of the fact that he washed up the dishes every night.

In 1960 the first oral contraceptive pill, *Enovid*, was approved for sale, and within a few years was universally available. Now women could determine if and when they would have children far more assuredly than before. This gave them freedoms that hitherto only men had enjoyed.

With a solid education, less time needed to run the home, and in control of their fertility, women in ever-growing numbers joined the work force. In 1963 President John F. Kennedy signed The Equal Pay Act, which ruled a woman must be paid the same as a man for the same work. Other developed countries soon passed similar legislation. Greater access to paid employment combined with improvements in women's pay meant that for the first time in human history women could support themselves and family members for whom they were responsible; they were no longer financially dependent on men.

These huge changes for women beginning in the 1960s took place in times of profound social disruption. The Vietnam War was raging, with its opponents marching in the streets. The African-American civil rights movement was in full swing. There were student riots in Europe. These events were the outworking of the belief, especially among the young, that social change was needed; the world could be made a better place; social equality was possible. This was fertile soil for the women's movement to erupt and prosper. As in the 1860s when women, most of them evangelical women, involved in the abolition of slavery movement began questioning their own subordinate status, so too did women involved in the civil rights movement of the 1960s begin questioning their subordinate status.

In this context, Betty Friedan in 1963 published her ground-breaking book *The Feminine Mystique*. For her, the "feminine mystique" was the post-Second World War supposition that a woman's role in society is to be a wife, mother, housewife, and nothing more. This, she discovered, had led large numbers of women to feel unhappy and unfulfilled. They wanted more than a husband, children, and a home. What the "mystique" did, Friedan concluded, was block women from developing a sense of their own worth and human potential as autonomous identities. Behind the "mystique," she pointed out, lay Sigmund Freud's belief that women are intrinsically childlike, needing male supervision. Nature had determined their destiny to be a wife, mother, homemaker, tender, and dependent on men.

In a short period of time, the book had sold a million copies. What Friedan said resonated with millions of white, middle class, educated women, many of them Christians. In 1966 the National Organization for Women (NOW) was formed with Betty Friedan as its first president. Those present at the first meeting agreed that "NOW is dedicated to the presupposition that women first and foremost are human beings, who . . . must have the chance to develop their fullest human potential."

By the 1970s women found themselves in a world never enjoyed by their sex before. They had been set free. The Western world had agreed women should be given equality before the law and equality of opportunity in all aspects of life. As a consequence, today we have women presidents and prime ministers of nations. Women are judges, politicians, professors, generals, and managing directors of large companies. They are physicians/doctors, lawyers, engineers, and computer designers. Women are plumbers, electricians, and carpenters. Now, almost by definition, the happiest and most mutually rewarding marriages are profoundly egalitarian.

In speaking of these huge changes, the fact that women still face challenges and are often disadvantaged must not be ignored. Men exert more political power and get most of the better jobs. Despite laws on equal pay men on average earn something like 20 percent more than women. Because most men are physically stronger than most women, men can use force to get their own way. It is women who bear children. This means for some years in their life they may be out of the workforce and fall behind men in their career path. The reality is that in our fallen world, gender equality, like all forms of social equality, remains an ideal to be pursued.

THE CHRISTIAN RESPONSE TO WOMEN'S LIBERATION

This monumental social revolution was not easy for women to work out in theory or practice. It has been extremely hard for many men to adjust to, difficult for businesses to implement, and overwhelming for many of the churches. The large mainline churches at first were entirely hostile to the women's movement even though it had its origins in the advocacy of nineteenth century Christian women. Their hostility is surprising because one might reasonably assume that all Christians would gladly endorse the primary presupposition of NOW, "that women first and foremost are human beings, who . . . must have the chance to develop their fullest human potential."

Many conservative Christians, most of whom had not read Betty Friedan's book, wrongly dismissed it as a frontal attack on Christian values. It was not. The primary message of *The Feminine Mystique* is that women should be set free to express their full human potential and be proud to be women. There is no mention of broader issues such as advocacy for abortion rights, endorsement of lesbianism, or any questioning of male-female differentiation.

Roman Catholics, and those of conservative evangelical and Reformed conviction, were the most hostile. They saw Friedan's book in particular and women's liberation in general as an attack on the "Christian family": a father who worked and earned the money, and a mother who bore and nurtured the children and ran the home. The problem with this view is that the so-called "Christian family" is a modern phenomenon, a consequence of the industrial revolution of the late eighteenth and nineteenth centuries. When people in huge numbers left villages and fields to go to the cities they created this new model of family where the men went out to work and the women stayed at home.

By contrast, in the Bible and for most of history, the family functioned as an economic unit. The whole family worked in the fields and cared for the animals. The home was a place where everyone ate and slept, and often the location for small-scale industry such as spinning, weaving, and joinery. In shops, and in businesses such as bakeries, every family member had a job to do. In this context, the wife usually managed household life. The mistaken view that the family consisting of a father who goes out to work and a mother who stays at home is "the biblical model" is still common in conservative Christian circles.

Many Christians were hostile to the women's liberation movement for a second reason, namely because it propounded the revolutionary idea that marriages should be equal partnerships where women "have the chance to develop their fullest human potential." This was taken to contradict the Bible's teaching on "male headship," the idea that men should be the leader and decision-maker in the home, and the pastor and leader in congregations.

Initially the Roman Catholic Church took the most intransigent position, but in 1987 Pope John Paul II issued his binding encyclical, *Mulieris Dignitatem: On the Dignity of Women*. In this he rejected the view held for centuries that in creation God subordinated women to men, insisting instead on their "essential equality." However, on the question of leadership in the church, he maintained the traditional view. Appealing to the fact that the twelve apostles were all men, and to the traditional Catholic idea that they were the first priests, he argued that women therefore could not be ordained in the Catholic Church. This has resulted in a very ambiguous Catholic position. Women cannot be church leaders because the twelve apostles were the first priests and they were all men, but they should be granted equality without any caveats in all other areas of life including marriage because this is the creation ideal, something endorsed by Jesus.

Liberal Protestants embraced with enthusiasm the liberation of women. For evangelicals it was far more difficult. They had accepted the view that prevailed until the mid-1960s that men are to be in charge in the home, the church, and the state. Most felt keeping to the old ways was what the Bible demanded but a few brave evangelical and Reformed souls came out boldly in support of women's liberation, arguing this is what the Bible envisages.[1] They were bitterly opposed by other evangelicals, mainly of Reformed persuasion, who argued that the Bible taught male "headship" and to deny this was to deny the authority of Scripture. This did not stop other evangelicals in ever-growing numbers from embracing the liberation of women and developing a "biblical case" for male-female equality. For the last twenty years, the social conservatives calling themselves "complementarians" have been in the ascendancy but now they are under huge pressure to change for reasons I listed in the last chapter.

FEMINISM

In what I have said so far in this chapter I have spoken of "women's liberation." I have avoided the loaded term "feminism."[2] For social conservatives, especially Christian ones, "feminism" is an evil and destructive philosophy that has caused all the ills of modern society; the increase in marriage breakups, the undermining of the Christian family, sexual promiscuity, the acceptance of homosexuality, gay marriage, abortion rights, the decline in church attendance, and much more. It is dismissed as a malevolent, monolithic movement seeking to overthrow society as it has existed across the ages. We can see why complementarians insist on calling evangelical egalitarians "evangelical feminists." To so name fellow evangelicals brands them as opponents of the Christian faith before they are allowed to speak.

---

1. The most influential evangelical book putting forth the biblical case for equality was Scanzoni and Hardesty, *All We're Meant to Be*, first published in 1974.

2. The online *Oxford Dictionaries* defines the word as, "The advocacy of women's rights on the ground of the equality of the sexes." https://en.oxforddictionaries.com/definition/feminism

In contrast, for me and many others, "feminism" is simply a name for those who want to see men and women given equal status and opportunity. It is entirely a positive word. Its roots lie in the nineteenth century emancipation movement, what late twentieth century historians call the "first wave of feminism." This was a movement led by evangelicals who believed the equality of men and women in Christ was clearly taught in Scripture. They were opposed to both slavery and the subjection of women. Among the leaders of the "first wave feminists" were the evangelicals William and Catherine Booth, the founders of the Salvation Army, Sojourner Truth, Amanda Berry Smith, Katherine Bushnell, A. J. Gordon, and Fredrik Franson. What this means is that feminism as it bloomed in the 1960s had deep evangelical and biblical roots. Sadly, in the late 1960s and early 1970s, very few evangelical Christians were at the forefront in efforts to see women granted equal status and opportunity, or the civil rights movement. Most fiercely opposed women's liberation.

Among those who gladly call themselves "feminists" there are profound differences. To depict feminism as unified philosophy with common aims is mistaken. What some feminists advocate other feminists oppose. They agree only that the primary agenda is that women be given equal status and opportunity, after this they take many paths. The assertion that post 1960s feminism is the cause of all the ills of modern society cannot be taken seriously. Whatever the downsides may be, the liberation of women has brought great good into the world. To see women flourishing in modern life in ways hitherto unknown and unimaginable is surely something very positive. The rewards of profoundly equal marriages that involve sharing household chores and child-rearing, and making decisions jointly, is also something to be commended. Much to my surprise and delight I found that the Köstenbergers, at least in one discordant paragraph, have a very similar view of feminism to mine. They write,

> There is no question that feminism—a movement concerned with the advancement of women's rights and with the achievement of women's complete parity with men in society, the home and the church—has had many positive results since its inception almost two centuries ago. Women's status and experience in the Western world, in particular, have been altered for the better in many ways. . . . In this way, justice has been served, and many women have been lifted from second-class status to genuine equality with men.[3]

3. Köstenberger and Köstenberger, *God's Design*, 294–95.

None of the ills of modern society can be attributed solely to feminism. They are rather a consequence of the profound social changes that have taken place in the last fifty years, of which the liberation of women is just one. For complementarians to claim that egalitarian evangelicals, because they are "evangelical-feminists," knowingly or unknowingly, are responsible in part for the increase in divorce, breakdowns in the family, for gay rights, and the acceptance of same-sex marriage, is nothing more than an attempt to blacken the name of their critics when their appeals to the Bible for their own views on women have collapsed.

Lastly I say to those who berate feminism, the only way to bring a halt to the liberation of women is to exclude them from higher education. It is education, more than anything else, that has empowered women.

WOMEN'S LIBERATION AND THE BIBLE

The debate about what the Bible says on the sexes is very much a contemporary one. It only became a red-hot question as a consequence of the revolutionary social changes outlined above. When the Western world affirmed the full equality of the sexes, *all* Christians were forced to reconsider what they thought the Bible said about women. For centuries Christians simply reflected and endorsed the prevailing cultural norms of society, arguing that women are to be subordinated to men in all spheres of life—the home, the church, and every part of society. Theologians and clergy along with everyone else until the 1960s generally spoke of women as "inferior" and of men as "superior," and the Bible was interpreted to teach just this.

It was women's liberation that forced all theologians to go back and consider afresh what the Bible taught on women, or better, on the male-female relationship. Such rethinking on what Scripture teaches when a profound social change takes place have happened many times in history. Let me give a few examples. When everyone thought the world was flat, theologians read the Bible to teach this. When everyone thought the sun revolved around the earth, the Bible was read to teach this. When everyone thought the world was created in seven literal days about 7,000 years ago, everyone believed this. Now most Christians do not think that the Bible teaches any of these things.

The closest parallels, however, to the contemporary change in thinking on what the Bible teaches on women are seen in the slavery and apartheid debates. In the nineteenth century in the American South, evangelical and Reformed Christians were of one mind, the Bible endorses the institution of slavery. Numerous weighty works were written putting the "biblical case for slavery," many by erudite Reformed theologians.[4] The Southern Baptist Convention was established in 1845 as a breakaway from the Northern Baptists over this very issue. The founders of the new denomination were agreed, the Bible teaches that slavery is acceptable to God. We see much the same thing in South Africa. For about fifty years learned theologians of the Dutch Reformed Church insisted that the Bible endorsed the doctrine of apartheid. In both cases there came a day when those who were claiming biblical support for the oppression of non-whites had to confess they had been wrong. They had quoted the Bible to support what the Bible condemned. Self-interest had corrupted their thinking, leading them to find in Scripture what advantaged them. In 1989 the Reformed Church of South Africa publicly acknowledged that to teach as they had that the white races should rule over other races is "heresy"; contrary to what the Bible actually teaches. It took Southern Baptists longer to publicly admit they had read the Bible wrongly on slavery. This admission only came in 1995.

These changes in how the Bible is understood do not speak of the rejection of any biblical teaching, only the rejection of an *interpretation* of the Bible that could not be substantiated in the light of new knowledge. The change in thinking on women is of this kind. We should not be surprised that Christians until modern times thought the Bible taught the subordination of women, because they lived in a cultural context where men ran the world, and because the Bible itself reflected a culture where male leadership was the taken-for-granted reality. Only when the world changed did most Christians see clearly for the first time that there were profound and principled statements in the Bible that spoke of the substantial equality of the two sexes in creation and in Christ.

In this book I set out, I hope in an accessible way, the biblical case for gender equality. I have been thinking about, writing on, and debating this issue on the world scene for over forty years. In what follows I outline chapter by chapter how the best of theologians, Catholic and Protestant, now interpret the key biblical passages that were once quoted to prove that God had made women "inferior" to men and thus excluded them from leadership in the world, the church, and the home. In doing this

---

4. In chapter 7 I will spell out the impressive "biblical" case for slavery.

I do not enter into detailed technical discussions of Hebrew and Greek words, except with the much disputed words, *kepalē* and *authentein*, or set out opposing views in *extensio*, or give long footnotes that list contending opinions on every disputed matter. To do so would lose too many of my readers. What I do is argue that the Bible makes the substantial equality of the sexes the creation ideal, as clearly and forcibly as I can, drawing on the best of scholarship, and always, as I mentioned in the last chapter, in response to the book, *God's Design*, written by Andreas and Margaret Köstenberger. In the many glowing commendations of this book by complementarians given on the first two pages, we are told that the Köstenbergers are "brilliant and respected" theologians who give the most scholarly, most comprehensive, and most up-to-date account of the complementarian position.

QUESTIONS FOR DISCUSSION

1. Give everyone the opportunity to tell their story on how they perceive the male-female relationships and of any change in thinking that has taken place for them over the years. A good commencement point for each person would be to start with how their parents related and what they learned from this. Allow each person to speak *without comment* at this point.

2. Ask those present how the male-female relationship can be discussed without hurting one another.

3. The argument was made above that profound social change tends to affect how Christians understand (interpret) the Bible. Metaphorically speaking, it gives them new glasses to see through. Discuss this idea.

4. In Western countries, in final high school results, on average girls get higher marks than boys and more women than men graduate from universities. What does this say about the world we live in?

5. Conversely, discuss the fact that despite claims of equality in society a very large percentage of the top 200 companies have no women on their board and few female executives. Despite laws that women should be paid the same for the same work, women on average are paid something like 20 percent less than men. Why do you think that there is such a gulf between the ideal and the reality for women?

6. Discuss the claim, "the best of marriages today are profoundly equal."

ADDENDUM: THE INVENTION OF THE COMPLEMENTARIAN POSITION BY GEORGE KNIGHT IN 1977

In the face of the growing impact of "women's lib" on society, the church, and on evangelicals specifically, one of the most creative, conservative Reformed theologians of the twentieth century, George Knight III, stepped forward with an answer. He reworded and reformulated what the theologians had taught for centuries on the male-female relationship. In his highly influential 1977 book, *New Testament Teaching on the Role Relationship of Men and Women*, he rejected the customary way of speaking of men as "superior," women "inferior" that had reigned until the middle of the twentieth century, arguing instead that men and women are "equal but different." Men and women are different because God has assigned to each sex differing "roles." These differing "roles" were given in creation before the fall. As such they give the ideal and are permanently binding. Knight was the very first theologian in history to differentiate men and women on the basis of God-given "roles." Paradoxically, in supposedly outlining the "historic" position Knight introduced a novel and very problematic way to indelibly differentiate men and women that all later self-designated "complementarians" followed.

Knight insists that what he is teaching is what the Bible teaches. How he appeals to the Bible is informative. He first argues that Gal 3:28 speaks only of "our spiritual equality";[5] it has no social application. He omits completely any discussion on what Jesus said and did in relation to women. His "biblical" case for what he calls "man's authority and headship over woman and woman's submission to man"[6] is essentially based on his interpretation of three texts: 1 Tim 2:11–14; 1 Cor 11:3; and 1 Cor 14:33b–38.

The first text, 1 Tim 2:11–14, is of huge importance to him because he argues this text unambiguously forbids a woman from teaching in church and having authority over a man[7] and it grounds the subordination of the woman in the created order.[8] In doing so Paul makes man's "dominion"[9]

5. Knight, *New Testament Teaching*, 20.
6. Knight, *New Testament Teaching*, 26.
7. Knight, *New Testament Teaching*, 30.
8. Knight, *New Testament Teaching*, 31.
9. Knight, *New Testament Teaching*, 31.

a transcultural and trans-temporal principle.[10] Breaking with the Authorized Version of the Bible, which translates the verb *authentein* in 1 Tim 2:12 as "to usurp authority," Knight argues that this verb, only found once in the New Testament, speaks positively of the authority a male pastor rightly exercises, an authority Paul denies to women.[11]

Next he appeals to 1 Cor 11:3. He says that Paul "begins his argument about the role relationship of men and women [in this passage] by placing it in a hierarchy of headships."[12] He says the Greek word, *kephalē*, translated "head," is used "to denote superior rank."[13] Thus he concludes that 1 Cor 11:3 is speaking of "the authority relationships that God has established between the Father and the Son, the Son and man, and man and woman."[14] He says the text speaks of "a chain of subordination."[15] In descending order of authority stand the Father, Son, man, woman. In making this argument Knight grounded the subordination women not only in creation but also in the life of God in eternity. Significantly, he concedes that his teaching on the subordination of the Son and women has "ontological" implications.[16] I agree with him on this.[17]

In arguing that the divine persons of the Trinity are in eternity hierarchically ordered, Knight openly but without admitting it broke with historic orthodoxy. The Athanasian Creed says, "In this Trinity none is before or after the other, none is greater or less than another . . . the three persons are coequal"; all three are "almighty" and all three are "Lord." The Belgic Confession of 1561 says, "All three [are] co-eternal and co-essential. There is neither first nor last: for they are all three one, in truth, in power, in goodness, and in mercy." The Second Helvetic Confession of 1566 says the "three persons [are] consubstantial, coeternal, and coequal," and then it condemns those who teach that any divine person is "subservient, or subordinate to another in the Trinity, and that there is something unequal, a greater or less in one of the divine persons." Why so few recognized that Knight was teaching a doctrine of the Trinity

---

10. Knight, *New Testament Teaching*, 29–32.

11. Knight, *New Testament Teaching*, 30, especially n. 1.

12. Knight, *New Testament Teaching*, 32.

13. Knight, *New Testament Teaching*, 32, n. 6.

14. Knight, *New Testament Teaching*, 57. See also 33.

15. Knight, *New Testament Teaching*, 33.

16. Knight, *New Testament Teaching*, 56.

17. On the heresy called "subordinationism," see Giles, "Defining the Error."

explicitly excluded by the Athanasian Creed and the Reformation confessions, and as he admits has unavoidable "ontological" implications, is a question that demands an answer. I will leave this answer to my readers.

Lastly he appeals to 1 Cor 14:33b–38.[18] This text, like 1 Tim 2 he argues, prohibits "women *teaching* men" in church,[19] and grounds this prohibition in the creation order. What it seems to do in fact is prohibit women from asking disruptive questions, and this directive is based not on creation, but "the law," which in this instance may allude to nothing more than Jewish oral law. No Old Testament law forbids women speaking in public. He does not mention that this text is textually doubtful.

Knight's novel and creative way of putting the case for the permanent subordination of women in the new cultural context gained almost universal endorsement by evangelicals opposed to the liberation of women. It is now how all complementarians put their case. The appeal of his rewording of the traditional position was that it obfuscated what was being argued and made it sound acceptable to the modern ear. Who could deny that men and women are different in significant ways and they tend to have different roles—women bear and feed babies, in most homes do the majority of the household work, and men put out the garbage and fix things—not that he was using the word "role" in this dictionary sense. Only one new development to his innovative theological work has occurred since he wrote. In a brilliant initiative, John Piper and Wayne Grudem in editing the symposium, *Recovering Biblical Manhood and Womanhood: A Response to Evangelical Feminism*, published in 1991, renamed the novel post 1970s case for the permanent subordination of women, "the complementarian position."[20] This is a self-serving designation because all evangelical egalitarians agree the sexes complement each other; man and woman *complete* what it means to be human. Thus, to call oneself a "complementarian" does not distinguish you from other evangelicals. At the same time as they gave their position this very positive nomenclature they negatively named those they were opposing "evangelical feminists." In socially conservative Christian circles a "feminist" is someone who is espousing an ideal that is counter to Christian family values.

18. Knight, *New Testament Teaching*, 36–38.

19. Knight, *New Testament Teaching*, 37. Italics added. This passage says nothing about teaching.

20. Grudem and Piper, *Recovering Biblical Manhood*. They tell us they coined this term to highlight "both equality and beneficial differences between men and women."

Note carefully: I am not arguing that Knight was the first to speak of differing "roles" for men and women. In the 1970s the changing "roles" of men and women was constantly being discussed. Women were going out to work, men were doing more child care and housework; women were doing work once reserved for men, men were doing work once reserved for women. Many Christians opposed this. What Knight did was give this much used word "role" new content. For him, a "role" was a creation-given power relationship, allocated on the basis of gender, which was the primary thing that differentiated men and women.

Knight's ideas are determinative for the Köstenbergers. Following him exactly they differentiate men and women primarily on creation-given "roles."[21] And like him they argue "the primary point in Gal 3:28 is spiritual" equality;[22] they ground woman's subordination in the created order and in the triune life of God;[23] assert that "*kephalē*" (head) means "authority over,"[24] and the verb *authentein* speaks positively of the authority that male pastors exercise.

THE INSIDIOUS USE OF THE WORD "ROLE"

I have already made the point more than once that no justification whatsoever can be found for predicating male-female differentiation primarily if not exclusively on creation-given "role" differences. No widely used English translation of the Bible uses the word "role"; a "role" in dictionary usage speaks of characteristic behavior that can change, and because complementarians deliberately use the word "role" to obfuscate what in fact they are teaching. For them, "role differences" undeniably speak of power differences. What primarily if not exclusively differentiates the sexes is that God has given men the leadership "role," women the obeying "role," and this can never change. Because of the monumental importance of this issue I must say more on it.

21. Köstenberger and Köstenberger, *God's Design*, 14, 18, 19,

22. Köstenberger and Köstenberger, *God's Design*, 168. On page 169 they say this again in other words. Galatians 3:28, they say, "relates primarily to how people relate to God, both in their salvation and in their sanctification." This is not to deny that the Köstenbergers contradict themselves by admitting the undeniable, this text "does have social implications" (p. 168). Through their book we find many similar contradictory assertions.

23. Köstenberger and Köstenberger, *God's Design*, 174–75.

24. Köstenberger and Köstenberger, *God's Design*, 174.

The modern English word "role," taken from the French word rôle, finds its late-nineteenth century origins in the theater and its early twentieth century academic usage in humanistic sociology. In dictionary usage and in sociological texts the words "role" and its synonym, "function," speak of routine behavior or acts and so we ask, for example, who has the role of gardening, washing clothes, doing the shopping, managing the finances, etc. in the home? In this everyday usage it is understood that roles and functions can change and do change. They are not fixed and person-defining. In the novel usage invented by Knight, and now entrenched in the evangelical world, a "role" is given an entirely different meaning found in no dictionary or sociological text. A "role" has nothing to do with routine behavior. It is a person-defining category, speaking of fixed *power relations* allocated on the basis of gender, not *role relations* that may change from place to place and from time to time. God the Father and men have the "role" or "function" of leading ("headship"); the Son of God and the women have the "role" of submitting—and this can never change. To prove that this so-called "role subordination" does not imply subordination in being or inferiority in person (ontological subordination)—which Knight conceded—post-Knight complementarians use carefully chosen illustrations seeking to get around this problem. They argue that the role differences such as that of the ship's captain and the crewman, the officer and the private in an army, and the manager and the worker do not imply the superiority of one party and the inferiority the other. This is true. I agree. These illustrations of differing "roles" do not imply ontological subordination or personal inferiority because first, the roles can change, and second because the higher position/role invariably has some basis in competence, training, age, etc. It is not ascribed by birth or gender. The problem is that these carefully chosen and selective illustrations in fact do not parallel what is being argued. The exact parallels to the distinctive complementarian usage of the terms "function" and "role," introduced by Knight, are to be found in classic aristocracy, the Hindu caste system, race-based slavery, and in apartheid where one's so-called "role" or "function" is ascribed by birth and it can never change. In this usage the one who rules is understood to be of a superior class or status and the one who obeys of an inferior class or status. In other words, "difference in role" speaks of an *essential and unchangeable* difference between persons, which is predicated on the premise that some are born to rule and some obey. The rulers and the ruled are not social equals and never can be. So what Knight and his followers are actually arguing is that the Son and women are defined by their subordination. The word "role" was deliberately chosen by Knight, and used by all complementarians to deliberately obfuscate what was actually being argued, namely that one party is permanently subordinated in authority to another.

When the word "role" is used in this novel sense to speak of what primarily and essentially differentiates the Father and the Son, the orthodox doctrine of the Trinity is denied. This would not be the case if the word was being used to speak only of the differing works or operations of the divine persons, as the dictionary definition of this word would suggest, but this is not the case. What is actually being argued is that what primarily differentiates the Father and the Son is differing authority; who rules over whom for all eternity. Because this difference is eternal and person-defining it speaks of the ontological subordination of the Son.[25]

We have already asked why theologians did not cry out in dismay when Knight hierarchically ordered the Trinity; now we ask why they did not cry out in dismay when he baptized the non-biblical word "role" into the holy discipline of exegesis. Knight's novel use of the non-biblical word "role" in the exegetical enterprise, cannot be accepted. Evangelical egalitarians have strongly objected to this use of the word "role," and made devastating critiques of it,[26] but their protests have been ignored or dismissed summarily. The Köstenbergers know these critiques of the use of the word "role" but they never mention them. This is inexcusable in a supposedly scholarly work.

25. Many complementarian theologians now recognize this. See my book, *Rise and Fall*.

26. So Groothuis, "Equal in Being"; Giles, *Trinity and Subordinationism*, 83–85, 158–60, 179–83; and Giles, "Genesis of Confusion."

4

In the Beginning: Genesis 1–3

In exploring what the Bible teaches on men and women, *no part of the Bible is more important than Gen 1–3.*[1] In his informed study of these chapters, Richard Hess says the importance of these chapters cannot be overemphasized in any study of the man-woman relationship. He writes,

> The account of creation, the garden of Eden and the fall in Genesis 1–3 may contain more doctrinal teaching concerning the nature of humanity as male and female, as well as the state of the fallen world, than any other text in the Bible.[2]

Similarly, the German conservative Old Testament scholar and complementarian Werner Neuer says, "Genesis 1–3 are the most fundamental chapters about man and woman in the Old Testament." These chapters, he adds, are of "supreme importance."[3] To these comments we may add the conclusions of Pope John Paul II in his authoritative encyclical *Mulieris Dignitatum: On the Dignity and Vocation of Women.*[4] He says that these opening chapters of the Bible, particularly what they say on man and woman, are "the basis of all Christian anthropology."[5] The

1. For an earlier form of this chapter see, Giles "Genesis of Equality."
2. Hess, "Equality," 79.
3. Neuer, *Man and Woman,* 59.
4. John Paul II, *Mulieris Dignitatem,* 11.
5. John Paul II, *Mulieris Dignitatem,* 22.

Köstenbergers agree: they say these chapters are "foundational" to what the Bible says on the sexes.[6]

When it comes to the specific and sharp debate between complementarians and evangelical egalitarians, these chapters are certainly of supreme importance. The whole complementarian case rests on the argument that before the fall the man ruled over the woman. Male "headship" is predicated in God's good creation before sin entered the world and for this reason it is transcultural and trans-temporal. It is not annulled by the death of Christ or overcome by the giving of the Spirit to believers. If this interpretation of Gen 1–3 is without merit and mistaken, then the complementarian case has no theological foundation and should be categorically rejected. Let me make this point even more emphatically, the complementarian case stands or falls on whether or not their distinctive interpretation of the opening chapters of the Bible is true or false. No text in the whole Bible is more important for their theological construct than Gen 1–3.

TWO CREATION ACCOUNTS, ONE STORY

Genesis 1–3, read in canonical context (i.e., as they are in our Bibles), give "a continual narrative."[7] They tell us that God created man and woman as the climax of his creative work and that he placed them in the garden of Eden. Tragically, however, the serpent enters and both the man and the woman fall into sin and as a consequence their relationships with God, each other, and the created world are damaged and they are banished from the garden. Christian theologians see this story as theologically foundational: It explains why there is sin in the world and why a savior and a renewed creation are needed. The story line makes sense, but we have in these three chapters two very different accounts of "the beginning." They are "a literary doublet."[8] In Gen 1, in repetitive and stylized language, God creates everything "good" in six days with the crown of his creative work, the creation of man and woman in his image and likeness. Chapter 2 gives a different account of the beginning in the form of a dramatic narrative interspersed with dialogue filled with symbolic elements (an idyllic garden "in the east," a forbidden tree, a talking snake, woman

6. Köstenberger and Köstenberger, *God's Design*, 23, see also 24.

7. Köstenberger and Köstenberger, *God's Design*, 26

8. Hess, "Equality," 82.

created from the man's side, expulsion from the garden, etc.) presented in seven "scenes," each marked out by a change of actors, situation, and activity.[9] Step by step God supplies what is needed in the garden; first vegetation, then water, then man/'adam to till the ground, and then a partner for him in the woman. In this garden "the serpent" appears and leads the woman and the man to disobey God's command not to eat of the tree of the knowledge of good and evil. The rest of this narrative tells of the consequences of their sin.

These two accounts of creation cannot be simplistically reconciled. Thus, how they are related is possibly the most important issue in establishing what the writer of Gen 1–3 in their present form was seeking to say. The Köstenbergers and I come to opposing conclusions on this matter. They argue that Gen 2 "supplements" Gen 1 by revealing that God has given to men and women "different roles"—to use their terminology.[10] "The man is ultimately responsible for leading in the marriage and the fulfillment of God's mandate [to rule the earth] while the woman is his partner, his suitable helper."[11] In what follows, they make it abundantly clear what they are arguing. Genesis 2 adds something that is *denied* in chapter one. Man and women are *not* essentially/substantially or "functionally"[12] equal, as they agree Gen 1 teaches; the man has the "function" or "role" of leading and directing, and the woman the "function" or "role" of being the man's subordinate helper who must follow his lead.

In stark contrast, I argue that Gen 2 "complements" Gen 1 by giving a second account of creation to make exactly the same point as ch. 1.

---

9. The seven scenes are as follows.
1. 2:5–7: narrative: God the sole actor, 'adam present but passive.
2. 2:18–25: narrative: God the main actor, 'adam minor role, animals passive, woman created to "complete" 'adam, marriage now possible.
3. 3:1–5: dialogue: serpent and the woman in dialogue.
4. 3:6–8: narrative: man and woman on center stage: God absent until the end of the scene.
5. 3:9–13: dialogue: God, man and woman on stage together.
6. 3:14–21: narrative: God main actor, he addresses serpent, woman, and man in that order.
7. 3:22–24: narrative: God the main actor, man and woman passive.
Brueggemann, *Genesis*, 44, speaks of four scenes.
10. Köstenberger and Köstenberger, *God's Design*, 23.
11. Köstenberger and Köstenberger, *God's Design*, 23.
12. Köstenberger and Köstenberger, *God's Design*, 30.

Man and woman are directly created by God in his image and likeness
and thus have the same dignity, status, and ruling function, yet one is
man, one woman. This reading of Gen 1 and 2 as saying the same thing
is how Jesus reads Gen 1 and 2. He quotes from both chapters as if they
are speaking with one voice (Matt 19:4–5; Mark 10:1–9). I think Jesus is
the best guide in how to relate Gen 1 and 2. Pope John Paul II in his binding encyclical comes to the same conclusion. He says, "The text of Gen
2:18–25 helps us understand better what we find in the concise passage
of Gen 1:27–28."[13]

The idea of marriage is mentioned for the first time in Gen 2:24.
Before this point it is man and woman in view not husband and wife. This
means that the Köstenbergers' assertion that Gen 2 primarily teaches "the
man's leadership in marriage and the wife's role as his suitable helper" is
not correct. The man and woman are first and foremost representative
man and woman. Thus if Gen 2 subordinates the woman to the man before the fall, then women in general in all creation, marriage, the church,
and the world are subordinate to men as God's unchanging ideal. This is
what in fact the Köstenbergers believe.

The Köstenbergers' assertion that God gives to man and woman in
Gen 2 different "roles" or functions also needs critical reflection. In complementarian speak the word "role," as we pointed out in the preceding
addendum, is not used as it is in everyday speech to talk about characteristic behavior that can change, but of what essentially differentiates men
and women and can never change, men have the ruling "role," women
the obeying "role." In arguing that Gen 2 distinctively adds the idea that
God has allocated in creation differing "roles" to men and women, in the
way that I have unpacked this term, the Köstenbergers set chapters 1 and
2 in conflict. They say in chapter 1 God gives to the man and the woman
the same ruling "function": "joint dominion."[14] In chapter 2 that God sets
the man over the woman. He gives him the ruling "role"; her the obeying
"role."

---

13. John Paul II, *Mulieris Dignitatem*, 22.

14. Köstenberger and Köstenberger, *God's Design*, 30.

THE AGREED INTERPRETATION OF GENESIS 1

There is virtually no scholarly debate over what Gen 1 says on the sexes. As the pinnacle of his creative work, God creates man and woman. In Gen 1:27–28 we learn four things:

1. God has created one species at the apex of his creative work, humanity, and this one species is either man or woman. Gen 1:27 reads,

> God created the *'adam* in his image;
> In the image of God he created them.
> Male and female he created them.

This verse is a threefold Hebraic poetic stanza. In the first line *'adam* is in the singular, in the second line the plural "them" appears, and in the third line the reason for the plural "them" is made plain, *'adam* is male and female.

The Hebrew "*'adam*" in this stanza must mean "humankind" because the *'adam* is the male and the female. In Gen 2 the word *'adam* can refer to the man in distinction to the woman and later become a personal name for the first man (Gen 4:25) but this does not question the meaning of "humankind" in Gen 1:27. Hebrew has no word for "humanity" other than *'adam*. What Gen 1:27 teaches is that humanity *is* male and female. God created one species, humankind, in two sexes. This means sexual differentiation is creation-given and good. And it implies that the two sexes *complement* each other. Man and woman are humankind; not man alone or woman alone. They are together more than the sum of the parts; they *complete* what it means to be human, especially so in marriage, the most intimate male-female complementary relationship.

I can safely say "the scholarly consensus" is that in Gen 1:27 the Hebrew word *'adam* refers to one species, humankind, that is always male and female. It is hard to see how it could mean otherwise. In their discussion of this text the Köstenbergers begin by affirming the scholarly consensus[15] but then at the end in one paragraph they move to the often-given exotic complementarian interpretation that here the word *'adam* means man (the male) in distinction to

---

15. Köstenberger and Köstenberger, *God's Design*, 28–31 line 8. Following this point they give the complementarian view.

woman.[16] On this view, it is from ʾadam, the man (male), emerge
the male and the female. The Köstenbergers conclude this suggests "male headship."[17] This is not serious scholarship. It is special
pleading.

2. Man and woman alike are made in the image and likeness of God.
This means first of all that man and woman have the same status and
dignity. Any denial of the essential equality of all human beings on
the basis of sexual identity, race, social status, caste, education, or
age is a denial of the God-given status and dignity of every human
being.

3. Man and woman together are to conjointly rule over God's creation.
The Köstenbergers argue that the expression, "made in the image of
God," indicates another truth: man and woman conjointly are given
the mandate "to rule the earth."[18] The God-given status of the man
and the woman makes them both God's vice-regents. I agree with
them, this is certainly the most likely interpretation of what "made
in the image and likeness of God" means, but this joint mandate to
rule is in any case explicitly given to man and woman in the words
following: "God blessed *them*" and said, "Have dominion . . . over
every living thing." In his book, *God, Marriage, and the Family*, Andreas concludes,

> By placing his image on the man and the woman and by
> setting them in a particular environment, therefore, God as-
> signs to them the mandate of representative rule. This rule
> is the joint *function* of the man and the woman.[19]

This is a surprising statement because for him the words "function" and "role" are synonyms.[20] In this comment Andreas is saying
that in creation God gave to the man and the woman the same ruling "role." Later, in the book he writes with his wife Margaret, *God's
Design*, they say the same: "Ruling the earth is a joint *function of*

16. They quote in support Ortland, "Male-Female Equality," 98. This "interpretation" is also given in Grudem, *Evangelical Feminism and Biblical Truth*, 34–36, and
many other complementarian publications.

17. Köstenberger and Köstenberger, *God's Design*, 31.

18. Köstenberger and Köstenberger, *God's Design*, 29.

19. Köstenberger and Jones, *God, Marriage, and the Family*, italics added; Köstenberger and Köstenberger, *God's Design*, 30.

20. Köstenberger and Jones, *God, Marriage, and the Family*, 23, paragraph 3.

the man and the woman. Humanity is conceived as plurality."[21] We agree completely; "Genesis [chapter 1] makes clear that humanity, male and female, was created . . . to rule the earth conjointly as God's representatives."[22]

4. To man and woman conjointly God gives the command "to be fruitful and multiply" (Gen 1:28). This is often called "the family mandate." The first readers of this text were aware, like us, that men impregnate and women get pregnant; procreation involves sexual complementarity, but the Genesis texts says nothing about this difference. What the author of Gen 1 wants to stress is that "the family mandate" is given to man and woman alike. It is a shared responsibility and privilege. Nothing is said about different "roles."

With this fourfold unambiguous and emphatic affirmation of the essential equality of the two differentiated sexes who complement each other ringing in our ears we now turn to Gen 2 and 3.

THE SUBORDINATION OF WOMEN INTERPRETATION OF GENESIS 2-3

It is obvious, as we noted earlier, that we have here a second account of the beginning. On coming to this chapter all evangelicals should be very wary of any interpretation of Gen 2 that denies what is unambiguously taught in chapter 1, namely that man and woman have the same status, dignity, and authority. We evangelicals cannot accept that texts, in this case standing side by side, could be teaching mutually exclusive truths. The Köstenbergers do not see this problem. They argue that Gen 2 "supplements" Gen 1 by introducing the idea of "man's leadership in the marriage and the wife's role as his suitable helper";[23] he is to lead, she obey. This chapter, in other words, teaches something that Gen 1 excludes.

On this interpretation of Gen 2, the Köstenbergers have much support from the past. For centuries, theologians read Gen 2 as "supplementing" chapter 1 in the sense that it added something not said in chapter 1, namely that God has set the man over the woman. Because these men lived in an entirely patriarchal culture, they unreflectingly read Gen 2 to be confirming what their everyday experience was; men rule, women

21. Köstenberger and Köstenberger, God's Design, 30.
22. Köstenberger and Köstenberger, God's Design, 23.
23. Köstenberger and Köstenberger, God's Design, 23, 33

obey. Many details in the story were taken to teach just this. I give the most common *inferences*[24] that were drawn to reach this conclusion, all of which the Köstenbergers endorse. Note carefully the text itself says none of these things; they are *inferences* made by male theologians in past times.

1. The man was created first and this means he is "first" in every way.

2. God created woman as man's "helper" (i.e., a subordinate).

3. Woman was made from and for the man, not vice versa.

4. God gave the command not to eat of the tree of the knowledge of good and evil to Adam, not to Eve, thereby making it clear that he was in charge in the garden.

5. Adam named the animals and Eve. Naming implies "authority over."

6. Eve was the one deceived by the serpent/devil. This demonstrates that women are more prone to sin and deception, and thus need the leadership of men.

7. After they had both sinned God spoke first to Adam, again showing that he had put him in charge.

In the historical and in the contemporary complementarian interpretation of Gen 2 and 3, the punishment God gives to the woman for her sin, namely that she will desire her husband but he will rule over her (Gen 3:16), introduces *nothing* new. Adam ruled over Eve before the fall. Gen 3:16 speaks of an intensification of that rule, or as Knight says, the imposition of an "autocratic and unloving rule."[25]

Absolutely basic to the contemporary complementarian position is the view that before the fall the woman was subordinated to the man, and all or some of the seven historic arguments just outlined are given as proof, admittedly usually worded more euphemistically than in past times. The Köstenbergers endorse and utilize all but number six in their discussion of Gen 2 and 3, and in their discussion of 1 Tim 2:14 they endorse number six.[26]

24. Payne, *Man and Woman*, 43–54, lists and discusses eleven such arguments and then gives twenty statements in Gen 1–3 that depict man and woman as equals (52–54).

25. Knight, "Family," 346.

26. Köstenberger and Köstenberger, *God's Design*, 211.

Because all complementarians ground the subordination of women in creation before the fall, it is for them the God-given ideal, a trans-temporal and transcultural norm. This "theological truth" explains for them everything said about the man-woman relationship in the New Testament. It is the "glasses" they wear to read the Gospels, Acts, and the Epistles.

In responding in some detail to each of these seven arguments for the pre-fall subordination of woman, which I am about to do, I note again first of all that each one of them is an *inference* drawn from details in the story. The text itself says none of these things. Drawing an inference from what is said in Scripture is theologically legitimate if the inference is plausible and it does not directly contradict what is unambiguously said in Scripture. In this case none of these inferences can be endorsed because as we will see they are all implausible and they all directly contradict what is said in the preceding chapter in Gen 1:27–28; namely that God has given to men and women in creation the same dignity, status, and dominion over all living creatures.

THE CONTEMPORARY SCHOLARLY INTERPRETATION OF GENESIS 1–3

The vast majority of scholarly commentaries on Genesis written in the last thirty years[27] and Pope John Paul II, following the best of Catholic scholarship, categorically reject the interpretation of Gen 2 and 3 just outlined. The Pope's interpretation is binding on the almost one billion Catholics. What follows is thus not an idiosyncratic evangelical egalitari-an reading of Gen 2–3, but what most contemporary Protestant scholarly commentators conclude, and what all Roman Catholic theologians teach.

This interpretation of Gen 2–3 presupposes that these chapters *complement,* not contradict, what is said in Gen 1. They do so primarily

27. In post-1980 commentaries see, Brueggemann, *Genesis;* Scullion, *Genesis;* Youngblood, *Book of Genesis;* Arnold, *Genesis;* Maher, *Genesis;* Amos, *Book of Genesis;* Brodie, *Genesis as Dialogue* ; Fretheim, "Book of Genesis"; Clifford and O'Carm, "Genesis"; Towner, *Genesis;* Kessler and Deurloo, *Commentary on Genesis;* Briscoe, *Communicator's Commentary;* Cotter, *Genesis;* Turner, *Genesis;* Hartley, *Genesis;* Walton, *Genesis.* For the same opinion in pre-1980 commentaries see Skinner, *Critical and Exegetical Commentary;* Cassuto, *Commentary on the Book of Genesis;* Vawter, *On Genesis;* Davidson, *Genesis 1–11;* Von Rad, *Genesis;* Speiser, *Genesis.* For virtually the same conclusions as mine on Genesis 1–3, see the essays by Hess, "Equality Without Innocence"; and Brauch, "Genesis."

in two ways. First, chapter 2 complements chapter 1 by *emphasizing* that God has made us man or woman. This is taught in chapter 1; now it is highlighted in chapter 2. The differentiation of the sexes is what Gen 2 emphasizes; it does not introduce the idea that the woman is subordinated to the man. Second, this narrative account of the beginnings complements chapter 1 by explaining why there is evil in the good world God created; why work and marriage have their challenges and why humankind's relationship with God is broken.

Having put aside the old patriarchal glasses, modern scholarly commentators, Protestant and Catholic, with the exception of those of complementarian conviction, are agreed, Gen 1 and 2 alike teach that God has created two sexes of the same dignity and status that complement each other because they are essential equals. The rule of the man over the woman is entirely a consequence of the fall.

Reading the Köstenbergers' book you would never suspect this is the contemporary agreed scholarly interpretation of Gen 1–3. Their "interpretation" of Gen 2 and 3 is given as if everyone is in agreement that the woman was subordinated to the man before the fall. *I find this deliberate ignoring of counter evidence or opinion in this chapter and every other chapter the most objectionable aspect of their book. It is an entirely un-scholarly methodology.*

We now critically assess the seven arguments the Köstenbergers give for the pre-fall subordination of women.

1. *Created second indicates that woman is second in status, or in complementarian terms, has the subordinate "role."* The chronological order in which creation takes place says nothing about who is socially "first." According to Gen 1, man and woman are created last and yet they stand at the apex of God's creative work. In Gen 2 man is created after the earth yet he is set over it. Often what is created second is superior, such as a later model of something. An old joke says, "God created Adam, took one look at him and said, 'I can do better than this,' and created Eve." John Calvin with his usual clear-sightedness said, the argument that woman is second in rank because she was created second does "not seem very strong for John the Baptist was before Christ in time, yet was far inferior to him."[28] Paul once mentions that man was created first, then Eve (1 Tim 2:13), but what he was inferring by this comment is to be

---

28. Calvin, *Paul's Second Epistle*, 217.

found in the literary context in which his words are found—i.e., in 1 Timothy, which we will consider later.

2. *Woman is taken "from man" and "for man."* This argument reflects what Paul says in 1 Cor 11:8–9, echoing exactly rabbinical teaching. In reply, we must first look at what Paul says following in verses 11–12, "Nevertheless, in the Lord woman is not independent of man or man independent of woman. For just as woman came from man so now man comes through woman." This is certainly a balancing comment, if not a self-given, corrective to what he says in verses 8 and 9. Now to the text of Genesis: in chapter 2 the woman is created "for man" because he is helpless and incomplete on his own and "from man" to make the point that she is "bone of my bones, flesh of my flesh"—just like me but woman. Neither of these reasons for why the woman was created *imply* the subordination of women; rather, they *imply* the substantial equality of the two sexes.

The argument that derivation necessarily implies subordination has no force. It is not true. The narrator of Genesis makes it clear that he does not believe this. In Gen 2:5 he tells his readers that "there was no one to till the ground" (*adamah*) and so God formed the *'adam* from the *adamah* (v. 7). Adam's derivation from the earth does not mean he is subordinate to it, just the opposite. What the narrator of Genesis intended to be understood in speaking of woman being made from the *'adam's* "side" is that alike both man and woman are God's creation and alike both have the same dignity, worth, and potential. Indeed many theologians have thought that taken from *'adam's* "side" indicates equality. Peter Lombard, just before he became Archbishop of Paris in 1157, wrote in his famous theological *Sentences*, "Eve was not taken from the feet of Adam to be his subordinate, nor from his head to be his master, but from his side to be his partner."[29] The Puritan commentator Matthew Henry gives the same conclusion in more colorful language.[30]

3. *The woman is created to be man's subordinate helper.* A "helper" is not necessarily a subordinate. Parents help their children.[31] A helper can be a superior, an equal, or an inferior. The Hebrew word *ezer* ("helper") is used twenty-one times in the Old Testament, fifteen

29. Lombard, *Theological Sentences*, 388.
30. Henry, *Matthew Henry's Commentary*, 1, 708.
31. On what follows see Payne, *Man and Woman*, 44–45; Hess, "Equality."

times of God, the sovereign helper of his people, Israel. Nowhere is it used of a subordinate helper. We thus must ask, what sort of helper does God provide for Adam? The text itself tells us that "the helper" is not a superior or a subordinate. The Hebrew word *kenegdo*, which qualifies *ezer*, defines the helper as one corresponding to him—literally "according to, or the opposite of."[32] The two words taken together thus speak of a fitting partner or companion for Adam.[33] The woman is his equal helper. The Köstenbergers' argument that the Hebrew is best translated "man's suitable helper" is unconvincing. Contrary to the evidence, they assert that the Hebrew word *ezer* speaks of a subordinate helper. They do not discuss how the qualifying word *kenegdo* defines the helper and they offer no scholarly support for their conclusions.

In an argument predicated entirely on their complementarian beliefs, the Köstenbergers say the author of Genesis could not be speaking of the woman as the man's *equal* helper because the Bible excludes the idea that "male-female roles [are] reversible."[34] This comment makes no sense. To conclude that Gen 2:18 is speaking of the woman as man's equal helper in no way questions male-female differentiation. The writer of Genesis speaks of Adam as helpless, incomplete, without the woman. The implication is that man and woman need each other to be fully human. Then we have the problem about speaking of irreversible "roles." The word "role" or the idea of "roles" is not found in the text. What justification can be given for introducing this modern sociological term into the exegetical enterprise at this point? None, I suggest. Then we have the problem of the logic of their "role argument." Are they saying that a man should never help a woman or his wife because to do so would be a reversal of male-female roles?

4. *God's command specifically to Adam not to eat of the tree of the knowledge of good and evil indicates that God had placed him in charge of the garden.* The major problem with this argument for male leadership in creation before the fall is that Eve did not exist at that time.

---

32. On the words used and their meaning see Payne, *Man and Woman*, 44–45.

33. Walton, *Genesis*, 177, thinks the best translation would be either "partner" or "counterpart."

34. Köstenberger and Köstenberger, *God's Design*, 35.

Also problematic for this argument is that later the author of Gen 2 and 3 says that the command was given to both of them (Gen 3:1).

5. *Naming indicates "authority over."*[35] This is simply untrue. If this were true Hagar's naming the Lord, *El Roi,* would indicate she had authority over God (Gen 16:13). To name someone or something is to distinguish one from another; to identify a person or place. To name someone "John" means he is not Bill or Mary. In the OT, the giving of a name often signifies something about the person. Jacob is given his name because he grabbed his twin brother's heel at birth and his name testifies to this fact. If name-giving does indicate authority over, it is anomalous that women most commonly name children in the Old Testament.[36] We should also note, in opposition to the Köstenbergers, that in Gen 3:23 Adam does not name Eve before the fall. He simply identifies her as woman (Heb *'ishah*) in distinction to man (Heb *'ish*). It is *after* the fall when he rules over her that he names her Eve (Gen 3:20). This argument that the naming of the animals infers Adam's leadership in the garden should not be accepted by any evangelical. It introduces a contradiction in Scripture. In Gen 1:28, man and woman together are given authority over all the animals. This means, if we do not want to set Scripture in conflict with Scripture we cannot believe that the naming of the animals indicates that man alone has been given the ruling "role" or function. The good thing is that we do not have to believe this because the text of Gen 2 does not say this. This opinion is simply an *inference* drawn by those wanting to support what they already believe.

6. *The serpent tempts the woman and she falls into sin. This demonstrates that women are more prone to sin and deception, and thus need the leadership of men.* If the serpent speaking first to the woman is indicative of something, then the differing order in which the actors come on stage in each scene, something we have noted is characteristic of how this story is told, then the chronological order in which characters appear in each scene would all need to be indicative of something. No one suggests this. We should also note that the narrator explicitly says, "And her husband was with her and he also ate"

---

35. Köstenberger and Köstenberger, *God's Design,* 48–49.

36. There are forty-six examples of child naming in the Old Testament, in twenty-eight cases the mother names the child, in eighteen the father. In Ruth 4:17, the women in the neighborhood name Ruth's son, Obed.

(Gen 3:6). They were both deceived and both disobeyed. A humorous explanation of this mute detail is that the serpent reasoned, "If I can deceive the woman, the man will be a pushover"! He was right. In 1 Tim 2:14, reflecting the situation in the Ephesian church where women had been deceived by the false teachers, Paul says, remember you women, it was Eve whom the devil first deceived.

7. *God addresses Adam first after the fall. This shows that he was in charge and ultimately responsible for their sin.* This inference has seemed compelling to male commentators for centuries and to complementarians today, but it is not. It is only one of many inferences or deductions that could be drawn. We could equally argue that God addressed Adam first because he was most culpable as another human being led him into sin, whereas Eve was less responsible because she was led astray by the serpent, a symbol of the demonic. Or we could infer the order in which Adam appears in this scene is no more significant than the order in which the other actors appear in other scenes.

We should also note that when God asks Adam why he ate of the tree, he replies that it was not his fault but hers. "She gave me the fruit from the tree and I ate" (Gen 3:8–13). In these words, Adam is depicted not as the master in the garden, but as someone weak who does not take responsibility for his own actions.

GENESIS 3:16

What the text of Gen 2–3 explicitly teaches is the substantial equality of the two creation differentiated sexes. The woman is *not* subordinated to the man in God's good creation. The argument that before the fall the man benevolently ruled over the woman and the fall introduces a malevolent expression of this rule, as complementarians characteristically argue, is without merit.[37] The Hebrew word translated "rule" (*mashal*) does not speak of despotic or malevolent rule. The word is frequently used of God's benevolent rule of his people.[38] Genesis 3:16 makes the rule of the man over the woman something new, a distortion or corruption of the perfect coequal relationship that the man and women enjoyed with each other before the fall. The rule of the man over the woman is

37. So Knight, "Family," 346
38. Payne, *Man and Woman*, 51.

depicted as *entirely a consequence of sin* and as such not pleasing to God and definitely not the God-given ideal. It is *descriptive* of life in a fallen world; not *prescriptive*.

The extraordinary thing is that because complementarians get their "exegesis" of Gen 1–3 completely wrong they make what is a consequence of the sin of Adam and Eve, the God-given ideal. What is not good in God's sight they make good. They argue God is pleased to see men ruling over women.

Until the rise of the complementarian movement all commentators took the "desire" of the woman for her husband mentioned in Gen 3:16b to be a desire for intimacy and/or a sexual relationship with her husband. The Köstenbergers adopt a post-1970s novel complementarian interpretation of this word.[39] They take the Hebrew *teshuqah* ("desire") to be speaking of a "desire to control."[40] They thus interpret Gen 3:16 to be teaching that following the fall the woman will "desire" to control her husband and as a consequence the husband and the wife will be caught up in a never-ending struggle. The pernicious logic of this argument is that all or most conflict in marriages arises because women will not submit to the godly rule of their husbands; they struggle against it as sinners. This novel understanding of the woman's desire, so popular among complementarians, has had many critics and recently suffered a death blow. Janson Condren, an Australian evangelical Old Testament scholar, in a compelling journal article, shows that this argument is "fundamentally misguided."[41] It is his conclusion that the Hebrew word *teshuqah* should not be translated as "desire." It speaks rather of "a returning to." Genesis 3:16 is saying, despite the man's rule over her and the pain of childbirth, the woman wants to *return* to her husband, seeking the perfect intimacy she enjoyed with him before the fall.[42]

---

39. First put forward by Susan Foh in her 1975 journal article, "What Is Woman's Desire?"

40. Köstenberger and Köstenberger, *God's Design*, 47–48.

41. Condren, "Toward a Purge." Walton, *Genesis*, 237, independently comes to the same conclusion. Another Australian, Marg Mowczko, has also heavily criticized Foh's argument. See Mowczko, "TESQUQAH."

42. Condren, "Toward a Purge," 244–45.

WHAT THIS ALL MEANS

The Köstenbergers and I are perfectly agreed. In any study of the man-woman relationship the right place to begin is Gen 1–3, and these chapters give the basis for everything else said in the Bible on the sexes. For the Köstenbergers and *all* complementarians, these chapters are of *utmost* importance because for them *their whole case* rests on the argument that in creation before the fall God subordinated the woman to the man. Because this hierarchical ordering of the sexes is located in God's good creation before sin entered the world, they conclude it lays down a trans-temporal and trans-cultural principle. Men are to lead.

What we have discovered is that this argument is special pleading. Genesis 1 and 2 teach the substantial equality of the two differentiated sexes. Genesis 3:16 makes the subordination of woman entirely a consequence of the fall. It is only after they have both sinned that the man begins to rule over the woman. This is not the creation ideal. It reflects life in our fallen world. *I say again, this is not an idiosyncratic egalitarian interpretation of Gen 1–3. It is what the majority of contemporary scholarly Protestant commentators conclude and what all Roman Catholic theologians and biblical scholars teach.*

If this is the case you need not read on. The subordination of women is not grounded in creation; the complementarian position is without any theological basis whatsoever.

A RIGHT INTERPRETION OF GENESIS 1-3 IS THE HERMENEUTICAL KEY TO A RIGHT INTERPRETATION OF ALL THAT THE NEW TESTAMENT SAYS ON THE MAN-WOMAN RELATIONSHIP.

The argument that the rule of the man over the woman is entirely a consequence of the fall and that it is not the creation ideal, is compelling and has extensive scholarly support; nevertheless, we do find Paul exhorting wives to be subordinate to their husbands and some New Testament texts that do or can be read to speak of the subordination of women. What this means is that New Testament texts can be quoted by both sides in support of their position. This has led to what I call a "text-jam" that has made reaching a common mind on what the Bible teaches on the sexes impossible to resolve. This problem must be faced and addressed.

Seemingly conflicting texts is not a problem only in the matter of the status and ministry of women. It is a problem for every doctrine.[43] What systematic theologians seeking to ground any doctrine in Scripture have to do is find what is primary and foundational in the varied comments in Scripture on the matter in focus. This problem was first recognized in the fourth century when Arius and Athanasius found themselves debating what in fact the Bible taught on the divinity of the Son. Arius quoted many texts that did or seemed to subordinate the Son to the Father. Athanasius argued in reply that individual texts must always be interpreted in the theological quest in the light of "the whole scope of Scripture." What Scripture as a whole teaches is Jesus Christ is God and the Lord.[44] To complete his argument Athanasius posited a hermeneutical rule, later Augustine would call it a "canonical rule,"[45] based on what Paul says in Phil 2:4-11. All texts that imply or speak of the subordination of the Son speak of him in "the form of a servant"; all texts that speak of him as God in all majesty, might, and authority speak of him in "the form of God."

When we come to the debate about the man-woman relationship, such a rule is demanded if one coherent doctrine of the sexes is to be given. Genesis 1-3 imply this rule.

All texts that imply or speak of the substantial and essential equality of the two sexes reflect the creation-given ideal; all texts that imply or speak of the subordination of women reflect the fall. They are not the God-given ideal. They either mirror the culture of the time or give practical time-bound advice to women living in a world where their subordination is assumed, or address an exceptional situation where the behavior of some women is causing offence.

All evangelicals who want to uphold the theological unity of Scripture should be pleased to embrace this rule.

QUESTIONS FOR DISCUSSION

1. Discuss the two opposing interpretations of Gen 2-3. Which do you think is the stronger? What fresh thinking or questions have you had as a result of this study?

43. I give the evidence for this assertion in my *Eternal Generation of the Son*, 43-51.
44. Athanasius, "Discourses Against the Arians," 3.29 (p. 409).
45. Giles, *Trinity and Subordinationism*, 74, 82, 99.

2. In the past, when patriarchy was taken for granted, what effect do you think this would have had on male theologians or pastors and on their interpretation of the Bible?

3. What do you think it means for men *and* women to be made in "the image and likeness of God"? How does this idea enlarge your view of humankind?

4. In Gen 1–3 gender equality and differentiation are both affirmed. Does this affirmation of gender difference support the idea that "men are from Mars, women from Venus"?

5. Does anything in modern life suggest to you that God has subordinated women to men?

6. Of what importance is it for evangelicals, Pentecostals, and charismatics that Pope John Paul II in 1987 ruled that the egalitarian reading of Gen 1–3, as outlined above, is binding on all Catholics?

ADDENDUM: MAN AND WOMAN IN THE FALLEN WORLD OF THE OLD TESTAMENT

The Köstenbergers *infer* from the fact that in the Old Testament all the patriarchs, the kings, the priests, and the written prophets were men, the principle of male leadership.[46] In contrast, I infer from these facts that the Old Testament accurately reflects a fallen world where the man rules over the woman. What is more, I am convinced their *inference* is mistaken because the Old Testament does not exclude women on principle from leadership. Below I will give a long list of significant women leaders mentioned in the Old Testament.

To argue that because all the patriarchs were men this signifies the principle of male rule is not much of an argument.[47] It is like saying all circles are round. The word "patriarchy" means the rule of the father, or more generally, the rule of older men. To be called a "patriarch" one had to be a man!

The appeal to the fact that in the Old Testament priests had to be men is also not much of an argument in support of the idea that men only should be leaders for all time among God's people.[48] Men only were

46. Köstenberger and Köstenberger, *God's Design*, 27, 57, 58, 59, 60, 61, 62, 69.
47. Köstenberger and Köstenberger, *God's Design*, 59–61.
48. Köstenberger and Köstenberger, *God's Design*, 64–65.

priests in Israel, but there was a reason for this and it was not the principle of male leadership. The Mosaic faith aimed to exclude any thought that the one and only God, Yahweh, was a fertility God, like the god(s) of their neighbors. In these religions there were women priests who were involved in fertility rites. Why, however, the maleness of the Old Testament priests is important for Christians escapes me. Jesus, the great High Priest, is the end of animal sacrifices and the need for priests to offer them (see the book of Hebrews). In the New Covenant he inaugurated all Christians, men and women, are priests who can come into the presence of God (1 Pet 2:4; Rev 1:6; 5:10; 20:6). Pastors, according to Reformers, are not priests but pastors and preachers. For them, pastors are the counterpart of the prophets, not the priests, and there were women prophets in the Old and New Testaments.

Deborah is the most telling reply to the Köstenbergers' claim that in the Old Testament leadership is a male preserve. She is said to be married, a prophet who speaks for God, and a judge (Judg 4:4). The Köstenbergers do all they can to make Deborah less significant than the text of Scripture indicates.[49] One argument they make to downplay the significance of Deborah is that the word "judge" in the Hebrew does not speak of a judge in the modern sense of this word.[50] I do not know who suggested it did. This comment is a red herring. The Old Testament scholar Daniel Block says, "The 'judges' functioned more as deliverers than as legal functionaries."[51] Then he adds, the Hebrew *shaphat*, "to judge," means "to govern administer, exercise leadership."[52] Like the other male "judges" God raised up Deborah to lead his people in a very dangerous time for them. When Israel is threatened by King Jabin of Canaan, Deborah "summons" Barak and puts him in charge of Israel's army (Judg 4:6). Barak, a renowned warrior, says he will only go into battle if Deborah comes with him (Judg 4:8). He needs her moral and prophetic support. Designating Deborah as a prophet marks her out as a leader among God's people. To be called a prophet, Block says, means the people recognized her as one who speaks for God "in the succession of Moses (cf. Deut 18:15-25)."[53] This high dignity is bestowed on Deborah, a woman.

49. Köstenberger and Köstenberger, *God's Design*, 67-68.
50. Köstenberger and Köstenberger, *God's Design*, 68.
51. Block, *Judges and Ruth*, 23.
52. Block, *Judges and Ruth*, 23.
53. Block, *Judges and Ruth*, 192.

Deborah was a never-forgotten national leader and hero; "the only woman in the distinguished company of the Judges."[54] We have her story in our Bibles to make it crystal clear that God can raise up women leaders and he is pleased to use them and bless their leadership.[55]

In the Old Testament we also find one Queen, Athaliah (2 Kgs 11:1–16). Again I suggest God raised her up to rule over Israel to make it plain that he could appoint a woman to be the ruler of the nation of Israel.

When it comes to prophets and prophecy women are far more prominent and far more significant leaders than the Köstenbergers allow.[56] God raised up prophets to lead his people by speaking for him. They were forthtellers of the word of God far more than foretellers of what was to happen in the future. In other words, they were God-appointed teachers of the people of Israel. Prophets could call priests and Kings to account. Many distinguished women prophets are mentioned in the Old Testament.

Moses' sister, Miriam, is described as a talented musician, a poet, and a prophet who speaks for God. When the Israelites safely made dry land after crossing the Red Sea, we are told "the prophet Miriam" took up a tambourine to rehearse God's mighty acts (Exod 15:20–21). The prophet Micah, looking back at this time, speaks of God "setting before you [i.e., as leaders] Moses, Aaron and Miriam" (Mic 6:40). Deborah, as noted above, is described as a "prophet" (Judg 4:4), a "judge/ruler" (Judg 4:5), a "mother of Israel" (Judg 5:7), and as "the wife of Lappidoth" (Judg 4:4). Huldah, the wife of Shallum, who lived in Jerusalem, is another example of a female prophet. In about 621 BC, King Josiah sent a delegation to her to inquire about "the book of the law" found in the temple during its restoration (2 Kgs 22:14; 2 Chr 34:22). Speaking in Yahweh's name, Huldah prophesied judgment on Jerusalem and Judah following Josiah's death, a prophecy that was fulfilled. Noadiah is another named woman prophet (Neh 6:14). The wife of Isaiah is said to be a prophetess (Isa 8:3),[57] and the prophet Ezekiel pronounces judgment against the daughters of Judah who prophesy falsely "out of their own imagination" (Ezek 13:17). In the Mishnah it is said, "Forty-eight prophets and seven women prophets prophesied in Israel."[58] To point out that all the classical

---

54. Cundall and Morris, *Judges and Ruth*, 82.

55. See the excellent article by Pierce, "Deborah."

56. Köstenberger and Köstenberger, *God's Design*, 66–67.

57. In this instance the title may simply allude to the wife of a prophet.

58. 6 Meg. 14a Bar.

prophets (those who wrote books) were men, as the Köstenbergers do, is of no significance.[59] Prophets like Samuel, Nathan, Elijah, and Elisha were great prophets and yet we do not have books in their name. What this means is that the Köstenbergers' claim that the Old Testament "consistently affirms" the "pattern of male-leadership,"[60] and that women were not in leadership, is simply not true. What we in fact see is a preponderance of male leadership, which is what we would expect in a traditional society and a significant number of women leaders to remind us that God has not excluded women from leadership.

BIBLICAL PATRIARCHY?

The Köstenbergers speak of Israel as a patriarchal society, where men were family, religious and societal leaders,[61] and they argue patriarchy is the biblical norm for all time. It is of concern to them, however that "in our day feminism has widely discredited the term ... by giving it a strongly pejorative connotation."[62] They wonder therefore if it would be better to designate "the normative" biblical pattern, "*patricentism*."[63] They tell us, nevertheless, that they are happy with the word "patriarchy" but what they want to insist on is "that patriarchy as an institution [in the Old Testament] was benevolent and beneficial rather than intrinsically abusive and oppressive."[64] "It provides a positive vision of the father's role as a blessing to those around him" in all cultures in all times.[65] It is what is needed today, says Russell D. Moore who writes in glowing terms of the Köstenbergers book on the first page. In addressing contemporary Christians he says explicitly, and I think the Köstenbergers would agree, "Patriarchy is good for women, good for children."[66]

---

59. Köstenberger and Köstenberger, *God' Design*, 57,

60. Köstenberger and Köstenberger, *God's Design*, 61, see also for the same claim, 57, 58, 59, 64, 69, 76, 77.

61. Köstenberger and Köstenberger, *God's Design*, 60, 61, 75, 76.

62. Köstenberger and Köstenberger, *God's Design*, 60.

63. Köstenberger and Köstenberger, *God's Design*, 60.

64. Köstenberger and Köstenberger, *God's Design*, 60.

65. Köstenberger and Köstenberger, *God's Design*, 61.

66. Moore, "After Patriarchy."

A TRADITIONAL SOCIETY YES, A PATRIARCHAL SOCIETY NO

In my opinion, calling ancient Israel a patriarchal society is not helpful if our goal is to historically and accurately describe family life in Old Testament times.[67] The words "patriarchy "and "patriarchal" were invented by nineteenth century anthropologists to designate societies where men exercised all the power and women were disempowered. This does not describe what we see in the Old Testament. Then we have the problem, as the Köstenbergers point out in relation to its use by some feminists, that it can be used to make sweeping negative evaluations of the lot of women. At the opposite extreme stand the Köstenbergers and many complementarians who use this term in entirely a positive way. Patriarchy is a benevolent institution that brings blessing and dignity to women and we modern Christians would be better off if we practiced it.

In ancient Israel, as in all traditional societies, men were normally community leaders, and certainly men had privileges and freedoms that women did not enjoy, but to argue that as a consequence things were all bad for women or an unqualified blessing has no historical foundation. The reality is much more complex.

When it comes to family life we must recognize that ancient Israel was a nation of farmers. In an agricultural economy the family unit is dependent on every member—each contributes in some way and none are powerless. On the basis of solid archaeological and literary evidence, Carol Myers says that in Old Testament days,

> Women's role in commodity production was essential for household survival, for ancient Israel lacked a developed market economy for most of the Iron Age. Ethnographic evidence strongly suggests that when women dominate indispensable household processes, they are positioned to exercise a considerable amount of household power. Those responsible for preparing life-sustaining food, for example, have a say in household activities relating to both production and consumption. They also control allocation of household space and implements. In short, depending on their age and experience, Israelite women had managerial roles, supervising the assignment of tasks and the use of resources in their own households and, in certain circumstances, across households. To put it another way, senior

67. I here follow Carol Myers, "Was Ancient Israel a Patriarchal Society?" 8–27.

women functioned as the COOs (Chief Operating Officers) of their households. They were hardly oppressed and powerless.[68]

This account of the Old Testament family explains so much of what we read of the ideal wife in Prov 31:10–31. She works from morning to night, managing the household, directing the servants, spinning and sewing, buying a field when needed, selling what the household produces, dispensing wisdom and teaching, and caring for the poor. For her industriousness and management skills her husband "praises her."

What Prov 31:10–31 makes plain is that what the Köstenbergers and other complementarians call the "biblical" understanding of the family and claim is the biblically prescribed "role" of wives, does not reflect anything said or described in the Old Testament (nor in the New Testament, as we will see). It reflects rather their own modern socially conservative conception of how families *should* operate and their ruling premise that God has subordinated women to men. In other words, they read into Scripture their own views.

LIFE FOR WOMEN IN ANCIENT ISRAEL WAS NOT ALL BLESSING OR BANE

The Köstenbergers are, nevertheless, right in saying that communal and family life in ancient Israel, which they call "patriarchal," was not necessarily oppressive for women, or worked always to their disadvantage.[69] Men in this context certainly had precedence and they had privileges and freedoms women did not enjoy. This was how things were. However, as Meyers shows, women had real power, and I would add that the Israelite family, the patriarchal family as the Köstenbergers call it, had rewards for women. The woman's father or husband provided protection and economic security for her and marriage gave women a status single woman did not have.

The problem is that in such societies, men all too often use their privileges and freedom to the detriment of women in general and their wives in particular. They exercise their power for selfish ends and this invariably has awful consequences for women. The Bible makes this

68. Myers, "Was Ancient Israel a Patriarchal Society?" 21.

69. On women in the Old Testament, see Myers, *Discovering Eve*; De Vaux, *Ancient Israel*; Neuer, *Man and Woman*, 81–87.

abundantly clear. The Köstenbergers cannot see this because they are wearing idealized patriarchal glasses.

Let me just give a few examples. The patriarch Abraham takes the slave girl Hagar as a wife when Sarah does not conceive (Gen 16:3). He has the freedom to do this. When Sarah becomes jealous of Hagar, Abraham puts Hagar, the mother of his son, Ishmael, out of his home knowing full well this might mean her death (Gen 21:8–19). This is neither benevolent behavior, nor a blessing for Hagar.

King David had many wives, yet lusts after the "beautiful" Bathsheba, a married woman, and sleeps with her (1 Sam 11:1–12). The Bible makes it absolutely clear that this displeases God, but the point I am making is that David's love life reflects the destructive consequences of male privilege and power. I give another example. In old age David takes "a beautiful" young virgin to bed with him (1 Kgs 1:1–4). She has no say in this; as a single woman she is powerless.

Then we can think of the story of Amnon, David's son, who raped his sister Tamar (2 Sam 13:1–22). His sin is condemned but he continued with his privileged life. In stark contrast, the consequences for Tamar in this traditional culture were devastating and life-long. She becomes a disgraced woman through no fault of her own who can never marry (2 Sam 13:20).

I now add a few other negative consequences for women mentioned in the Old Testament. According to the law, a women could not inherit property, divorce her husband,[70] or be trusted to make a vow (Deut 21:16–17; 24:1–4; Lev 27:1–8). Daughters were considered the property[71] of their fathers and could be either sold into slavery to pay off debt or married for a bride price (Gen 29:1–10; Exod 21:7; Neh 5:5). Wives were considered the property of their husbands, although they held a higher status and more privileges than slaves and concubines (Exod 20:17). Marriages were typically arranged by the father before a girl reached puberty.

The German complementarian Old Testament scholar, Werner Neuer, says, "The generally high place given to women in the Old

---

70. De Vaux, *Ancient Israel*, mentions two exceptions. See Deut 22:13–19; 22:28–29.

71. De Vaux, *Ancient Israel*, uses this term, but he says the bride price (the *moha*) should not be understood as the buying of a wife. Neuer, *Man and Woman*, 86, says, "Legally the man counted as the 'owner' of the wife (cf. Exod 21:3, 22; Deut 24:4; 2 Sam 11:26), and the woman her husband's 'possession' (Gen 20:3; Deut 22:22)."

Testament was spoiled by legal rules and traditions which led to their oppression and denied their equality."[72] They put them at a "disadvantage."[73]

Nowhere is the downside for women in ancient Israelite society seen more painfully than in the case of the widow. When a woman's husband died she found herself in a very precarious situation. She could not support herself and her children because she could not work for a living. The Mosaic Law recognizes this reality and demands that provision be made for widows and others in a similar situation (Exod 22:22–24; Deut 14:29; 16:11, 14; 24:17). This may have kept widows from starving but it did not overcome their unhappy lot in life. The book of Ruth is a story of two widows.

AND LASTLY

The Köstenbergers, along with many other complementarians, may want us to believe patriarchy is prescribed by God and is inherently benevolent, good for women and children, but I am not convinced on either matter. It is certainly good for men—well at least at one level. In patriarchy all the privileges and power are enjoyed by men. I can understand why so many evangelical men want to believe this is what the Bible mandates, but there are three insurmountable problems with his argument.

First, as I have just argued, their understanding of patriarchy has little if any relationship with the historical reality we see in the Old Testament. In ancient Israel women on occasion could be communal leaders and in the home there was a high degree of mutual dependence and women managed daily life; they were the head of the home.

Second, the lot of women in traditional societies and ancient Israel is one example where men have more power than women; women are disadvantaged. Men commonly use their power to further their own ends and women suffer. Benevolence is more the exception than the rule.

And third, we must dispute the Köstenbergers' argument that what is *described* in the Old Testament is *prescriptive* for all places and for all times; or in their terms, the patriarchal family is the God-given norm. This inference is untenable. If everything described in the Old Testament were *prescriptive* for modern life we would need to abandon all the comforts of contemporary life. What is more, we would need to embrace the good and the bad aspects of communal life in ancient Israel.

72. Neuer, *Man and Woman*, 86
73. Neuer, *Man and Woman*, 85.

5

Jesus, the Best Friend Women
Have Ever Had

BEFORE WE LOOK AT what Jesus said and did in regard to women, four
introductory points need to be made.

1. There are compelling arguments for beginning any study of what the
   Bible says on the man-woman relationship with Gen 1–3. There are
   equally compelling reasons when coming to the New Testament for
   beginning with the Gospels. They are placed first in the New Testament because they are of first importance. They give an account of
   the life and teaching of Jesus, the founder of the Christian faith. The
   Köstenbergers agree that the Gospels have a certain priority in New
   Testament revelation.[1] We should not set Jesus and Paul in conflict,
   but if we find tensions between Jesus and Paul, we should read Paul
   in the light of what Jesus says. We are followers of Jesus Christ, not
   of Paul. The teaching of Jesus should have priority.

2. Jesus was a man of his age. He did not drive a car, watch TV, or go to
   shopping malls, and never imagined a time when more women than
   men would have university qualifications, be leaders in all spheres
   of society, and be able to support themselves. In his day, a woman
   was dependent on a man (father, husband, eldest son, guardian)
   all her life. Jesus took for granted the social realities of his day. He
   never questioned arranged marriages or even the law that a brother

1. Köstenberger and Köstenberger, *God's Design*, 80.

76

of a deceased man should take his wife as his own and have children by her (Mark 12:18–23 and parallels). This means we should not depict Jesus as a modern-day feminist.[2] And it means that we should not expect Jesus to say anything on such modern questions as women and higher education, women in the work force, women in business and political leadership, self-supporting single women, let alone women and ordination.[3]

3. What Jesus did was *subvert* the prevailing view of women held by the Jewish leaders of his day. I say the "leaders," because in the daily village life of Palestine in the first century where men and women worked side by side in subsistence farming and in small businesses, male-female relationships were far less structured and prescribed than the rabbis would have liked.[4] It is in this context that most of what Jesus said and did in general, and in particular in relation to women, is to be placed.[5] In what he did and said he affirmed

2. So Elliott, "Jesus was not an Egalitarian." However, Elliott over-states his case. See in reply Beavis, "Christian Origins."

3. Köstenberger and Köstenberger, *God's Design*, 81, say little has been written by evangelicals on Jesus and women. This is simply not true. What is true is that complementarians have shown virtually no interest in Jesus and women, except for the fact that the twelve apostles were all men. Jesus' teaching and example cannot be reconciled with complementarian theology. The Köstenbergers are somewhat of an exception. In Margaret Köstenberger's book, *Jesus and the Feminists*, and in the book *God's Design*, which she and Andreas write, they do consider what Jesus says on women, but as we will see they ignore his most important teaching on women and they domesticate everything else he says on women. On Margaret's book see the review by the New Testament scholar, Aida B. Spencer, "Book Review," 26–29. She calls *Jesus and the Feminists*, "a very simple book" (26). Now to other evangelicals on Jesus and women; my first published journal article was, "Jesus and Women," in *Interchange*, 131–36. In my books, *Women and Their Ministry*, 17–28; *Better Together*, 17–24; and *Patterns of Ministry*, 26–32, I discuss Jesus and women in detail. I have a chapter titled "Jesus and Women," 89–110, in Clifton and Grey, *Raising Women Leaders*. There are in fact many evangelical works on this topic. See Witherington, *Women in the Ministry of Jesus*; Bauckham, *Gospel Women*; Scholer, "Women," 880–87; Spencer, "Jesus' Treatment of Women in the Gospels;" Spencer, *Beyond the Curse*, 43–63; Bailey, *Through Middle Eastern Eyes*, 189–275, etc.

4. In his seminal study on "The Social Position of Women" in Judaism at the time of Jesus, Jeremias in his, *Jerusalem at the Time of Jesus*, 359–76, sets Jesus in contrast with the teaching of the rabbis. These were an elite group of theologians and what they say on women in many cases expresses their views, not the reality of life in first century Palestine villages. The Jewish scholar, Ilan, *Jewish Women,* I think also errs to a lesser extent in doing this.

5. See Kraemer, "Jewish Women."

mutual and respectful relationships between men and women and he excluded any devaluing of women. He never openly denounced demeaning views of women but by his words and actions made them unacceptable to his followers. This is very similar to how he responded to other matters the Jewish leaders held dear; he subtly subverted them. Thus, he did not directly attack the central institutions of Judaism. He did not tell people to keep away from the temple or denounce its worship, but what he taught on the temple undermined its centrality and significance for Christians. He never told his hearers not to observe the Sabbath; but what he said about and did on the Sabbath led the early Christians to abandon Jewish Sabbath observance. He never abrogated the Law of Moses, but he freely interpreted it, majoring on the principles it implied (Matt 5:21–43). It is the same with women. What he said and did undermined the prevailing idea that women were the subordinate sex.

4. Jesus said not one word on how the church was to be organized after his departure to heaven. Church leadership structures were worked out as the church gradually took institutional form in the culture of that time and later. The apostles, we should carefully note, are never depicted as pastors set over congregations. They symbolize that the church, the world-wide Christian community, is the new or restored Israel.[6]

We now turn to the Gospels.

WOMEN DISCIPLES

In contrast to his Jewish counterparts, Rabbi Jesus had female disciples. His call, "Come follow me," was in the first instance addressed to the men who travelled with him as his close companions. He called them "the twelve," "the twelve disciples," and on a very few occasions, "the apostles" (Mark 1:16–20; 6:7; cf. 6:30). However, Jesus also gave the same invitation to men and women without distinction (Mark 8:34). In the Synoptic Gospels, those who accept his invitation to become his disciple are said to "believe" (Mark 1:15; Luke 8:12–13; Matt 18:6). In John's Gospel, a "believer" and a "disciple" are synonymous terms (John 1:12; 2:11; 6:28–29;

---

6. At the end of this chapter I study carefully why Jesus chose twelve *male* apostles.

JESUS, THE BEST FRIEND WOMEN HAVE EVER HAD   79

21:23). The historic disciples were not a "men's club" on a male-only walking excursion: women disciples were numbered among them.

JESUS AND HIS RELATIONSHIP WITH WOMEN

How Jesus related to women, given the cultural context, is astounding. In first century Judaism, men did not talk to women who were not their wives or family in public (John 4:27)—let alone touch them. Jesus freely did both. He healed the woman who breached the purity laws by touching him, offering not one word of criticism of her. Rather than chastising her for her actions, he sent her away with his blessing, "Daughter, your faith has made you well; go in peace and be healed of your disease" (Mark 5:34). Another time, he went gladly to a sick little girl's home, "took her by the hand" and healed her (Mark 5:41). When a Syrophoenician woman begged him to cast out a demon in her daughter, he first rebuffed her because she was a Gentile by saying, "Let the children [of Israel] be fed first, for it is not fair to take the children's food and give it to dogs." To this hard reply to her request she daringly says to Jesus, "Even the dogs under the table eat the children's crumbs" (Mark 7:27–28). Jesus took no offence at her cheeky response to his words. His ego was not dented by the woman answering him back. Rather, he commends her and heals her daughter as she has asked (Mark 7:29). At another time, when he met a grieving mother, "he had compassion on her and said, 'Do not weep.'" He then raised her son (Luke 8:11–17).

JESUS AND WOMEN: FOUR TELLING ENCOUNTERS

When a woman cried out in the crowd, "Blessed is the womb that bore you and the breasts that nursed you," Jesus replied, "Blessed rather are those who hear the word of God and obey it" (Luke 11:27–28). In Jesus' eyes, as important as mothering might be, the highest calling for men and women is to hear and obey the word of God. The Köstenbergers do not mention this important comment by Jesus.

The longest narrative of an encounter between Jesus and a woman is in John 4, which takes place by a well in the village of Sychar, which you can visit today. I have drunk from that well. Jesus spoke with a woman about her life and "living water," revealing himself to her as the Messiah. When the male disciples who had temporarily left him returned, John says, "They were astonished that he was talking with a woman" (John 4:27). Jesus does not discuss with her the weather, the weight of the water jars, or what women should wear. He had a theological conversation with her. This woman then goes to her village and tells the men what Jesus had said. John says, "Many believed in him [Jesus] because of the woman's testimony" (John 4:39). In this passing comment, John allows that women can lead men to faith by preaching. Jesus had no reservations about talking theology with, or evangelizing women, or about women evangelizing men!

The Köstenbergers say, "This narrative really *only* indicates that the woman bears witness to others about Jesus." It "lends support to the notion that women, like men, should passionately share their faith."[7]

Another meeting between Jesus and women was in his visit to the home of Mary and Martha (Luke 10:38–42). When Jesus entered the home, Martha greeted him and got busy with domestic chores. Her sister, in contrast, "sat at the Lord's feet and listened to what he was saying." She took the male *role*, where men sit and listen to guests, while women prepare food in the kitchen. This still happens, I discovered when visiting a home in rural Jordan some years ago. Nothing much has changed. Not surprisingly, Martha became quite angry. She said to Jesus, "Lord, do you not care that my sister has left me to do all the work by myself? Tell her then to help me." Instead of rebuking Mary, as the first readers of Luke's Gospel would have expected, Jesus commended her for choosing "the better part" and chided Martha for being "worried and distracted by many things." This is a story about "role reversal." Joseph Fitzmyer says this story

> makes listening to the "word" the "one thing" needed. Priority is given to hearing of the word coming from God's messenger over preoccupation with all other concerns. Martha wanted to honor Jesus with an elaborate meal, but Jesus reminds her that it is more important to listen to what he has to say. . . . Moreover, Luke in this scene does not hesitate to depict a woman as a disciple sitting at Jesus' feet.[8]

One sits at a teacher's feet to learn, and one learns in order to teach others.

---

7. Köstenberger and Köstenberger, *God's Design*, 103. Italics added.
8. Fitzmyer, *Gospel According to Luke*, 2, 892.

The Köstenbergers tell us that this story tells of "a conflict that arose historically between two sisters," nothing more, and it "illustrates Jesus' affirmation of women receiving spiritual instruction."[9]

Another significant narrative is the account of Jesus' anointing by a woman. This was an important story in the early church; one of the few stories in all four Gospels, albeit in variant forms.[10] Mark sets his version of the story immediately before the Last Supper—thereby adding significance to it—and he has the woman anoint Jesus' head. In the Old Testament, a prophet anointed the head of a Jewish king. The implication is that this unnamed woman prophetically recognizes that Jesus is the long-awaited Messianic king. Jesus is not embarrassed by her action, and allows no criticism of her. He is in fact so taken by her action that he says, "Truly I tell you, wherever the good news is proclaimed in the whole world, what she has done will be told in remembrance of her" (Mark 14:9). Has this been done? No, she has been forgotten. Of the three disciples that figure most prominently in Mark's passion story, one of them, Judas, betrays Jesus. He is remembered today and demonized. Another, Peter, denies him. He is remembered today and lionized. The third, a woman, who publicly anoints him as the Messiah and is commended by him, is not remembered or even named.

The Köstenbergers mention this story once in passing but do not discuss it.[11]

JESUS ON MARRIAGE

Jesus' teaching on marriage is also startling (Matt 19:3–9). When he was asked the androcentric question, "Can a man divorce his wife *for any cause*," he replied by pointing his questioners to the original creation. For Jesus, this gives the God-given ideal before sin entered the world. First, he quotes from Gen 1. He asks them, "Have you not read that the one who made them at the beginning 'made them male and female'" (Gen 1:28). Then he quotes from Gen 2, "What God has joined together let no man separate" (Gen 2:24). This was revolutionary teaching. It made marriage equally binding on the man and the woman. Men have no

9. Köstenberger and Köstenberger, *God's Design*, 105.

10. Matt 26:6–13; Mark 14:3–11; Luke 7:37–50; John 12:1–8. There may have been more than one anointing.

11. Köstenberger and Köstenberger, *God's Design*, 113.

special privileges or freedoms. His questioners then asked him, "Why then did Moses command to give a certificate of dismissal and divorce her?"— alluding to Deut 24:1–4. In reply to this question, Jesus says, "It was because you were so hard-hearted that Moses allowed you to divorce your wives but from the beginning it was not so" (Matt 19:8).

How Jesus deals with this question on divorce is very significant. He answers in terms of the God-given nature of marriage. In doing so he makes a contrast between the creation ideal and the realities of fallen existence, and gives priority to the creation ideal. The creation ideal he locates in Gen 1 and 2. God has created us man and woman and marriage is a lifelong union. This means that neither a man nor a woman should divorce. Men have no special privileges. Moses was simply giving guidelines on what to do when a marriage fails, not endorsing divorce.

What is to be carefully noted is that Jesus quotes from Gen 1 and 2, presupposing that the two chapters are teaching the same on the man-woman relationship. Nowhere in either chapter 1 or 2 of Genesis, as we have shown, is there any suggestion that the woman is subordinated to the man in creation before the fall. It is after the fall that the man begins to rule over the woman (Gen 3:16) and marriages begin to break down. Neither male "headship" nor divorce are conceivable before sin entered the world.

We should also note the hermeneutic Jesus uses. He allows that not every text in Scripture has the same theological weight. He makes the creation ideal given in Gen 1 and 2 weightier than a comment given by Moses dealing with the realities of life in a fallen world.

Jesus' teaching on divorce is hugely important. He wants his disciples to make the creation ideal their ideal for their marriages; a lifelong union between a man and a woman who have the same responsibilities, rights, and privileges.

The Köstenbergers mention that Jesus prohibited divorce but they have no discussion of this text[12] and make no mention of the fact that Jesus parallels the teaching of Gen 1 and 2, or on his hermeneutic.

JESUS ON LEADERSHIP

In the all-too-often heated debate about women in leadership in today's church, many evangelicals argue that women should not be allowed to

---

12. Köstenberger and Köstenberger, *God's Design*, 101, 53.

exercise authority over men, because God has given headship/leadership to men. We therefore ask what would Jesus say to such people? On six occasions, we hear his verbal answer: *those who would lead in my community are to be servants, not rulers* (Matt 20:26–28; 23:11; Mark 9:35; 10:43–45; Luke 9:48; 22:24–27), and once we observe him demonstrating how leadership is to be exercised in his washing of the feet of the twelve (John 13:4–20). He said, unbelievers like to "lord it over others . . . but it is not to be so among you." A leader in my community is "one who serves" (Luke 22:25–26). Evangelicals, who seek to exclude women from leadership in the church, and thus ordination, have completely misunderstood the nature of leadership in the Christian community. They think it is about exercising *authority over* fellow believers, whereas Jesus taught it was about costly, *humble service for others*. Thus, the right question to put to Jesus is not, "Can men *and* women be leaders exercising authority over God's people?" But rather, "Can men *and* women be leaders who give themselves in costly, humble service for God's people?"

The Köstenbergers do not discuss these six or seven texts, although they quote them a few times. Why do they fail to do this we must ask? It is a breathtaking omission. The answer I suggest is that what Jesus teaches on leadership and how the Köstenbergers understand leadership in the Christian community cannot be reconciled. They consistently depict leadership in terms of "authority over," not costly, humble, sacrificial service. True, they speak frequently of "servant-leadership," but in a give-away sentence they tell us how they understand this: "Servant-leadership is biblical, but not a leadership drained of all notions of authority"![13] Christian leaders, they add, "have real authority to which others are called to submit."[14]

JESUS COMMISSIONS WOMEN AS "APOSTLES TO THE APOSTLES"

Surprisingly, the risen Jesus chose to appear first to women whom he then sent to tell the frightened male apostles that he had risen from the dead (Matt 28:1–10; Mark 16:1–8; Luke 24:1–12; John 20:1–18). St. Thomas Aquinas called these women "apostles to the twelve apostles."[15]

13. Köstenberger and Köstenberger, *God's Design*, 188.
14. Köstenberger and Köstenberger, *God's Design*, 189.
15. For the reference to Thomas and the endorsement of Thomas's words by

Noting that Jesus appeared first to Mary Magdalene, the Köstenbergers helpfully say, "By appearing first to a woman, the risen Jesus implicitly challenged the patriarchal culture of his day that did not consider women as viable legal witnesses."[16] I could not say it better.

LUKE AND WOMEN

All four Gospels say something distinctive on women yet they all confirm the fact that Jesus had the highest possible view of women. The Köstenbergers summarize this information in a homely way,[17] and it is done in a scholarly way in a number of other publications.[18] I write here only on Luke's contribution to the Gospel tradition. I agree with the Köstenbergers that Luke adds the most on women.[19]

For centuries it has been noted that Luke is particularly concerned to emphasize Jesus' positive and affirming stance toward women.[20] He names thirteen women who do not appear or are not named in the other Synoptic Gospels;[21] he has three parables that positively mention women not found in the other Gospels;[22] and he gives women a very prominent place in the birth stories.[23] He depicts Elizabeth and Mary as women who speak in the power of the Spirit and explicitly calls Anna a "prophet"

Pope-John Paul II see his, *Mulieris Dignitatum*, 60 and note 38.

16. Köstenberger and Köstenberger, *God's Design*, 107.

17. Köstenberger and Köstenberger, *God's Design*, 108–12.

18. In my chapter on "Jesus and Women" in *Raising Women Leaders*, 104–8, I summarize these findings and reference works on each evangelist.

19. Köstenberger and Köstenberger, *God's Design*, 113.

20. A huge amount has been written on Luke and women. The general consensus is that Luke is consistently positive about women, yet constrained by first-century parameters. Some, however, have challenged this consensus. The most comprehensive bibliography on Luke and women and the most balanced assessment of the debate just mentioned is given by Keener, "Luke's Perspective," 597–638. For a positive view of Luke and women by two Australian scholars who use narrative criticism to show how the many Lukan stories and comments on women cohere, see Forbes and Harrower, *Raised from Obscurity*.

21. Luke 1:5; 2:36; 3:19; 4:26; 7:11–17; 8:1–2; 10:38–42; 11:27–28; 15:8–10; 18:1–8; 24:19.

22. Luke 13:20–21; 15:8–10; 18:1–8.

23. He makes no mention of "the wise men" but he has three "wise women": Elizabeth, Mary, and Anna. They are key players in the Christmas story according to Luke.

(Luke 2:36–38).[24] For him, Mary the mother of Jesus is always strong in faith (Luke 1:26–56; 8:19–21; Acts 1:14). She is "a model believer."[25] In Acts, Luke has the Spirit poured out on men and women believers alike, and as a consequence they alike speak in the power of the Spirit (Acts 2:17–18).

In material unique to Luke's Gospel, we also find a consistent and deliberate pattern of pairing male and female characters,[26] something also found frequently in the Book of Acts.[27] The Köstenbergers list fourteen examples from the Gospel,[28] there are certainly more.[29] We see this pairing in parables (11:5–13 and 18:1–8; 15:3–7; 15:8–10; 13:19 and 13:21), and in healings (4:26–27 and 4:31–39; 7:11–17 and 8:40–56; 13:10–17 and 14:1–6) and also in word ministry. Luke wants to make it clear that both men and women spoke the word of God in the power of the Spirit (Luke 2:25–38; Acts 2:17–18; 21:9–11).The Köstenbergers conclude that this pairing suggests something "similar to Paul's reference to 'no male and female' in Galatians 3:28," which for them only relates to equality in salvation, the spiritual dimension.[30] In contrast, the German theologian Helmut Flender says,

> Luke deliberately extended and developed male-female parallels to emphasize that in the new community founded by Christ man and woman stand side by side before God. They are equal in honor and grace, they are endowed with the same gifts, and they have the same responsibilities.[31]

What Luke says on women is of critical importance. He goes out of his way to mention women and to extol their leadership in deed *and* *word*. In any discussion of what the New Testament says on women, Luke

24. "The Magnificat" is a prophetic oracle (cf. Luke 1:67). On prophecy in Luke's Gospel see Forbes and Harrower, *Raised from Obscurity*, 40–41

25. Forbes and Harrower, *Raised from Obscurity*, 59.

26. Köstenberger and Köstenberger, *God's Design*, 113.

27. D'Angelo, "(Re)Presentation of Women," 183–84, gives nineteen examples. Spencer, "Book Review," 28–29 gives more examples.

28. Köstenberger and Köstenberger, *God's Design*, 114. Luke 1:15–23/1:26–56; 2:25–35/2:36–38; 4:27/4:26; 4:31–37/4:38–39; 6:3–16/8:2–3; 7:11–17/8:40–56; 10:25–37/10:38–40; 11:5–13/18:1–8; 11:32/11:31; 14:1–6/13:10–17; 19:9/13:16; 15:3–7/15:8–10, 13:9/13:21; 24:13–35/24:1–11.

29. D'Angelo, "(Re)Presentation of Women," 182–23, lists eighteen examples.

30. Köstenberger and Köstenberger, *God's Design*, 113.

31. Flender, *St. Luke*, 10.

is a very important voice. He champions the equal status, dignity, and word ministry of men and women. A doctrine of male headship not only cannot be found in Luke-Acts, it is antithetical to the author's whole way of thinking about men and women in the Kingdom of God that has dawned in the death and resurrection of Jesus Christ and the giving of the Holy Spirit to all God's people.

Luke contributes almost a third of the New Testament. His voice must be given a hearing in any discussion of *what the Bible actually teaches about women.*

JESUS WAS A MAN

I must mention, as I draw this chapter to a conclusion, one argument the Köstenbergers put in support of the abiding principle of male leadership that does not arise from anything said in the Gospels.

They argue *the fact* that Jesus was a man, not a woman, is of profound theological significance. From it they *infer* male headship.[32] This *inference or deduction* is not endorsed by orthodox theologians writing on Christology. Their conclusion is given by the Köstenbergers themselves in a sentence that stands counter to their thesis, "It was Jesus' humanity, not his maleness that was essential for our salvation."[33] For Athanasius, Jesus is designated "the Son" because a son implies a father, and sons and fathers are of the same nature or being.[34] When it comes to the title "Son" (of God) in the Gospels, this title identifies Jesus Christ as the long-awaited messianic Son of the King of Kings, who is destined to rule forever in all might, majesty, and power.[35]

To be the incarnate Son of God Jesus had to be a man or a woman, and for reasons not revealed, he was a man. This *fact* does not *imply* God has a preference for men. This would be bad news for women.

WHAT IS NOT SAID IN THE GOSPELS

What we *do not find* on the lips of Jesus, or on the pages of any of the four Gospels, is one word on "male headship." The idea is never mentioned

32. Köstenberger and Köstenberger, *God's Design*, 82–83.

33. Köstenberger and Köstenberger, *God's Design*, 83.

34. Giles, *Jesus and the Father*, 136.

35. Frame, *Doctrine*, 658.

explicitly or implied by any of the teachings or stories we have just discussed. What is more, a fair reading of the Gospels shows that much of what Jesus said and did implicitly excludes this idea. When it comes to church leadership, Jesus again says not one word on who should or should not lead but in prescribing leadership in his community in terms of lowly, costly service he undeniably threw open the door to women. They seem to be better at serving than men! In reply complementarians cry out in anguish, "But Kevin, what about the twelve apostles, they were all men?" To this matter we now turn.

THE TWELVE APOSTLES WERE ALL MEN

The twelve apostles were all men; this is a historical fact. The dispute is over the significance of this fact. What should be *inferred* from this moot fact?

In the many books I have on my shelves written by complementarians almost without exception they say little if anything on Jesus and women, except for one matter, the twelve apostles were all men. The Köstenbergers' book on this matter and many others stands apart. They have a whole chapter on Jesus and the Gospels, even if they shamelessly depict the Savior as a nice man who speaks respectfully to women while always upholding the principle of male headship. For them, the principle of male leadership is unambiguously underlined and endorsed by the fact that Jesus chose twelve apostles who were all men. They give more space to this matter than any other in their chapter on Jesus and the Gospels—not surprisingly, for this issue is of huge importance for their case.

No one ever has disputed the twelve were all men. What evangelical egalitarians dispute is that this *implies* the principle of male headship. They think the appointment of twelve men *implies*, rather, a traditional culture where men were usually leaders in the public sphere. In the ancient world and up to very recent times, men were leaders in the home, the church, and the state. They therefore see nothing noteworthy in the fact that Jesus chose twelve men to be the nucleus of the new community he was founding.

What complementarians need to do to substantiate their distinctive *inference* is to give some evidence that Jesus taught or endorsed the principle of male leadership—and that is what they cannot do. Jesus never said, "I am choosing twelve men to be my apostles *because* I believe men should be leaders." What he said and did *implies*, rather, that he believed men and women were of the same dignity and status and had the same leadership potential. Not once does he mention, let alone endorse, "male headship," and much of what he said and did suggests he did not accept this idea. This means their *inference* runs counter to what is revealed in the Gospels.

Before considering specific reasons why Jesus chose twelve men to be his first apostles we must make a clear distinction between what Jesus did *and* taught. Jesus travelled mainly by foot, but this does not indicate that he was opposed to other forms of travel. Jesus dressed like other men of his day but this does not mean we must dress like him. Jesus chose twelve men who were all Jews, but this does not prove that all priests/pastors must be Jews. What Jesus *did* is not prescriptive; his teaching is. If Jesus wanted his future followers to understand that only men should be leaders in the community he founded, we would expect him to *say* something on this. He never does; not one word.

There are a number of concrete reasons why Jesus chose twelve men and no women. I give a number of them, all of which I think played a part.

1. To be numbered among the twelve, Luke says, one must have followed Jesus from the time of his baptism until his ascension (Acts 1:21–22)—to have been his constant companion throughout his ministry. In the cultural context of first century Judaism, it was not possible for women to travel for weeks on end and to sleep, often in the open, with men. Luke, it is true, speaks of women literally following Jesus (Luke 8:1–2); but possibly this was only while he was in a town or moving from one town to another.

2. Luke says the most about the twelve apostles, asserting that their primary work was *to bear witness* to the ministry, teaching, death, and resurrection of Christ (Luke 24:48; Acts 1:21–23; etc.). In Judaism, the witness or testimony of women in support of factual matters was generally rejected.[36] The Köstenbergers concede this fact.[37] Thus Paul, when recounting the resurrection witnesses in 1 Cor 15:5–11, does not mention the women who were first to the empty tomb and first to see the resurrected Christ. For this reason, to appoint women as factual witnesses was not an option for Jesus.

36. See Ilan, *Jewish Women*, 163–66.
37. Köstenberger and Köstenberger, *God's Design*, 113.

3. The twelve apostles had to be men because, for Jesus, the number twelve indicated that he was calling into existence the new or restored Israel, the church (Matt 19:28; Luke 22:30).[38] If his Jewish audience were to see this symbolic paralleling, the twelve had to be men like their Old Testament counterparts—the twelve sons of Israel. In this symbolism the twelve are not proto-pastors but proto-church. Their maleness is not what is important; it is that they are *twelve in* number.

4. Lastly, I raise a somewhat humorous objection to the argument that the maleness of the twelve is prescriptive of which gender should be in church leadership. In Acts 6:3, Luke says that the apostles recommended that seven *men* (Luke uses the specifically male term, *anēr*) should be appointed to manage the food for the Hellenist widows. If the maleness of the twelve apostles is *prescriptive for church leadership*, then is the maleness of the seven who were to look after the food supplies also prescriptive? Men and men only are to *man* the church kitchen?

Any appeal to the fact that the twelve were all men to prove that Jesus endorsed the principle of "male headship," is special pleading. This *inference* runs counter to what Jesus plainly says and does in regard to women.

THE RESTORATION OF EDEN

What we have learned from our study of the Gospels is that Jesus related to women as if the fall had never taken place. He saw them as they were created by God, standing alongside man, head erect, with the same dignity and leadership potential as men (Gen 1:27–28). The idea of a pre-fall subordination of women that reveals an abiding principle that men should lead finds no place in his teaching, and much to the contrary. He says not one word on male headship. The theologian Helmut Thielicke explains why:

> According to the Synoptics [the first three Gospels] Jesus dealt with women as human beings or sisters. When he addressed them, as they were originally meant to be in God's creation, he was looking beyond the disturbed relationships spoken of in the

38. The Köstenbergers agree. See Köstenberger and Köstenberger, *God's Design*, 94

story of the fall. . . . The despised status of women in rabbinic
Judaism, as well as in the contemporary Greek world is actually
a kind of paradigm of this disturbance of the created order of
the sexes, and Jesus' attitude to it is really a protest against it.[39]

FINALLY, I COMMEND THE KÖSTENBERGERS FOR INCLUDING A CHAPTER ON JESUS AND WOMEN, BUT WITH RESERVATIONS

I commend Andreas and Margaret for including a chapter on Jesus and
women. This is a topic most complementarian books avoid completely,
mentioning only that Jesus chose twelve *male* apostles. The problem with
their chapter is that the Jesus they speak of, who they confess as the Son
of God, never challenges the views on women that they already hold.
Anything he says or did that could disturb their complementarian view
of women is ignored or "domesticated." Paradoxically, they say, "domesti-
cating" what the Bible says "is a form of abusing God's word by robbing it
of its authority."[40] They are deaf to the fact that the Gospels, in their own
words, "may be saying something other than what [they] already believe"
about women.[41]

ADDENDUM: THE AUTHORITY WE SHOULD SEEK

As I have just noted, on six occasions, Jesus said, *those who would lead
in my community are to be servants, not rulers* (Matt 20:26–28; 23:11;
Mark 9:35; 10:43–45; Luke 9:48; 22:24–27), and once he illustrated this
principle by his own actions in washing the feet of his disciples (John
13:4–20). Unbelievers, he said, like to "lord it over others . . . but it is
not to be so among you." A leader in my community is "one who serves"
(Luke 22:25–26).

Jesus contrasts two types of leadership—one where someone has
power over people, demanding obedience, and servant leadership, where
power over others is not involved. The former, Jesus says, is how leadership is exercised in this fallen world; the latter should be how leadership

---

39. Thielicke, *Ethics of Sex*, 8.
40. Köstenberger and Köstenberger, *God's Design*, 326.
41. Köstenberger and Köstenberger, *God's Design*, 326. I quote their own warning.

is exercised in the Christian community. Many Christians, especially evangelicals of Reformed persuasion, somehow cannot hear what Jesus is saying on leadership. They believe God has given to husbands in the home and pastors in the church *power over* those they lead. So the Köstenbergers say, "Servant-leadership is biblical, but not a leadership drained of all notions of authority."[42] Christian leaders have "real authority to which others are called to submit."[43]

In the early nineteenth century the brilliant pioneer sociologist Max Weber (1864–1920) argued that leadership can be expressed in one of two ways—by exercising power over others or by an innate authority that others recognize.[44] Leadership predicated on power commands and others must obey. Employers, managers, officers in the army, policemen, and parents of young children exercise this kind of power. The leader who exercises power says, "Do as I command, I am in charge around here, I will tell you what to do." Or, "I am the pastor, you need to accept what I say and teach." "I am your husband and 'head': do as I ask you." Leadership expressed as power needs no legitimation. People believe the one exercising power should be obeyed and there will be dire consequences if obedience is not rendered.

Leadership based on innate authority is different: it is something recognized and freely accepted. It evokes in others a desire to follow and listen. It is transactional. One person exercises leadership and others accept it gladly. Jesus exemplified and commended such authority. He was not a recognized rabbi, and he was not an old man or of noble birth, who could expect to be obeyed. He could not impose his views and wishes on others; yet when he spoke, people recognized an authority that could not be ignored (Matt 7:29; Mark 1:22; 1:27).[45] People heard him speak, and those with ears to hear wanted to follow him and do as he said. This kind of authority implies respect and influence.

Weber said that authority, unlike power, needs legitimation. People must recognize in some way the person leading is legitimately leading.

42. Köstenberger and Köstenberger, *God's Design*, 188.

43. Köstenberger and Köstenberger, *God's Design*, 189.

44. See Weber, *Economy and Society,* and the helpful introduction to his work by Parkin, *Max Weber.*

45. It is also to be noted that the Gospels also use *exousia*/authority to mean "power over." So the rulers of this world are said to have "authority over" others (Matt 21:23; Luke 9:1; 19:17; 20:20; 22:25) and Jesus gives his disciples "authority over" sickness and demons (Matt 10:1; Mark 3:15; Luke 9:1).

Legitimation, he argued, may be given in one of three ways, although he accepted that in real life a particular leader may have a combination of these three. In traditional societies, noble birth or age gives people authority. In bureaucracies, legitimation is by appointment: someone high up says who shall lead and others accept this directive. Third, Weber spoke of "charismatic" authority signaled by a compelling personality. Subsequent discussion has added "expertise" as an important legitimating factor. People accept the leadership of those who they believe know what they are talking about. I would add moral qualities, especially when it comes to leadership in the Christian community. People accept the leadership of those who exemplify the values and virtues they espouse.

What confuses matters is that in everyday English the words "power" and "authority" can be used synonymously. We can say a policeman has power or authority over the public, and mean the same thing. We see this confusion when we speak of "coercive authority." In Weber's terms, this is power.

Making a contrast between *extrinsic* and *intrinsic* authority solves this problem. "Extrinsic authority" is, in Weber's terms, the exercise of power. One person commands and others obey. "Intrinsic authority," on the other hand, is what Weber calls, without any qualification, "authority." One person exercises leadership and others freely accept this leadership because they think it is "legitimate" authority.

THE AUTHORITY OF PASTORS, HUSBANDS, AND WOMEN

When the Köstenbergers speak of the authority God has given to men, and excluded to women, they always have in mind extrinsic authority—power over others. Wives should do as their husbands ask, pastors should be obeyed and women should not preach or lead churches because God has forbidden women authority in the church (quoting 1 Tim 2:12). In exercising extrinsic authority, one person plays the role of the parent and others play the role of the child. I read Jesus to be saying this kind of authority is not an option for his disciples. Leaders are to be servants, not seeking power over others but serving them.

In giving ourselves in service of others we gain intrinsic authority. A husband who gets up to a crying baby at night, cleans the toilet, puts his income into a joint account, never speaks in a derogatory way to his wife, and listens to her views, has intrinsic authority. His wife wants to do as he asks, and he will do what she asks because of his respect for her and her influence over him. Pastors who visit the sick and troubled, play with children, speak nicely to people, are not judgmental and harsh, are genuinely prayerful, know the Bible well, and show psychological and spiritual maturity, have intrinsic authority.

When people see these qualities in their pastor(s), they respect them, listen to and learn from their sermons, and gladly follow, recognizing their (intrinsic) authority. I know this to be true from forty years as a pastor. This authority is earned, not given by ordination or by ecclesiastical appointment. It is earned by years of faithful ministry. One of the Alban Institute books is titled, *Growing in Authority, Relinquishing Power.*[46] These words capture what pastoring is all about.

Finally, we come to the authority women may rightly exercise in the home and the church. Nothing in Jesus' teaching affirms the exercising of *extrinsic* authority by men or women in the home or in the church. What Jesus wants to see in his community, in men and women, is *intrinsic* authority. Disciples who set an example of self-giving service, humility, godliness, prayerfulness, and love that others want to follow. Women and men should both seek this kind of authority.

Far too many evangelicals, and virtually all complementarians, have got it wrong. They think God has given to men "power over" their wives and pastors "power over" their congregations. They exclude women from exercising such power. In reply to them, Jesus says in effect, "You're mistaken. If you want to be my disciple, leadership is about costly service. In my community don't seek power over others. It is the same for my male and female disciples."

46. Hahn, *Growing in Authority.*

6

Was Paul a Misogynist?

POSSIBLY NO ONE HAS had more bad press than St. Paul when it comes to women. He is often accused of being a misogynist. Did he not tell women to cover their heads and keep silent in church and submit to their husbands, and suggest that women are more prone to sin than men? If this is what he said, from a twenty-first century perspective, most would say "guilty as charged." The problem is that Paul was a first-century man and the evidence brought forward is very one-sided. He also said things about women no one except Jesus had ever said. In many ways, as far as women are concerned, he was revolutionary in his teaching and practice.

PAUL ON THE CHRISTIAN LIFE IN THE "IN-BETWEEN" TIMES

Paul was never in doubt that he lived in a fallen world. Life was hard and brutal for most people. Life expectancy was short and any injury or illness could spell death. A very few were privileged and held great power; most people were relatively powerless. About a third of the population in the Roman Empire were slaves. When the Roman legions went to war, those captured were made slaves, sold like cattle, and were forced to work by the whip. Most women were restricted to the home in towns, but in this context they exercised a lot of authority. They managed the affairs of the home.[1] Women as a general rule were not educated, except in

---

1. See following in this chapter my discussion on the home in the ancient world.

94

domestic duties. Their husband was chosen for them and they had to obey him. Wealthy women, especially wealthy widows, in contrast, had freedoms that other women did not enjoy. They managed business, were "the head of their home" and were often patrons with men and women dependent on them.[2] Phoebe was such a woman (Rom 16:1); Lydia was another (Acts 16:11–15). Possibly most, or at least many, of the women Paul singles out and commends for their ministry were such women.[3]

It was in this world that Paul lived and ministered; yet after his encounter with Jesus Christ on the Damascus road, he knew that God was at work to change this world for the better. In the death and resurrection of Jesus Christ and the giving of the Holy Spirit a new age had dawned, or as he called it, "a new creation" that awaited a final consummation (2 Cor 5:17; Gal 6:15). In all of Paul's writings and theology, we find a tension between the now and the not yet. His is a theology of the "in-between times." In this present time, the believer and the church know in part the blessings of the new creation; but they also know the struggles and frustrations of living in this fallen creation. Paul recognized that for the Gospel to succeed the early Christians had to accept the taken-for-granted social realities of their day.[4] So we note he never denounced the institution of slavery. Rather, he exhorted Christian slaves to accept their lot in life, albeit asking their Christian masters "to treat their slaves fairly and justly" (Col 4:1). Similarly, he exhorted Christian wives to be subordinate to their Christian husbands, albeit asking these men to love their wives like their own bodies (Eph 5:28, cf. Col 3:18). We can thus rightly say Paul accepted the subordination of women and slavery as taken-for-granted facts of life in the first century yet, as we will see, sought to subvert these cultural norms in his teaching and practice. In this chapter, I discuss two examples where Paul does this, first in gender relations and second in ministry. In the next chapter I discuss a third example, Paul's attempt to transform marriage into an equal partnership. What is said in this chapter and the next will show that Paul was not, in regard to women, an uncritical supporter of the status quo, let alone a misogynist.

---

2. On patronage in general and women as patrons in particular see Cohick, *Women in the World of the Earliest Christians*, 285–320.

3. See further, Cohick, *Women in the World*.

4. Westfall, *Paul and Gender*, 13.

PAUL'S THEOLOGY OF LEADERSHIP IN THE CHURCH

In 1 Cor 12–14, Rom 12:3–8, and Eph 4:11–12 Paul spells out his theology of ministry.[5] Peter is of much the same opinion (1 Pet 4:11–12). Paul is emphatic: all ministry flows from the empowering and enabling of the Holy Spirit. He says to "each is given a manifestation of the Spirit for the common good" (1 Cor 12:7), meaning that a ministry is given by the Spirit to every believer, for the building up of the church (1 Cor 14:1–5). It is impossible to read into Paul's theology of ministry any social, racial, or gender issues. For Paul, the Spirit is non-discriminatory in bestowing the spiritual or grace gifts (*charismata*) that make ministry in the church possible. In each of the passages listed above, Paul likens the church to a human body where each part has a contribution to make of equal value. One is like a foot, another a hand, another an eye—and one cannot do without the other. I say again; it is impossible to read racial, social, or gender issues into this teaching.[6] Spirit-gifting is the sole basis for all ministry/leadership.

He names about thirty ministries but it is clear that his lists of ministries are not exhaustive. Any ministry that builds up the church he would be glad to call a *charisma*—a gift of grace. Helping, encouraging, giving generosity are gifts and so too are teaching, prophecy, and apostleship (1 Cor 12:27–28). His theology of ministry does not envisage one person out front as "the minister" or pastor who does all the more important ministry. This is a much later development not envisaged in the New Testament.

Paul avoids giving people lofty titles, so common in the Greco-Roman world and in the Judaism he knew.[7] A leader is for him a servant—a *diakonos*. This word immediately catches our attention. In the footsteps of his master, Paul defines all leadership in the Christian community in terms of *diakonia*/service. He uses the *diakon* . . . words about forty times. A number of these references link the *diakon* . . . words with preaching, and so table waiting is not in mind, but in all of them the cost of ministry is in the foreground.[8] Paul's acceptance of his lowly status as a servant of

5. See my 250-page book, *Patterns of Ministry*, for more on church and ministry in the apostolic age.

6. In more detail see Giles, *Patterns*, 33–41.

7. Giles, *Patterns*, 34–36.

8. Collins, *Diakonia*, argues that *diak* . . . word group does not have as its primary meaning, "waiting on tables," and thus humble service, but he concedes that on the lips

Christ is shown in his willingness to speak of himself as a slave (*doulos*) (Rom 1:1; Gal 1:10; Phil 1:1; Col 1:7; 4:7; Titus 1:1). In the Greco-Roman world, slaves were right at the bottom of the social order.

We can only understand Paul's theology of ministry when we understand that in the first and second centuries virtually all Christian gatherings were in homes and the large home of a wealthy person would have held at the maximum forty people. Probably most house-churches would have had about a dozen in attendance.[9] When Paul writes to the church (*ekklesia*) in Corinth, Thessalonica, or wherever he is addressing all the Christians in that city who met in little house-churches.[10] The house-church setting determined to a large degree what took place when the church assembled. It encouraged wide participation and informality. In this setting the gifts of ministry he lists were exercised, especially that of prophecy and the testing of prophecy by those who heard the prophecy (1 Cor 11:4–5; 14:1–39; 1 Thess 5:19–20). This context explains why Paul so often speaks of people ministering to one another.[11] In house-churches, the Lord's Supper was celebrated in the context of a shared meal (1 Cor 11:17–22). This made church a bit like a dinner party. No one person was the counterpart of the pastor of today. Pastors and teachers (in the plural) are one of the Spirit-given ministries given to the church along with apostles, prophets, and evangelists (Eph 4:11). Declarative, half hour long sermons by a trained pastor do not fit this house context. If someone came with teaching (1 Cor 14:26) it would have been discussed and questions asked (1 Cor 14:35).

Amazingly, the Köstenbergers make no mention of Paul's charismatic understanding of ministry or of the fact the early Christians met in homes in small numbers. This is a very serious omission but what is worse is that because they fail to acknowledge these facts they read into

---

of Jesus and Paul it does speak about lowly service. See further Giles, *Patterns*, 80–81.

9. On house-churches see, Giles, "House Churches"; Gehring, *House Church and Mission*; Simson, *Houses that Change the World*; Banks, *Going to Church in the First Century*; Banks and Banks, *Church Comes Home;* Osiek and McDonald, *Woman's Place*; Campbell, *Elders*, 117–18, 151–52; Osiek and Balch, *Families in the New Testament World*; Verner, *Household of God*; Adam, *Earliest Christian Meeting Place*

10. For more on this see, see Giles, *What on Earth is the Church?*

11. Paul, or one of the other apostolic writers, tell the recipients of their epistles to minister to one another (Gal 5:13; cf. 1 Pet 4:10); to build up/encourage one another (Rom 14:19; 1 Thess 4:18; 5:11; cf. Heb 10:25); to instruct/teach one another (Rom 15:14; Eph 5:19; Col 3:16); to speak the truth to one another (Eph 4:25; Col 3:1); to bear one another's burdens (Gal 6:2); to care for one another (1 Cor 12:25); etc.

the New Testament their own modern cultural understanding of church and church leadership and then appeal to this to support their conclusions on what should be prescriptive for church life today. The result is that what they claim the Bible teaches on leadership in the church is in fact what they believed before they turned to the New Testament.

The Köstenbergers' primary thesis is that the Bible consistently "exhibits a pattern of male leadership."[12] We have seen that the text of the Old Testament excludes this conclusion and nothing in Jesus' teaching supports this thesis. The Köstenbergers claim Paul similarly endorses "a pattern of male leadership."[13] They frequently speak of "Pauline circle" of predominantly male leaders.[14] They say, "it is clear that the nucleus of Paul's missionary leadership team was composed of "faithful men" (2 Tim 2:2)." We now examine this argument.

PAUL'S PRACTICE OF MINISTRY: HE ENDORSES THE LEADERSHIP OF WOMEN

Paul's *practice* of ministry reflects closely his *theology* of ministry. The number of women in leadership in the early Pauline churches, given the cultural context, is breathtaking. Nowhere is this more obvious than in the sixteenth chapter of his epistle to the Romans. In this chapter, he mentions ten women; he names eight of them, and commends the ministry and leadership of seven. Most of them were almost certainly women of some social standing.[15] If we consider all the early Paulines, more than one-quarter of the leaders Paul mentions by name are women, twelve in number.[16]

Phoebe: Romans 16:1–2

Phoebe is mentioned at the head of the list and singled out for extended commendation (Rom 16:1–2). Paul warmly speaks of her, asking that the

12. Köstenberger and Köstenberger, *God's Design*, 69, 74, 115, 121, 190, etc.

13. Köstenberger and Köstenberger, *God's Design*, 121, 190.

14. Köstenberger and Köstenberger, *God's Design*, 123, 124, 125, 132, 143, 144, 157.

15. So Köstenberger and Köstenberger, *God's Design*, on Lydia, 138–39, and on Phoebe, 150.

16. Gehring, *House Church*, 211.

church in Rome receive her. It is likely he commends her first because she is to carry his epistle from Corinth to Rome.[17] Letters in the Roman Empire were generally personally delivered. There was no public mail system.

The Köstenbergers rightly say, "Phoebe was clearly a woman of some importance and stature."[18] The two titles Paul gives to Phoebe indicate that she was not just an ordinary female member of the church at Cenchreae, the eastern port city of Corinth. Paul calls her a *diakonos* and a *prostatis*. The first term is correctly translated "deacon" (the feminine form "deaconess" does not appear in the New Testament). What this title implies at this point of time is disputed but we need to note that Paul calls himself and Apollos *diakonoi* (1 Cor 3:5) and he gives this title to Tychius, Epaphras, and Timothy (Eph 6:21; Col 4:7; 1:7; 1 Thess 3:2; 1 Tim 4:6). I thus argue it is best to translate this word as we would if a man was so designated. She was "a minister": *a servant leader* in the church at Cenchreae. I am not suggesting she was *the* pastor of the church in Cenchreae; churches led by one person of any name were unknown in the first century. What I am arguing is that this title marks her out as church leader.

Second, Phoebe is designated a *prostatis*. This is the only time this noun is used in the New Testament. Literally the word means "to stand before." It speaks of someone in a leadership position. Verbal forms of this word are frequently used by Paul to designate church leaders.[19] Shortly before in Romans 12:28, he speaks of "those in leadership (*ho proistamenous*). The noun in extra-biblical literature is often used of presidents of associations.[20] The word in this context, may, however, mean "patron." A patron was someone of some social standing who aided others by providing such things as housing, financial support, and by representing their interests before local authorities. Patrons were prominent and well-to-do citizens, and they could be women. Many synagogues had patrons, a few women. The best conjecture is that Phoebe was a house-church leader and as such was seen as the patron of the Christians that met in her home.

17. Moo, *Epistle*, 913; Köstenberger and Köstenberger, *God's Design*, 150.

18. Köstenberger and Köstenberger, *God's Design*, 150.

19. Rom 12:8; 1 Thess 5:12; 1 Tim 3:4, 5, 12; 5:17.

20. See Payne, *Man and Woman*, 63.

Priscilla: Romans 16:3–5

The next woman mentioned in Rom 16 is Priscilla (Paul always gives her the more respectful name Prisca),[21] along with her husband Aquila. Professor Murphy O'Connor calls them "the most prominent couple involved in the first century expansion of Christianity."[22] Defying cultural custom, Priscilla is named before her husband in four of the six references to them (Acts 18:18, 26; Rom 16:3; 2 Tim 4:19). This unusual detail must mean that she had some preeminence in the marriage. This may have arisen because she came from a noble family, or because she was the stronger Christian leader in this couple relationship, or both. Her giftedness in ministry certainly seems to have been a factor. In the four places she is mentioned first, the ministry of the couple is in focus. This suggests that she took the lead in instructing Apollos because she is named first in this story (Acts 18:18, 26). The Köstenbergers say it is "a fact that this instruction of Apollos took place in a private setting," by which they mean a home.[23] They make this point to discount the significance of Pricilla teaching Apollos. This teaching did not take place "in a public setting," a church gathering.[24] "A woman may instruct someone privately as long as their husband is present"[25]—this is of course their view; Paul does not say this. They seem oblivious of the fact that all church gatherings were in homes. Later they discount their own argument by saying, "Wherever this couple went they had a church meeting in their home [in which] they taught people such as Apollos."[26] In Rom 16:5 Paul speaks of the church in "their" home, using the plural form of the possessive pronoun (cf. 1 Cor 16:19). Priscilla and her husband Aquila were the co-leaders of their house-church.

Paul calls this couple "*sunergoi*" (fellow-workers or coworkers), saying "they risked their necks for my life" (Rom 16:3). Paul uses the same noun, *sunergoi*, of outstanding male leaders: Timothy (Rom 16:21), Apollos (1 Cor 3:9), Titus (2 Cor 8:23), Epaphroditus (Phil 2:25), Clement and others (Phil 4:3), and Urbanus (Rom 16:9). For this woman to be called a "fellow-worker" with Paul and other notable Christian leaders

21. Priscilla is a diminutive form of Prisca.

22. Murphy-O'Connor, "Prisca and Aquila," 40.

23. Köstenberger and Köstenberger, *God's Design*, 140.

24. Köstenberger and Köstenberger, *God's Design*, 140.

25. Köstenberger and Köstenberger, *God's Design*, 140.

26. Köstenberger and Köstenberger, *God's Design*, 148.

is a great honor. It marks her out as a member of what the Köstenbergers call "the Pauline circle" of leaders, who they wrongly claim were all men.[27] This designation, *"sunergoi"* (fellow-workers or coworkers), is closely associated with the term *diakonos*. In 1 Cor 3:5 Paul first speaks of himself and Apollos as *diakonoi* and then in 3:9 as *diakonoi* and *sunergoi* (cf. 2 Cor 6:1, 4). This suggests that the two words are virtual synonyms in Paul's epistles. These *sunergoi* were recognized leaders/ministers and Paul demands that Christians be subject "to every fellow worker" (1 Cor 16:16). Consequently, the Köstenbergers greatly reduce the force of the word *sunergoi* because it is used of a woman when they say it "simply indicates partnership in ministry."[28]

Junia: Romans 16:7

Another woman in this list is Junia, almost certainly a woman apostle;[29] she was not one of the twelve apostles, but rather an apostle like Barnabas, Apollos, James, and Timothy.[30] Because the existence of a woman apostle would completely undermine the argument that women cannot be priests in the Catholic tradition, or church leaders and teachers in the Reformed tradition, male commentators have tried valiantly to find reasons to reject what the text says. They have argued that:

1. Paul here speaks of a male apostle called Junias.

2. Paul is only saying Andronicus and Junia were esteemed by those who were apostles.

3. Andronicus and Junia were not apostles like Barnabas, Apollos, James, and Timothy.

1. The first objection to Junia being a woman apostle is the argument that the name *Iounian* given in the Greek text of Rom 16:7 refers to a man. It is sometimes alleged that this is a contracted form of a Greek transliteration of the Latin name *Junianus* shortened to *Junias*. Despite exhaustive searching, not one example of the contracted

---

27. Köstenberger and Köstenberger, *God's Design*, 123, 124, 125, 132, 143.

28. Köstenberger and Köstenberger, *God's Design*, 145.

29. See on what follows, Epp, *Junia*.

30. On the two kinds of apostles see Giles, *Patterns*, 127–48.

male name, Junias, has been found. There is no such name.[31] For this compelling reason, virtually all recent commentators have conceded that here Paul speaks of a woman, almost certainly the wife of Andronicus. The Köstenbergers concede this point,[32] as does Douglas Moo who is also totally opposed to the leadership of women in the church.[33]

2. The second objection to Junia being a female apostle is that the Greek translated as "of note among the apostles" (*episēmoi en tois apostolois*) can mean one of two things: either that Junia and Andronicus were highly esteemed *as* apostles, or that they were held in high esteem *by* the apostles. Again, virtually all modern commentators agree that in this context the Greek most naturally means that Junia and Andronicus are commended by Paul as esteemed apostles.[34] Their faith and work as apostles was noteworthy. Since Paul adds that they were "in Christ before I was," it seems likely they were Jewish believers, and it is possible that they were eye witnesses of the resurrection (1 Cor 15:7). In the light of Paul's high estimation of them and their work the suggestion that he mentions them simply because the true apostles held them in high esteem is implausible.

3. The third objection to Junia being a female apostle in the same sense as Barnabas, Apollos, James, and Timothy is a dogmatic one. Women cannot be church leaders; therefore, Junia cannot be an apostle like Barnabas, Apollos, and so on. Moo who has to admit that the name Junia is a female name, as noted above, takes this route. He arbitrarily concludes that here Paul uses the title "apostle" in a "looser" sense, definitely not of an "authoritative leadership position."[35] The Köstenbergers have another solution. They argue Andronicus and Junia were simply "an outstanding missionary couple."[36] They certainly were, but this comment is just a play on words; a smoke

31. Thorley, "Junia," argues the name cannot be found because it would not be the proper contraction of *Junianus*.

32. Köstenberger and Köstenberger, *God' Design*, 153.

33. Moo, *Epistle*, 923.

34. A dissenting voice is Bure, "*Episēmoi en tois Apostolos*," who argues that the Greek taken in isolation can mean "well known to the apostles," which I think no one denies. It just does not make sense in the context of a warm commendation of Andronicus and Junia.

35. Moo, *Epistle*, 923.

36. Köstenberger and Köstenberger, *God's Design*, 155.

screen. The Greek word *apostolos* means "a sent one." To send in Latin is *missio* and via this root we get the English word "missionary." A missionary is a sent one. Thus, the Köstenbergers are in fact agreeing that this couple were outstanding missionaries like the other first-century post-Easter apostles who were evangelists and church planters. Finally, in seeking to minimize what Paul says in Rom 16:7 about Junia, the Köstenbergers say this reference to Junia simply "indicates the noble calling for a woman to be a missionary wife and serve in cross cultural ministry alongside her husband"![37] What a put down of missionary women. And then they add, her ministry "was with other women,"[38] something not even hinted at in Scripture, or plausible (cf. Acts 18:6).

The Early Commentators on Romans 16:7

Every commentator on Rom 16:7 before the thirteenth century took it that Paul was speaking of a woman apostle. In his commentary on Romans, the erudite Roman Catholic scholar, Joseph Fitzmyer, lists sixteen Greek and Latin commentators from the first Christian millennium who all take Paul in Rom 16:7 to be speaking of a woman apostle.[39]

I give some examples; Chrysostom, who lived in the fourth century and is ranked among the most learned of the Greek Fathers, unambiguously and profusely says of Junia:

> To be apostles is something great. But to be outstanding among the apostles—just think what a wonderful song of praise that is! . . . They [she and Andronicus] were outstanding on the basis of their works and virtuous actions. Indeed, how great the wisdom of this woman must have been that she was even deemed worthy of the title of apostle! [40]

In the next century, Theodoret (393–458), bishop of Cyrrhus, speaking explicitly of Andronicus and Junia says,

37. Köstenberger and Köstenberger, *God's Design*, 155.
38. Köstenberger and Köstenberger, *God's Design*, 155.
39. Fitzmyer, *Romans*, 737–38. See also Epp, *Junia*, 32–33.
40. The English translation is taken from Epp, *Junia*, 32.

To be called "of note" not only among the disciples but also among the teachers, and not just among the teachers but even among the apostles is amazing.[41]

Still later John of Damascus (675–749) says,

And to be called "apostles" is a great thing . . . but even among these of note, just consider what great encomium this is.[42]

It was not until the thirteenth century that Junia was given a "sex change" and from then on commentators began arguing that in Rom 16:7 Paul was commending two male apostles. Interestingly, Calvin showed his usual independence of thought in his treatment of this verse. He conceded that here Paul commends a man and a woman, calling them both apostles, in the sense of missionaries and church planters.[43]

Lastly we note that in the second century other women were called apostles. This is attested by the apocryphal, *Acts of St. Paul and St. Thecla*.[44] This work is a popular story that had wide circulation in the post- apostolic period. It is first quoted in the second century AD. Here we meet Thecla, a woman apostle and companion of Paul who teaches, baptizes, and is eventually martyred for her faith in Christ. This story is certainly fiction, but it does suggest that second-century Christians saw no problem with a woman apostle.

This almost certain mention of a woman apostle in Rom 16:7 is of huge significance. All arguments that Paul excluded women from church leadership and teaching on the basis of theological principle are demolished if Junia is an apostle, and the overwhelming evidence indicates just this. Paul says apostles, and he is not speaking only of the twelve, are "first in the church" (1 Cor 12:28). Later, in writing to the Ephesians he says that along with the prophets, the apostles are "the foundation" on which the church is built (Eph 2:20). They are the ones that begin churches and teach the first converts. Everyone agrees apostles taught. It is not at all surprising to find women apostles in the early church. Jesus appeared first to women and sent them to proclaim the good news to the twelve male apostles he had risen from the grave (Matt 28:7; John 20:17). And

41. Epp, *Junia*, 33.

42. Epp, *Junia*, 33.

43. Calvin, *Epistle of Paul the Apostle to the Romans*, 322.

44. An English translation of this work is found in Hennecke, *New Testament Apocrypha*, 2, 353–64.

Paul's theology of the *charismata* (see 1 Cor 12:1–31) envisages that every ministry is open to men and women without distinction.

It would almost seem that God in his infinite wisdom put the story of Deborah in the Old Testament, and in the New Testament Paul's commendation of Junia, to remind us that he can raise up outstanding women leaders and bless their ministry. Both Deborah and Junia unambiguously tell us that the complementarian thesis that leadership pleasing to God is male is false.

Mary, Tryphaena, Tryphosa, and Persis: Women Who "Labor in the Gospel," Romans 16:6, 12

Next in Rom 16, Paul singles out for commendation Mary (Rom 16: 6) of whom the apostle says she "has worked hard among you." The word translated as "worked hard" is the Greek verb *kopiaō*. It is also used of "those workers in the Lord Tryphaena and Tryphosa" and "the beloved Persis," whom he mentions a little later in verse 12. We can discuss the ministries of these four women together. Paul frequently uses the verb *kopiaō* when speaking of the ministry of those involved in teaching and preaching. The Reformed New Testament scholar Herman Ridderbos says that this word "specifically denotes work in the Gospel and in the church."[45] In 1 Cor 15:10 Paul says of his own preaching, "I worked harder (*kopiaō*) than any of them;" in 1 Cor 16:16 Paul exhorts the church in Corinth to be "subject" to "every fellow worker and laborer" (*kopiaō*); in 1 Thess 5:12 in a similar vein he says, "respect those who labor (*kopiaō*) among you and are over you in the Lord and admonish you"; and in 1 Tim 5:17 we read of the elders who "labor (*kopiaō*) in preaching and teaching." Paul's consistent use of the word explains why he commends these four women. Each one of them has served the Lord faithfully in preaching and teaching.

In direct opposition to what Paul's terminology indicates, the Köstenbergers conclude these women were involved in "a variety of good works, which are the hallmark of committed, mature, pious women in the first century."[46] This "interpretation" of what Paul says about these three women has no basis in the text of Scripture and indeed it seems to run counter to what Paul actually says.

45. Ridderbos, *Paul,* 461.
46. Köstenberger and Köstenberger, *God's Design,* 152.

Euodia and Syntyche: Philippians 4:3

Turning to Paul's letter to the Philippians, we meet Euodia and Syntyche (Phil 4:3) who Paul honors by calling them *"sunergoi"* (fellow-workers or co-workers). Possibly they worked with Paul in founding the church in Philippi. When Paul writes, these two women are at loggerheads with each other. The dispute does not concern us, but what Paul says about them is important. He describes them as having "struggled side by side with me in the Gospel together with Clement and the rest of my *coworkers."* The Greek verb *synathleō,* translated as "struggled," means "to compete in a contest." It suggests an athletic event in which the contestants strain every muscle to win. Euodia and Syntyche had been involved in strenuous and ongoing Gospel ministry. Certainly they were evangelists proclaiming the Gospel, but this implies they were also church planters and as such teachers of their converts. Besides these two women, only a few of Paul's most trusted companions are called "coworkers": Clement, who worked with these two women at Philippi; Epaphroditus (Phil 2:25); Timothy (1 Cor 4:12); and Titus (2 Cor 8:23). Again, the Köstenbergers discount the significance of these two women. They say they were probably unmarried and thus "serve as a source of inspiration particularly for unmarried women today to make an important contribution to the ministry of the Gospel in and through their local church."[47] This conjecture is just pious platitude. Nothing in the text of Scripture indicates they were single women or that they simply contributed to the ministry exercised by men.

Women Prophets

In Acts we are told that Peter recognizes Joel's prophecy—in the last days God would pour out his Spirt on all his people, young and old, men and women, and they would prophesy—had been fulfilled on the day of Pentecost (Acts 2:17–21). In these words Spirit endowment and prophecy are intrinsically connected. Later, Luke tells us that when Paul arrived in Caesarea he went to the home of Philip the evangelist who had four unmarried daughters who prophesied, in other words who were prophets (Acts 21:8–9).[48] In 1 Cor 11:4–5 Paul speaks positively of men and women

47. Köstenberger and Köstenberger, *God's Design,* 156.

48. Luke's use of the present tense of the participle indicates they prophesied on a regular basis. It was a gift and a ministry. On what follows see Giles, "Prophecy,

leading in prayer and prophecy in the church so long as the women cover their heads and men do not. We will look at this passage in some detail in a moment. We note here only one thing, this text unambiguously speaks of men and women leading the church in prayer and prophecy and this is acceptable to Paul. For Paul, prophecy is the most important ministry in the congregation (1 Cor 14:1–19). He only once speaks of women leading in prophecy (1 Cor 11:5), but his theology of the *charismata* implies that all gifts were given indiscriminately. The Spirit could empower both men and women to prophesy or to exercise any other ministry.

For Paul, the ministry of the prophet is "second" in importance behind that of the apostle and before the teacher (1 Cor 12:28; Eph 4:11), and it is of great value because in prophecy the church is "built up, encouraged and consoled" (1 Cor 14:3), and the hearers "learn" (1 Cor 14:31). We will return to prophecy and women prophesying when we come to discuss 1 Cor 11:3–16 shortly.

Women House-Church Leaders

The first Christians met in homes.[49] This gathering was for them what we would call today a coming together of the local church, the congregation. These house congregations were the primary unit of the church in the apostolic and post-apostolic age. It seems that Paul invited those of some social standing who had been converted to host these little churches, because they had larger homes and because they could act as quasi-patrons to those who gathered in their home on the first day of the week. When the believers met in a home, the owner would have presided much like the ruler of the synagogue did in house synagogues.[50] Whether a man or a woman was the leader of a house-church, they were not the counterpart of the modern-day pastor. Like the ruler of a synagogue it seems they were charged with facilitating ministry by those present. In Acts, Lydia, the seller of purple cloth, was a host to a house-church in Philippi (Acts 17:11–15). Later, in writing to the Colossians, Paul commends another women house-church leader named Nympha (Col 4:15). Very likely,

Prophets, False Prophets," 970–77.

49. I have fully documented this matter earlier in this chapter.

50. In meeting in homes the early Christians followed Jewish practice. Many if not most of the early synagogues were in homes. See further Giles, *Patterns*, 3–4.

Chloe is another example (1 Cor 1:11). Prisca and Aquila are a couple who conjointly lead a house-church (Rom 16:5; 1 Cor 16:19).

THE HOME IN THE ANCIENT WORLD

In the ancient world a sharp divide was made between the public sphere (*polis*), which was the domain of men, and the home (*oikos*), which was the domain of women. The male head of the family was the *paterfamilias* and his wife the *materfamilias*. The *materfamilias* had the responsibility of managing the home, educating the children, directing and disciplining slaves, and paying the bills, etc. Philo, the first century Alexandrian Jew, describes the situation:

> For the nature of communities is twofold, the greater and the smaller: the greater we call cities and the smaller households. As to management of both forms, men have obtained that of the greater, which bears the name of statesmanship, whereas women have obtained the smaller, which goes under the name of household management.[51]

Later we find the Christian John Chrysostom expressing much the same ideas:

> Our life is customarily organized into two spheres; public and private. . . . To women is assigned the presidency of the household; to man, all the business of the state, the marketplace, the administration of justice, government, the military and all other enterprises. [A woman] cannot express her opinion in the legislative assembly, but she can express it at home.[52]

Against this backdrop, Paul's advice to young widows to marry and *manage or rule* their households well (1 Tim 5:14) makes sense. The Greek verb translated by the NRSV as "manage" is *oikodespotein*, literally meaning "house despot." In this text Paul speaks of the woman as what we would call today "the head of the home."

Once we realize that this is how public and private life was understood and contrasted in Greco-Roman society, we can see that dogmatic assertions that women could not have had leadership positions in the early house-churches is not convincing. Not only were some wealthy

---

51. Philo, *Special Laws*, 3.170, 280.

52 Chrysostom, "Kind of Women Who Ought Be Taken as Wives," 36.

women, usually widows, leaders of extended families, but also in the home setting married women had an authority denied to them in public life. What this means is that we should expect women participated fully in the house-church setting, and see the complete exclusion of women as a consequence of the church becoming a public institution when church buildings began to appear late in the second century AD.

This account of the home in the Greco-Roman world also is a warning not to read into the New Testament the home life we know in the twenty-first century, which is to be more contrasted than compared with that of the first century.

I have already made the point more than once and I now make it again. The Köstenbergers and virtually all complementarians *infer* that when the New Testament uses the word church/*ekklesia* what is being spoken about is a public gathering where significant numbers are present and there was one or more male office bearers who did all the teaching/preaching at the front. This is simply not true. All or virtually all church gatherings in the first century were in homes, a setting that encouraged informality and wide participation, including the participation of women and no one had the "role" of the modern-day pastor.

THE "PAULINE CIRCLE" OF PREDOMINANTLY MALE LEADERS

Again, this time in reference to Paul, we have found the Köstenbergers' primary thesis that the Bible consistently "exhibits a pattern of male leadership"[53] is without foundation and contrary to what the Bible says. The "Pauline circle" of leaders includes some very noteworthy women. Their bold assertion that "it is clear that the nucleus of Paul's missionary leadership team was composed of 'faithful men' (2 Tim 2:2)" is simply not true. As we have seen, Paul commended the leadership of many women. Their appeal to 2 Tim 2:2 is special pleading. This text does not speak of "faithful men," but of faithful men and women.[54] Paul uses the generic *anthropoi* that is inclusive of men and women (it is used explicitly of women in 1 Pet 3:4!). The New Revised Standard Version, which I have chosen as my translation for this book, rightly translates this verse as what you

53. Köstenberger and Köstenberger, *God's Design*, 123, 124, 125, 132, 143, 144, 157.

54. Payne, *Man and Woman*, 330–31.

have heard from me (Paul) "entrust to *faithful people* who will be able to
teach others."

THE CONTESTED TEXTS

Galatians 3:28

Paul writes, "There is no longer Jew or Greek, there is no longer slave or
free, there is no longer male and female; for all of you are one in Christ."
I agree with the Köstenbergers that here Paul is primarily speaking about
equality in salvation.[55] These words come at the end of his argument that
Jew and Gentile alike are saved by faith in Christ and thus they are Abraham's [spiritual] offspring.

I also agree with them that Paul is definitely *not denying racial, social, or sexual differentiation.*[56] Evangelical egalitarians, like them, do not
interpret this verse to be teaching "undifferentiated equality,"[57] or that
all gender distinctions "have been abolished in Christ."[58] To claim this
is what evangelical egalitarians teach is just polemic, without any factual
basis. We are in agreement: in becoming a Christian, someone does not
cease to be Jew or Gentile, slave or free, male or female. What Paul is denying is that these differences are of any consequence in the new creation
realized "in Christ." We are one in Christ, even if in (fallen) Adam we are
divided in innumerable ways.

The Köstenbergers say here Paul teaches that we are "one in Christ"
not equal in Christ.[59] True, Paul uses the Greek word *hen* (one) and not
isos (equal) but surely if we are one in Christ what divides is excluded. We
are equal in a profound way. In Galatians, Paul clearly shows this oneness
in Christ is not exclusively soteriological; "spiritual" as the Köstenbergers
would have us believe.[60] The historical occasion for this teaching was
Peter's treatment of Gentiles as second-class citizens even though "God
shows no partiality" (Gal 2:6). Paul writes, "But when Cephas came to

55. Köstenberger and Köstenberger, *God's Design*, 164, 167, 168.

56. Or in the Köstenberger's complementarian speak, "The obliteration of all gender roles in the home, the church and society." Köstenberger and Köstenberger, *God's
Design*, 162.

57. Köstenberger and Köstenberger, *God's Design*, 162, 165.

58. Köstenberger and Köstenberger, *God's Design*, 162.

59. Köstenberger and Köstenberger, *God's Design*, 164.

60. Köstenberger and Köstenberger, *God's Design*, 168.

Antioch, I opposed him to his face because he stood condemned" (Gal 2:11). Paul calls Peter a hypocrite (Gal 2:13) for acting "contrary to the Gospel" (Gal 2:14). This carries over to chapter 3: "O foolish Galatians, who has bewitched you?" Galatians 3:26 continues this link, "For in Christ you are *all* sons of God through faith. For as many of you as were baptized into Christ, have put on Christ. There is no Jew/Greek division; there is no slave/free division; there is no male/female division, for you are all one in Christ Jesus." For Paul, "being baptized" and "putting on Christ" have practical social implication in how Christians relate to one another. Furthermore, the wording of Gal 3:28 directly opposes the common Jewish, with parallel Hellenistic, thanksgivings: "Blessed art Thou, O Lord our God, King of the universe, who has not made me a heathen . . . a bondman . . . or a woman."[61] The divisions Gal 3:28 repudiates are all social divisions, so to interpret Paul's repudiation of them as irrelevant to these social divisions is to miss their obvious application as well as their historical and cultural contexts.

With the master-slave division, virtually all Christians now agree that Paul recognized that oneness in Christ had a social dimension. He did not openly attack slavery in his day, but what he said to masters and slaves eventually so undermined the institution, that when the time was right, Christians concluded that slavery was neither pleasing to God, nor a reflection of the creation ideal where each person is of equal status and worth (Gen 1:27–28). So we note that Paul exhorts both the master and the slave to give to each other their due (Eph 6:5–9; Col 3:22–24), and asks Philemon to consider Onesimus his slave a "brother" (16).

With women, Paul's linking of spiritual and social oneness takes yet another turn. Because men and women are one in salvation they are one in receiving the Holy Spirit. And if they have the Spirit, then they have a ministry/*diakonia* and a gift of grace/*charisma* (1 Cor 12:7). In the world in which Paul ministered, women as a general rule were to keep silent in public and were excluded from leadership in the public sphere; but in the church, he allowed that women could lead in prophecy and prayer (1 Cor 11:5), be house-church leaders and minister to all present in many ways, and be coworkers alongside male apostles.[62] Paul's acceptance of the leadership of women in the house-churches must be seen as a social

---

61. See Payne, *Man and Woman*, 84.

62. In a moment we will document these assertions.

implementation of what it means to be "one in Christ" in the new creation, spoken of in Gal 3:28.

I return to the Köstenbergers: in a totally unexpected comment at the end of their discussion of this text they seem to contradict themselves. They say, "While Paul's primary point in Galatians is spiritual [I would say soteriological], the passage does have social implications."[63] I agree.

1 Corinthians 11:2–16

The Köstenbergers admit that "this passage is difficult to interpret."[64] Paul's arguments for why women should cover their heads and men not, when *leading* in a house-church in prophecy and prayer are very hard to understand for us moderns in a totally different cultural context. At least twice Paul appears to correct himself (1 Cor 11:8–12). It is almost as if Paul is in dialogue with the Corinthians and himself, trying one argument after another to make his case on head coverings.[65] This means that taking any one verse or comment in this passage in isolation may well lead to a wrong conclusion.

Before considering what Paul actually says I give the Köstenbergers' summary of what this passage teaches. It teaches, they say, "the abiding principle of woman's submission to male authority."[66] And, "First Corinthians 11:2–16 teaches that a woman may participate in praying and prophesying in church *under male spiritual leadership and authority*."[67] Does it? Where does it say this? They also say that in this passage "Paul affirms the differences and distinctness of male and female in the created order."[68] On this we agree. No evangelical egalitarian denies that God has made us man or woman and we are distinct in many ways, most profoundly in our bodies. To suggest otherwise is disingenuous. *We agree this passage affirms male-female differentiation; we disagree this passage teaches the permanent subordination of women.*

---

63. Köstenberger and Köstenberger, *God's Design*, 168.

64. Köstenberger and Köstenberger, *God's Design*, 172.

65. Conzelmann, *1 Corinthians*, 182, boldly states Paul himself is "somewhat confused" in his arguing.

66. Köstenberger and Köstenberger, *God's Design*, 176.

67. Köstenberger and Köstenberger, *God's Design*, 160. Italics added.

68. Köstenberger and Köstenberger, *God's Design*, 176.

Verse 3

Paul begins his discussion on head coverings with a play upon the word "head" (*kephalē*). He says the Son, men, and women all have a metaphorical "head," before speaking of what men and women should have on their literal "head." This verse is accurately translated, "The head of every man is Christ, and the head of the woman is the man, and the head of Christ is God." The most contested issue in this whole chapter is the meaning of the Greek noun, *kephalē*, translated into English as "head." The Köstenbergers are emphatic: speaking specifically of 1 Cor 11:3, they say whenever *kephalē* is used "with reference to human relationships" it carries the "primary . . . sense of authority," not "source."[69] In making this claim they stand in opposition to the overwhelming majority of contemporary commentators and theologians.[70]

In seeking the meaning and force of the metaphorical meaning of any word, the literary context is always what is most important. To argue that *kephalē* means head/authority over in 1 Cor 11:3 is implausible. Paul immediately goes on to say that as long as a woman has her head covered she can *lead* the church in prayer and prophecy. Why subordinate woman to man and then immediately say that women can lead in church? It makes no sense. The well-established metaphorical meaning of "source," in the sense of "source of life," does make sense of this introductory comment.[71] Paul is saying Christ is the *kephalē* of all humankind—as the co-creator; man (Adam) is the *kephalē* of the woman (Eve) in her creation, a point Paul makes in 1 Cor 11:8 and 12, and God [the Father], is the *kephalē* of Christ (the Son), in his eternal generation or incarnation. This interpretation of verse 3 avoids reading it to be teaching the error of subordinationism, the hierarchical ordering of the divine persons, which the Köstenbergers embrace.[72] After the Köstenbergers published *God's Design for Men and Women* in 2014, many of their complementarian friends came to agree with me that to interpret 1 Cor 11:3 to be teaching the Father is "head over" the Son just as man is "head over" woman

69. Köstenberger and Köstenberger, *God's Design*, 170.

70. Payne, *Man and Woman*, 117–18, n. 7, lists forty scholarly works that argue that *kephalē* means "source" in 1 Cor 11:3. This book was published in 2009; the list is now far longer. In the 2016 evangelical civil war over the Trinity, many complementarians abandoned this interpretation of 1 Cor 11:3 and of the word *kephalē* because they recognized it reintroduced the Arian error in new wording. See Giles, *Rise and Fall*.

71. See further on *kephalē* the addendum at the end of this chapter.

72. Köstenberger and Köstenberger, *God's Design*, 37–39, 174–75.

depicts the Trinity hierarchically and thus implies the Arian heresy.[73]
Here it should be carefully noted that in this text Paul does not speak
of a fourfold hierarchy, Father-Son-man-woman, but of three paired relationships in which in each instance one party is the *kephalē*. Christ is
mentioned first and last.

That *kephalē* does not mean "head over/authority over" in verse 3
is confirmed by what Paul says in verse 10. The Köstenbergers argue that
verse 10 speaks of the authority the man has over the woman.[74] It does
not. In the New Testament the Greek word *exousia* (authority) is used
103 times, and nine times in 1 Corinthians. In every instance it alludes
to the authority one possesses.[75] This text speaks of the authority women
have in the new creation. It is rightly translated, "The women ought to
have authority over (her) own head." Paul could not have said this if he
believed women were set under the authority of men as the creation ideal.

Lastly, I make the point that translating *kephalē* as "source" in 1 Cor
11:3 is not a novel egalitarian idea. The native Greek-speaking church
fathers, Cyril of Alexandria, Theodore of Mopsuestia, Athanasius, and
Eusebius, also in this instance took *kephalē* to carry the meaning of
"source."[76]

Verses 3–4

Now Paul comes to the specific questions the Corinthians had asked him
about. It presupposes a debate about head covering among Christians
in the cosmopolitan city of Corinth. Why Paul asks women to cover
their heads and men not to, when leading in worship (1 Cor 11:4–5), has
evoked a lot of debate but no consensus. In no other epistle does Paul
make this demand. The Köstenbergers dogmatically assert that "women's
wearing of head coverings is clearly a cultural practice" that symbolizes
"submission to authority."[77] They offer no documentation or evidence for
this *inference*. In contrast, Cynthia Long Westfall, who comprehensively
documents her evidence, notes that slaves, prostitutes and freed women

73. Giles, *Rise and Fall*, 35–43.
74. Köstenberger and Köstenberger, *God's Design*, 176–77.
75. See in more detail, Payne, *Man and Woman*, 182–83.
76. Payne, "Evidence," 21–25
77. Köstenberger and Köstenberger, *God's Design*, 173, 178.

were forbidden in the Greco-Roman world from veiling.[78] Married wom-
en covered their heads as symbol of their married status, modesty, and
chastity.[79] Their head covering spoke of their honored status. What Paul
wants, she argues, is that *all* women (v. 5) when they lead the church in
prophecy and prayer cover their heads to symbolize that they are *all* honored alike in the church, even the women who are denied honor outside
the church.[80] This ruling makes a lot of sense in a Christian community
where not many were wise, powerful, or of noble birth (1 Cor 1:26).

The argument Paul uses for this ruling is that women should cover
their head and not men because to do otherwise is to dishonor one's metaphorical head. In these words Paul alludes to an honor/shame culture
foreign to us.

The Köstenbergers say not one word on the significance of Paul's
endorsement of women prophesying in church. Indeed, when they sum
up their conclusions on this passage they omit any reference to it. They
say that in this passage Paul is telling women how they are to "worship
and pray, at the church's worship gatherings."[81] This interpretation would
lead to the traditional demand that all women cover their heads when
they go to church!

For Paul, prophecy is of "second" importance in the life of the
church (1 Cor 12:28) and to be highly prized because it edifies the church
(1 Cor 14:1–5).[82] Charles Hodge, commenting on 1 Cor 11:4–5, says
prayer and prophecy were "the two principal exercises in the public life
of the early Christians."[83] Paul twice speaks of teachers as distinct from
apostles and prophets (1 Cor 12:28; Eph 4:11), but in his writings and in
the rest of the Bible the ministries of the prophet and the teacher overlap. In 1 Corinthians Paul says that when prophets prophesy they "build
up, encourage and console" the assembled church (1 Cor 14:3) and their
hearers "learn" (1 Cor 14:31), which is what happens when people teach.
In Acts 13:1 we read of one ministry, the prophet and teacher. In Rev

78. Westfall, *Paul and Gender*, 25.

79. Westfall, *Paul and Gender*, 27.

80. For the whole argument read ibid., pages 24–36

81. *God's Design*, 178. It should be noted that in this sentence the Köstenbergers leave out any comment about women prophesying in church; they only mention
praying.

82. I have a full chapter on prophets and prophesy in the Bible in my book, *Patterns of Ministry*, 149–173.

83. *First Corinthians*, 208

2:20 we read of Jezebel "who calls herself a prophet and is teaching and beguiling my servants." In this verse a prophet, albeit a false prophet, is said to teach. In his important study on prophecy in the apostolic age, David Hill argues that prophecy is basically Spirit-inspired teaching.[84] All this is very difficult information for the Köstenbergers and all other complementarians because to admit that Paul ranks prophecy higher in importance than teaching and that prophecy and teaching can overlap would undermine their dogma that 1 Tim 2:12 excludes all women for all time from teaching/preaching in church.

Over a hundred and fifty years ago, Catherine Booth, the wife of William Booth, the founder of the Salvation Army, came to a very different conclusion to that of the Köstenbergers. In her wonderful little 1859 booklet, *Female Ministry: Or, the Right of Women to Preach the Gospel,* she argues that 1 Cor 11:5 is "the most prominent and explicit passage in support of women preaching," with Acts 2:17–21 in confirmation.[85] She defines prophecy as St. Paul does, as "the edification, exhortation and comfort of believers" (1 Cor 14:3) and thus equates it with preaching.

Verses 6–7

In verse 6 Paul develops the shame theme he has just mentioned. For a woman not to cover her head is shameful—in that cultural setting In verse 7 he introduces the idea that men and women have different glories, which again is a very difficult idea for us moderns. This verse needs a lot of unpacking and a good scholarly commentary should be consulted. What Paul is affirming is male-female differentiation. God has made us men and women.

Verses 8–12

Having spoken of the creation in verse 7 Paul continues with this matter. He says, "Indeed man was not made from woman, but woman from man. Neither was man created for the sake of woman, but woman for the sake of man." Complementarians love to quote these verses in isolation to prove that Paul subordinates woman to man. Paul in fact does not do this. In verses 8 and 9 he only says what Gen 2 says. To claim these words teach

84. *New Testament Prophecy.*
85. Booth, *Female Ministry,* 4.

the subordination of women is an *inference,* not a reflection of anything Paul actually says. The bigger problem is that while complementarians love to quote these words, they ignore completely what Paul says following as his own warning against any devaluing or subordinating women. Quite unexpectedly and counterintuitively, Paul then says in verse 10, "For this reason . . . a woman ought to have authority over her head." I discussed this verse above. Following this aside, Paul then says, looking back to verses 8 and 9, "Nevertheless"—the Greek *plen* is an adversive to make a point emphatic[86]—"in the Lord [that is for us Christians], woman is not independent of man, or man independent of woman for just as woman came from man, so man comes through woman."[87] In these words, Paul excludes the thought that in the new creation, women are dependent on or subordinate to men.

Now to Sum Up

What we have in 1 Cor 11:3–16 is exceptional teaching addressing an exceptional debate. Nowhere else in the Bible is there teaching on head coverings for men and women. What Paul says fits a specific cultural and historical context. For this reason, no evangelical scholar today argues that this Pauline directive, predicated on references to the creation, lays down a universally binding rule. We should, however, see in what Paul says a binding theological principle. This is implied in verses 4 and 5: men and women should be free to lead in church assemblies. God has made us man or woman, gender differentiation is God-given and good, and for this reason the church needs the contribution of men and women to be whole.

Yes, there are difficult things to understand in this passage but one thing is crystal clear: in Corinth men *and* women were leading in prayer and prophecy when the church assembled, the most important ministries for the earliest Christians, and Paul approves of this.

86. Payne, *Man and Woman,* 189.

87. Payne, *Man and Woman,* 190–91, argues that the Greek word *chōris* translated above as "independent of" should be translated "separate from." He makes a strong case for this.

1 Corinthians 14:33b–36

The Köstenbergers next turn to 1 Cor 14:33b–36 where they find the words, "Women should keep silent in the churches." This they read as restricting in some way what women can do in church because they are subordinated to men. The Köstenbergers opt for the explanation, made by Don Carson, that what is forbidden is the judging of prophecies.[88] I can see no merit in this opinion whatsoever. It is just a guess. The text itself says if the women have anything to ask, "let them ask their husbands at home" (1 Cor 14:35). The explanation that Paul is forbidding women from asking disruptive questions in the little house-churches is exegetically far more plausible.

But there is a bigger issue; it is highly likely that Paul did not write these words; they were added by a later scribe. This has long been argued as a possibility but in recent years Philip Payne has put forward compelling evidence for their omission in the earliest written manuscripts.[89] Without any discussion on the evidence Payne amasses, the Köstenbergers quickly pass over this problem in a dismissive footnote. This is not academically acceptable. Payne's evidence is compelling. It cannot be simplistically or arbitrarily dismissed. It cannot because an agreed evangelical rule is that if there is serious doubt on the textual authenticity of any text in the Bible, it should not be quoted in support of any doctrine.

1 Timothy 2:8–15

Complementarians are agreed, the interpretation of 1 Tim 2:12 is absolutely crucial to their case. Their position stands or falls on whether or not this text speaks of a transcultural and universal prohibition on women teaching/preaching and exercising authority in church because the command is predicated in the creation order.

Because of the huge importance of this one passage for complementarians, it has been the most disputed text among evangelicals for the last forty years. Whole books and innumerable articles have been written on this passage and still there is no consensus. Andreas Köstenberger has been one of the most prolific contributors to this debate and all his

88. Carson, "Silent in the Churches."

89. See Payne, *Man and Woman*, 217–70, and more recently with added evidence, Payne, "Vaticanus Distigme-Obelos Symbols," 604–25.

arguments have been critically evaluated and found wanting.[90] In *God's Design* he basically ignores his critics, at best dismissing them in a very brief footnote.[91]

Before we consider what is said in this passage I must respond to the Köstenberger's claim that evangelical egalitarians cannot interpret this text correctly because they have embraced the ungodly culture of our age; accepted the world view of radical feminism, and rejected the clear teaching of Scripture by arguing for "undifferentiated male-female equality,"[92] thereby denying "male-female role distinctions."[93] It is hard to know what to say in reply to such absurd charges. All the better known and most published egalitarian evangelicals have a high view of Scripture, and never set culture over Scripture. No evangelical egalitarian denies God-given male-female differentiation and none holds to or advocates "undifferentiated male-female equality." True, evangelical egalitarians do not speak of "male-female *role* distinctions;" because "role" distinctions are never mentioned in the Bible and nowhere in the Bible are men and women differentiated by their supposed "roles." The word "role" is not found in any of the most common translations of the Bible. The complementarian use of the word "role" is a disingenuous and deliberately obfuscating way of saying men and women are differentiated on the basis that men rule, women obey. We evangelical egalitarians do not endorse this way of differentiating the sexes. We believe God has differentiated the sexes primarily by giving them different bodies, not by giving them different "roles." If "roles" can change, as sociologists insist, this is a very inadequate, if not dangerous, way to differentiate men and women.

90. In 1995 Köstenberger, Schreiner, and Baldwin edited and contributed to a series of essays on 1 Tim 2:9–15 published in the book *Women in the Church*. I subjected this book to a lengthy and detailed critique. See Giles, "Critique," in two parts. Andreas made a reply to me ("Women in the Church," 205–24) and in answer I wrote, "Dear Professor Köstenberger." Far more telling has been the response to Andreas' linguistic work by the erudite Phillip Payne. Most of this is found in his large book, *Man and Woman*. As a result of this trenchant criticism by me and Payne, Andreas was forced to republish *Women in the Church* in a second "edition" in 2005. The most damaging chapter for their case by Daniel Doriani was deleted.

91. He seldom interacts with his critics and in three brief footnotes dismisses the work of Payne.

92. Köstenberger and Köstenberger, *God's Design*, 196.

93. Köstenberger and Köstenberger, *God's Design*, 196.

1 Timothy 2:8–15

In studying this contentious text we must find an agreed approach. I am happy to accept the methodology that the Köstenbergers enunciate.[94] It involves three steps, all emphasizing context. Here I recall the often heard maxim attributed to various people, "a text without a context is a pretext for a proof text." Nowhere is this truer than with 1 Tim 2:12.

First, the historical context: in exegesis, the Köstenbergers and I agree, the goal is to determine the historical meaning of what we find written in Scripture. To do this we need to place ourselves as far as we can in the world of the people addressed. The historical context in which the epistle of 1 Timothy is set in brief is as follows. This epistle was written sometime in the later part of the first century, when Christians were meeting in small house-churches, leadership in the Christian community was fluid, and all believers were thought to have a ministry. In this epistle and in 2 Timothy and Titus, which were written roughly at the same time, Paul charges Timothy and Titus with the work of opposing the false teachers who were tearing the Christian communities in these two cities apart (1 Tim 1:3–7, 19–20; 4:1–2, 16; 6:3–5; 2 Tim 2:14–19; 3:10–16; Titus 1:10–16; 2:1–2; 3:8–10). Writing to Titus in Crete where the false teachers were active, Paul tells his young deputy to silence the *men* who are "upsetting whole families" by teaching "what is not right to teach" (Titus 1:10–11). Writing to Timothy in Ephesus, Paul makes plain, the false male teachers had a field day among the women. They had forbidden them to marry (1 Tim 4:3), led some to "follow Satan," and as a result some women were "going about from house to house [house-church to house-church] . . . saying what they ought not say" (1 Tim 5:13–15). The prohibition on women teaching in 1 Tim 2:12 fits into this historical context. The Köstenbergers assert that "at an historical level" all the false teachers were men; women are depicted as "the victims of false teaching."[95] This is simply not true. The very last quote just given speaks of women going from house to house [church] "saying what they ought not say" (1 Tim 5:13–15).

The second context of huge importance is the literary context. The immediate literary context of Tim 2:12 are verses 8–15. What we discover here is that something abnormal, exceptional, is present. Almost everything said in verses 8–15 have no parallels in the rest of the New

94. Köstenberger and Köstenberger, *God's Design*, 329.
95. Köstenberger and Köstenberger, *God's Design*, 204.

Testament. Nowhere else do we read of men being forbidden to pray "without anger or argument"; how women should dress *when they pray* in church;[96] a command that *only* women need to be taught; women prohibited from teaching; the word *authentein*; significance given to the fact that Adam was created first; Adam was not deceived but Eve; and a promise that women "will be saved by bearing children."

This brings us to the third context the Köstenbergers prescribe. They call this the "theological" context. I would call it "the canonical context," but I think we are talking about the same thing. Every verse must be interpreted in the light of all of Scripture—the canon. Or, to put it the other way, no verse can be interpreted so that it contradicts what is clearly revealed in other parts of Scripture. The Reformers made the same point when they insisted that "Scripture must be interpreted by Scripture."[97] Evangelical exegetes should always keep this rule in mind, but it is mainly the responsibility of systematic theologians who have to find in the varied comments in Scripture, some seemingly in contradiction to what is said elsewhere, a unified answer to the theological question before them.

Affirming and practicing this rule in the case of 1 Tim 2:12 is of vital importance. We evangelicals must find a way to interpret this prohibition so that it does not deny what is so clearly taught elsewhere in Scripture. We must find an interpretation that does not make what is said in this verse contradict Gen 1–2, which with one voice teach the substantial or essential equality of the two differentiated sexes; or contradict Gen 3:16, which makes the rule of the man over the women a consequence of the fall; or question that Deborah was a ruler over Israel; or marginalize the prophets, men and women, who spoke for God in the power of the Spirit; or leave us all puzzled as to why Jesus said not one word on male "headship" and much to the contrary; or stand in opposition to Paul's *theology of ministry* that teaches the Spirt gives a ministry to every believer irrespective of gender and his *practice of ministry,* which allows and affirms the leadership of women, and specifically women leading the church in prophetic ministry, a form of preaching.

96. The Greek *hōsautōs* at the beginning of verse 9 suggests the word "prayer" is implied: men are to pray . . . likewise, women are to pray in church. In 1 Cor 11:5 Paul accepts that women led in prayer in church. True, 1 Pet 3:3–5 also asks women to dress modestly, but this is not specifically related to church assemblies as it is in 1 Timothy. This is the least significant exceptional fact.

97. Köstenberger and Köstenberger, *God's Design,* 330. The Köstenbergers endorse this canonical rule.

An Evangelical Interpretation of 1 Timothy 2:12

What we are seeking, therefore, is an evangelical interpretation of this text that does not set it in contradiction to what is clearly and repeatedly said elsewhere in Scripture. First, I consider the linguistic issues that have been fiercely debated.

The most contested issue is the meaning of the word *authentein*, found only in this verse in the New Testament. The question is, does this word speak of the authority a male pastor may rightly exercise that is excluded to women, or of a kind of authority that is not right for a man or woman to exercise in the church? For the complementarian case, it is absolutely essential that it means the former; it speaks of rightful authority that God gives to male pastors, denied to women. The verdict is now in. The standard New Testament Greek dictionary says the word means, "to assume a stance of independent authority."[98] In other words, it speaks of illegitimate authority. I set out the evidence for this conclusion in addendum 3 at the end of this chapter. Complementarian linguistic scholars have not been able to find one example where *authentein* around about the time of Paul or earlier simply means authority in a positive sense. We must conclude therefore that Paul is forbidding women from exercising authority of a kind not allowed in the church, whoever exercises it. In using this exceptional word, Paul makes it plain that he is speaking of an exceptional situation.

Whether Paul forbids one thing, teaching in an *authentein* way (by seizing authority or dominating), or two things, teaching *and* acting in an *authentein* way, is also contested. It is obvious that the two prohibitions are very closely related, but the question just stated remains.[99] Andreas Köstenberger has put a huge amount of effort into arguing 1 Tim 2:12 prohibits two things,[100] but Payne, and Belleville independently, have shown his arguments are without merit. The prohibition forbids one thing, teaching in an *authentein* manner.[101]

Now to a detail in 1 Tim 2:12 that is seldom discussed. Paul's prohibition is in the singular, "I forbid *a* woman teaching; from dominating or

98. Bauer, Arndt, Gingrich, and Danker, *Greek-English Lexicon*, 150.

99. See further on this addendum 3 following.

100. Köstenberger, Schreiner, and Baldwin, *Women in the Church*, 81–104; Köstenberger and Schreiner, *Women in the Church*, 53–84.

101. I set out the evidence for this assertion in an addendum at the end of this chapter.

usurping authority over *a* man." If Paul was forbidding all woman from teaching/preaching in a church setting as we know it today we would expect him to say, "I forbid women to teach men." But he does not say this. A house-church setting explains the singular. Paul is addressing the specific problem that he mentions in 1 Tim 5:13–15 of women giving false teaching in house-churches one-on-one. Paul is not forbidding all woman from teaching/preaching in church like a man or woman might do today; he is forbidding individual women from taking aside individual men and browbeating them with their views—in other words, teaching them in an *authentein* way. The house-church setting is presupposed throughout the New Testament, including the Pastorals.[102] In the house-churches of the first century ministry was freely exercised; there were no pastors set over every church who gave most if not all the teaching, like there are today. There was no pulpit and declarative preaching was not a characteristic part of house-church meetings.[103] In 1 Cor 14:26 Paul describes what took place when Christians met in a home context. "When you come together, *each one* has a hymn, a lesson, a revelation, a tongue or an interpretation." Innumerable times Paul speaks of the one another ministry that took place in these house-churches.[104] Several times he tells believers in their house-churches *to teach one another* (Rom 15:14; Col 3:16) and to speak the truth to one another (Eph 4:25). Women cannot be excluded from this one another ministry; Paul's theology of ministry has the gifts of ministry allocated on the basis of the *charisma* given by God, not on the basis of gender. Undeniably women led in prayer (1 Tim 2:9; 1 Cor 11:5), prophesied (1 Cor 11:5), and ministered in many ways in the house-churches of the first century. It is in this home setting that the Köstenbergers envisage Priscilla and Aquila teaching Apollos.[105] In this specific setting where everyone is free to speak and teach Paul prohibits women who have been "deceived" from teaching men individually, seeking to impose their ideas on them. They are to be quiet and learn.

In the second addendum at the end of this chapter I will explain the various titled ministries we find mentioned in the New Testament but it is probably helpful at this point in discussing the house-churches

102. On this see Giles, "House Churches," 6–8, and my earlier discussion in this chapter on house-churches in the first century.

103. Giles, *Patterns*, 190–92.

104. Giles, *Patterns*, 39. See also 190–92 where I discuss the dialogical nature of teaching in the house-churches.

105. Köstenberger and Köstenberger, *God's Design*, 140.

that I say something about Christian communal leadership in the apostolic age. To understand what is said on leaders in the New Testament we must accept that neither Jesus nor the apostles, or Paul in particular, prescribed how the church was to be led. How and who lead in the Christian community emerged to meet the need of the time. We find many titles for leaders that reflect in most cases their function and we see development with the passing of time. When the Pastorals were written, the title bishop (1 Tim 3:1) seems to have become the title given to the host of the house-church and the title deacon to one or more assistant leaders. The bishop as the respected host of the house-church often would have given teaching (1 Tim 3:2), and if one or more of the elders from the city-wide (Titus 1:5) "council of elders" (1 Tim 4:14) were members of a particular house-church and were gifted in teaching (1 Tim 5:17), they too would have given instruction from time to time. Nowhere in all of Paul's epistles is it ever suggested that teaching is the preserved domain of named office bearers. Teaching others was what better informed Christians did Heb 5:12; James 3:1). The Pastorals make this truth emphatic; there were many people teaching in Ephesus and Crete, some giving false teaching. In Ephesus, women going from house to house teaching what they ought not teach was a big problem (1 Tim 5:13–15).

One of the most common errors that contemporary Christians make is that when they find the word church/*ekklesia* in the New Testament they give content to this word in terms of their modern experience of church. The Köstenbergers do this consistently. The truth is church in the New Testament is more to be contrasted than compared with church in the modern world. I say again, a church *gathering* in the apostolic age was in the context of a home where informality and mutual ministry prevailed. This is the historic phenomenon that 1 Tim 2 envisages. The Köstenbergers never acknowledge this fact. For them, "church" in the first century is like church today, a large public gathering with one or more appointed leaders[106] who have "institutional authority,"[107] and are responsible for all teaching/preaching.[108]

I do not believe that in 1 Tim 2:12 Paul is forbidding all women from teaching/preaching in church or leading in church, but should any reader disagree with me please note that this text is not forbidding women to

---

106. Köstenberger and Köstenberger, *God's Design*, 194.

107. Köstenberger and Köstenberger, *God's Design*, 57.

108. Köstenberger and Köstenberger, *God's Design*, 218.

preach/teach in a church like we know today. Paul is forbidding individual women from teaching one-on-one in little house-churches, *not* from teaching as an office bearer (pastor) in a large structured church as we know today. Thus, how to apply today Paul's prohibition, however understood, I am sure you can see, is by no means clear. The Köstenbergers certainly overstate their case when they dogmatically conclude that what Paul says in 1 Tim 2:12 means today that a woman should never teach a man "in a public church setting."[109] I cannot see that it does.

If I am correct in arguing that the Köstenbergers read their twenty-first century understanding of church into 1 Tim 2:8–15, then in doing so they break the hermeneutical rule they lay down, which they say "guards the authority of Scripture";[110] namely, to avoid at all cost reading into the historical text the contemporary interpreter's own horizon and agenda.

Verses 13–14

These two verses are the most important for any interpretation of 1 Tim 2:11–12. It is agreed they give "dual rationale" for Paul's prohibition.[111] They tell us why the apostle makes this ruling. Three interpretations of these dual rationales have been given. First, there is the historic interpretation that virtually all the great theologians across the ages articulated.[112] This is accurately given and endorsed by the Australian evangelical scholar Leon Morris, in his 1957 Tyndale commentary. Women are not to speak in public, especially in church, and not to exercise authority in the state, the church, or the home, because verse 13 reveals "the true order of the sexes." "Man's priority in creation places him in a position of superiority over women."[113] In other words, *chronological order* in creation indicates that man is "first" in rank, woman second. The second rationale given in verse 14: "woman must submit to man, because 'Adam was not deceived, but the woman.'" In these words Paul teaches "the greater aptitude of the weaker sex to be led astray."[114] This interpretation of 1 Tim 2:13–14, the

109. Köstenberger and Köstenberger, *God's Design*, 218.

110. Köstenberger and Köstenberger, *God's Design*, 337.

111. Köstenberger and Köstenberger, *God's Design*, 210.

112. Doriani, "History of the Interpretation," 213–68. Giles, *Trinity and Subordinationism*, 145–55.

113. Marshall, *Pastoral Epistles*, 77.

114. Marshall, *Pastoral Epistles*, 77.

complementarian theologian Daniel Doriani says, is predicated on the "ontological" inferiority of women.[115] In a cultural context where it was almost universally believed that God had made men "superior," women "inferior" this interpretation exactly reflected what everyone believed and was not questioned.

In the 1970s this interpretation became untenable. The huge change introduced by the women's movement forced all theologians to abandon the historic interpretation. No longer could anyone say openly that they believed God had created women "inferior" to men and that they were more prone to sin and error. First, to give a new interpretation of these verses was George Knight III in his 1977 ground-breaking book, *New Testament Teaching on the Role Relationship of Men and Women*. He gave what Doriani calls a "reinterpretation" of 1 Tim 2:13–14. In creation, before the fall, God gave to man the "role" of leading, woman the "role" of obeying. These "roles" reflect the hierarchical *social order* God established in creation and can never change. They are the God-given ideal.[116] The Köstenberger's put it this way, "Because Adam was created first, *the creation order* indicates that authority rests with Adam." "According to Paul, priority in creation entails primacy with regard to the exercise of authority."[117] Knight, the Köstenbergers, and all complementarians find verse 14 much more difficult. Only very brave complementarians admit that this verse says women are more prone to sin and deception.[118] Most follow Knight's creative solution. Eve's sin was one of "role reversal." God had put Adam in charge and so when Eve took it upon herself to speak to the Satan on her own she usurped his headship. Knight says, "When the roles established by God in creation were reversed by Eve, it manifestly had a disastrous effect."[119] The Köstenbergers put it this way: in verse 14 "Paul reminds his readers what happened historically when woman acted apart from man, leading him into disobedience, rather than the man fulfilling his role and leading woman."[120] This is not exegesis but *eisegesis*. Adam was with Eve when they sinned (Gen 3:6) and by his own decision he ate of the tree. For this reason, God held them both fully

115. Doriani, "History of the Interpretation," 258.

116. On this see Doriani, "History of the Interpretation," 258–59, especially n. 180.

117. Köstenberger and Köstenberger, *God's Design*, 211. Italics added.

118. See Doriani, "History of the Interpretation," 258–59, 264–66. Payne, *Man and Woman*, 406–7, gives other examples.

119. Knight, *New Testament Teaching*, 31.

120. Knight, *New Testament Teaching*, 31.

accountable for their sin. Adam and Eve's sin was not "role reversal; it was disobedience of the command of God. Nowhere in Gen 1 and 2 is man set over the woman, let alone given the leadership "role." The text of Genesis emphasizes that man and woman have the same status, dignity, and leadership potential before the fall. The rule of the man over the woman is entirely a consequence of the fall as Gen 3:16 makes explicit. Then we have the unpardonable sin of introducing the sociological term "role" into the supposedly exegetical enterprise when neither the idea nor the term is found in Scripture.

Evangelical egalitarians at the same time as complementarians realized that the historic interpretation of 1 Tim 2:13–14 had to be rejected because it has no basis in the text of Gen 1 and 2 and because it horribly demeaned women, who like men are created in the image and likeness of God and conjointly appointed by God to rule over the world, not the man over the woman. Because they had to think deeply, had no help from the past, and complementarians were constantly attacking them as liberals, this took some time.[121] I outline what I now consider to be the best and soundest way to understand what Paul is saying in these two verses. He is not giving his interpretation of Gen 1–3, or quoting any words given in these chapters, but simply making an analogy or seeing a parallel between what happened in the garden of Eden and what has happened in Ephesus. He is saying no more than the garden of Eden illustrates how disastrous the consequences can be when a woman is deceived by Satan (as women have been in Ephesus, see 1 Tim 5:15) and then takes it upon herself without proper authority to teach men. Just as in the garden, woman put herself first and was deceived by the serpent, so the women in Ephesus have put themselves "first" having been "deceived" by Satan.

On this interpretation of 1 Tim 2:13–14, Paul is not arguing that man is "first" in rank because he was in *chronological order* created first and that women are more prone to sin and deception because Eve sinned first, nor is he appealing to a past *hierarchical social order* given in creation before the fall that subordinates all women to all men for all time—something never mentioned in the Bible. Rather, he is alluding to the *heresy-created disorder* in the church at Ephesus. If this is the case, then Paul's prohibition on women teaching and leading in church, however understood, is not grounded in a supposed pre-fall subordination of the woman, and thus universally binding. It is an exceptional ruling,

121. I find this interpretation first clearly articulated in 1992 in Keener, *Paul, Women and Wives*, 117.

addressing an exceptional problem in a church of the first century. Paul is saying no more than, it is you women, like Eve, who have been deceived, stop teaching your false doctrines. Women, it is true, are singled out by Paul and forbidden to act in a certain way to men. For women to set themselves over free men in Paul's cultural context was totally unacceptable.[122] We must never divorce Paul from his historical and cultural context.

The great strength of this interpretation of 1 Tim 2:13–14 is that it does not impose on the text of Gen 1–3 an interpretation that the writer of Genesis seeks to exclude. It is his view that in creation before the fall man and woman, two differentiated sexes, are substantially and essentially equal.

Verse 15

Immediately following his comment on Eve's deception, Paul says, "Yet she will be saved through childbearing" (NRSV). Undeniably this final comment is related to the issues addressed in this section of 1 Timothy. The idea that women will be saved through childbearing would seem to contradict the doctrine of justification by faith and thus, not surprisingly, a huge amount has been written on this text. The Köstenbergers tell us that there are at least seven different interpretations of this verse. They do not give these or carefully exegete the text; instead, they imperially say, "women will be spiritually preserved if they devote themselves to their God-given role in the domestic and familial sphere."[123] This is not exegesis but rather a reading of modern socially conservative ideas into the text.

I do not intend to give an interpretation of Paul's words in verse 15 because I think we lack vital information. There must be a reason why Paul made this exceptional comment that is so difficult. What we do know is that the false teaching at Ephesus had an ascetic strain. The false teachers were forbidding people from eating certain foods and from marrying (1 Tim 4:3). It is against this backdrop, I suggest, these words must be understood. Paul is countering what they are teaching.

122. Westfall, *Paul and Gender*, 75.

123. Köstenberger and Köstenberger, *God's Design*, 216.

What we do learn from this text, and there can be no missing this point, is behind all that is said in 1 Tim 2:8–15 lies an exceptional situation, of which we know very little.

CONCLUSION

I conclude that the evidence is compelling; in principle (Gal 3:28) and in practice Paul affirmed the equality of the sexes as far as he was able in his first century cultural context. The number of women involved in leadership positions he mentions and commends is quite breathtaking given the first century setting. To read 1 Tim 2:12–14 as a universal prohibition of women teaching/preaching and leading in church as we know it today is simply not an option for an evangelical who wants to uphold the ultimate unity of Scripture. In the next chapter we will consider what Paul says on the marriage relationship and we will again discover that he is subversive of the prevailing cultural norms. It is his belief that *Christian* husbands and wives should give themselves to each other in costly sacrificial love and service like Christ gave himself for the church in costly sacrificial love and service.

QUESTIONS FOR DISCUSSION

1. Because the early churches were located in homes, the numbers were small and formality at a minimum. In this context, the Lord's Supper was celebrated as part of an ordinary meal (1 Cor 11:17–22). How does this information help us understand what Paul says about ministry/leadership in the church? How might it suggest some difficulty in applying what Paul says about church in the first century to the twenty first century?

2. In the New Testament we find no example where one man or one woman is the sole pastor/minister. What are some disadvantages of solo leadership in today's church? How/why might women be disadvantaged by it?

3. What do you think many able, godly women who have leadership positions in society feel about their exclusion from leadership in many of our churches? Could this teaching be a hindrance to such women becoming Christians?

4. In many, if not most, evangelical and Pentecostal churches today, there are large worship services and small home groups. Have we got the best of both worlds?

5. What do you understand by the expression, "servant-leadership"?

ADDENDUM 1: A PERENNIAL ERROR: ABSOLUTIZING ONE TEXT

Virtually all evangelicals who argue that women should not teach/ preach or lead in the church say 1 Tim 2:11–14 is conclusive. We need look no further than this one text to discover what the Bible says on the man-woman relationship. We are told that this one text is "decisive,"[124] "fundamental,"[125] the "primary,"[126] or "the most important text to consider"[127] in any examination of what the New Testament teaches on the man-woman relationship. Outlining the two sides in this debate, James Beck and Craig Blomberg, the editors of the book *Two Views on Women*,[128] say the interpretation and application of 1 Tim 2:11–14 is "the most determinative" issue in this debate.[129] In other words, who wins this debate depends more than anything else on how this *one* passage is interpreted. To place all the weight on the *interpretation* of this *one* text in determining whether or not half the human race is subordinated to the other half, and excluded from teaching/preaching and leading in church seems precarious, especially since competent evangelical New Testament scholars are not agreed on its interpretation. Egalitarian evangelicals with the highest view of Scripture argue that this text speaks to an exceptional situation and thus gives exceptional teaching. It therefore does not exclude all women for all time from teaching/preaching and leading in church.

What few Christians are aware of is that majoring on one text that seems to contradict much else in Scripture has been toxic to the life of the church from earliest times. It is a perennial mistake that has always

---

124. Jensen, *Sydney Anglicanism*, 128.

125. Schreiner, "Women in Ministry," 218.

126. Saucy and TenElshof, *Women and Men*, 291. So also John Piper on the back cover of the book, Köstenberger, Schreiner, and Baldwin, *Women in the Church*, 1995.

127. Clark, *Man and Woman*, 192.

128. Beck and Blomberg, *Two Views*, 17.

129. Beck and Blomberg, *Two Views*, 307.

led to error and division. The best theologians have consistently rejected such "proof-texting." They are agreed that the primary rule in appealing to Scripture to establish doctrinal norms is that the mind of God is revealed in *the whole of Scripture*. Texts that seem to contradict the whole must be interpreted so that this is not the case. "Scripture must interpret Scripture."

I just give a few examples where majoring on one text has led the church into error:

In the fourth century, Arius argued that God the Father is uniquely God and that the Son, while above all others, was created in time. He quoted Prov 8:22: "The Lord created (*ktizō*) me at the beginning of his works" as proof. He said no text could be plainer or more explicit. Athanasius could not accept Arius' teaching on the Son, nor his interpretation of Prov 8:22. For him, the Scriptures were clear; Jesus Christ the Son of God is God in all might, majesty, and power, and as such is not a creature. In his famous *Discourses Against the Arians*,[130] Athanasius gives far more space to seeking an alternative interpretation of Arius' proof-text than he does to any other specific issue.[131] His most profound and primary reply is that an interpretation of one text that contradicts what "the whole scope of Scripture" teaches, cannot be accepted.[132] For Athanasius, no matter how explicit the teaching of one text may seem, what it seemingly says can never negate what is primary and fundamental to all of Scripture, in this case, that Jesus Christ is God in all might, majesty, and power, without any caveats. After a long and bitter debate, the church agreed with Athanasius. The Nicene Creed of 381 says the Son "is not created," but eternally begotten of the Father and on this basis he is "God from God, Light from Light, true God from true God, one in being with the Father."

In the sixteenth century, Luther addressed the same problem. His Roman Catholic opponents insisted that salvation is based on works, quoting Jas 2:24: "A person is justified by works and not by faith alone." They said this text is clear and unambiguous and they pointed to a few other passages where they thought the same thing was taught (Matt 25:31–46; John 5:29; 2 Cor 5:10). Luther made a radical reply. He concluded that what James taught on salvation was "in direct opposition to

130. Schaff and Wace, *Nicene and Post-Nicene*.
131. Some thirty-six pages in Schaff and Wace, *Nicene and Post-Nicene*.
132. Athanasius, "Discourses Against the Arians," 3.29 (p. 409).

St. Paul and all the rest of the Bible," and "I therefore refuse him a place among the writers of the true canon of the Bible."[133] Luther took this decisive stance because he could not allow that one verse in the epistle of James could be permitted to contradict what he believed was primary and foundational to all the epistles of Saint Paul, namely that we are justified by faith in Christ alone by grace alone. Modern evangelical commentators have found a less drastic solution. They conclude James is not rejecting Paul's teaching on justification by faith, but a false understanding of Paul's doctrine. We should note the logic of this argument: what James says on face value does contradict Paul; therefore, we must find a way to interpret James so that what he says in this one verse does not contradict Paul.

A twentieth-century example of the error of majoring on one text is found in Professor Oscar Cullman's book, *The State in the New Testament*.[134] After the Second World War, the question before the church was, why did so many German Christians support Hitler? Cullmann's answer was that the Germans in the post–First World War period longed for a strong state that would bring back honor to the German people and establish political stability. When Hitler achieved this, they found in one text, Rom 13:1, a biblical basis for obeying Hitler, no matter what he did. In this text Paul writes, "Let every person be subject to the governing authorities, for there is no authority except from God, and those authorities that exist have been instituted by God." Hitler's supporters said nothing could be plainer: rulers are appointed by God, Hitler is our ruler, therefore we should be subject to him. Cullman's reply to this argument is that if Rom 13:1 is read to definitively sum up all that the Bible teaches on the state, then this one verse stands in "flagrant contradiction to the teaching of Jesus. It would also contradict the other New Testament authors as well, chiefly the author of the Johannine apocalypse. Above all, moreover, Paul would contradict himself."[135] Jesus limits the rule of the state to its own domain (Mark 12:17), and Rev 13 teaches that the state can become an instrument of the Devil. Cullmann concludes that only by adopting a holistic hermeneutic that makes the whole of Scripture primary, can a truly biblical understanding of the state be established. When this approach is not adopted, and all attention is given to one verse, then the

133. Dillenberger, *Martin Luther*, 36.
134. Cullman, *State*.
135. Cullman, *State*, 46.

Bible is made the servant of our preconceived commitments. Its voice is silenced and human presuppositions prevail. Indeed, Cullmann goes so far as to argue that "the fountainhead of all false biblical interpretation and all heresy is invariably the isolation and absolutizing of one single passage."[136]

When I was writing this chapter I thought this post–Second World War example was very much past history. Before sending the manuscript of this book to the publisher I was invited at short notice to teach a week-long post graduate course in the Philippines. The academic who I was working with said at our first meeting, "Do you know what the most quoted verse in the Philippines today is?" I shook my head. She said, "Romans 13:1. The majority of Christians in the Philippines quote this text in support of President Rodrigo Duterte who they say, following Paul, has "been appointed by God." For this reason they believe he should be commended for his decisive actions against drug dealers who the police freely shoot."

I now give two examples where the absolutizing of one verse or passage has caused a sharp division among evangelicals. Seventh Day Adventists believe Christians should worship on the seventh day of the week. They say this is the explicit teaching of the Ten Commandments and the Sabbath commandment is grounded in the creation order revealed in Gen 1. Most Christians reject this reasoning. They say Jesus did not teach this and Paul says that one day is as good as another (Rom 14:5). The first day of the week is to be preferred because this is the day Jesus rose from the grave. We should note again the logic of this argument. Yes, the fourth commandment clearly teaches the seventh day is holy, but on the basis of much else in Scripture, most Christians believe a change to the first day is acceptable to God. They argue that one text, even if it is in the Ten Commandments and is predicated on creation, does not settle the issue.

When I was a young Christian in the 1960s, the Pentecostal movement was in its heyday. Pentecostals were teaching that every believer needed to be "baptized in the Spirit," and speaking in tongues was the evidence for this "second blessing." In every conversation I had with my Pentecostal friends, I was taken to Acts 8:4–24 where we read of how the Samaritans first believed in Christ, but when Peter and John arrived and laid hands on them they received the Holy Spirit. Nothing could be

---

136. Cullman, *State*, 47.

plainer; the Samaritans believed and then later were baptized in the Holy Spirit. This is what this text says. When I asked my wise pastor what I should think, he said to me, "Kevin, what we have to decide is whether what took place in Acts 8 is normative and prescriptive or something exceptional. Opening his Bible he pointed out to me that in Acts 2, Luke, quoting Peter's Pentecost sermon, makes believing, receiving the Spirit, and water baptism what is involved in becoming a Christian (Acts 2:38). A second or subsequent gift of the Spirit is not envisaged and speaking in tongues is not mentioned. Then turning to Paul's epistles, he pointed me to texts where Paul is emphatic that being in Christ and having the Spirit are two sides of one coin (Rom 8:9–17; 1 Cor 12:12; Gal 3:2–3). I thus concluded, long before I had begun to think about 1 Tim 2:12–14, that no one text taken in isolation—however clear it seemed—could settle any question. My guide to Christian living should be, as I later learned from Athanasius, "the whole scope of Scripture."

In this argument I have just made, it is important to note that I do not differ from the Köstenbergers. They say, "Not everything in the Bible has equal weight."[137] I am sure they agree with me that James 2:24 (justified by works, not faith) is not of the same theological weight as Rom 3:24 and Eph 2:8 (justified by grace through faith, not works). I hope I have convinced them that 1 Tim 2:11–12 with its entirely unique prohibition and wording is not of the same theological weight as Gen 1:27–28, the teaching and example of Jesus on women, and Paul's teaching on ministry in the church given in 1 Cor 12:4–31, Rom 12:3–8, and Eph 4:11–12.

In conclusion, I sum up the argument I have just put in three sentences.

1. The most important context to be considered by the evangelical theologian in the interpretation of any one verse is the whole Bible.

2. When what the Bible as a whole actually says about women is understood, the evangelical theologian cannot with integrity interpret 1 Tim 2:11–12 to be an absolute prohibition on women in leadership or teaching/preaching.

3. If one verse that is discordant with the overall teaching of Scripture is absolutized, the church is divided and damaged, and often heresy follows.

---

137. Köstenberger and Köstenberger, God's Design, 345.

ADDENDUM 2: SERVANT-LEADERSHIP IN THE APOSTOLIC CHURCHES

Behind the contemporary intramural evangelical debate over women in church leadership lies a more profound debate about whether or not the New Testament dictates how the church should be led. Some Christians believe passionately that the Bible prescribes how the church should be governed and others that the Bible does not do this; no one pattern is more "biblical" than another. Presbyterians have traditionally been the most dogmatic, arguing that the presbyterian system is *jure divino*—given as divine law.[138] The Köstenbergers are of this opinion. They say the Bible prescribes how the church should be led. They write, "We believe that Scripture teaches a plurality of local church leadership in the form of a team of pastors or elders and allows for (though does not demand) a group of deacons,"[139] excluding women from all leadership positions where authority is exercised.[140]

I am of the opposite opinion and I have written a book of over 250 pages, *Patterns of Ministry Among the First Christians*, making the point that neither Jesus nor any of the apostles, certainly not Paul, prescribed how the church was to be led. What we see in the New Testament is the emergence of differing forms of leadership, each given a name that in most cases reflect function, and the development of these ministries with the passing of time. This development was from less structured forms of leadership to more structured forms, a process called "institutionalization." What this means is that we do not find in Scripture any one church order and for this reason we cannot claim "our" church order is what Scripture mandates. Below I will outline what the various leaders with different titles did but before I do this I make one telling point in relation to women in church leadership. Most complementarians insist that no woman should be the solo-pastor of a church with 50 to 500 people, but such churches did not exist in the first century and mono-ministry was unknown. There is no mandate for a man or a woman to take such a position. In the apostolic age, Christians met in homes in small numbers, there were no ordained leaders and wide participation was the norm in this informal setting (see 1 Cor 14:26). In house-churches, the owner of

138. See further on this Giles, *Patterns*, 96–97.

139. Köstenberger and Köstenberger, *God's Design*, 194.

140. Köstenberger and Köstenberger, *God's Design*, 194. This is the primary thesis of their book.

the home gave formal leadership but as the Spirit moved other people were free to minister to one another. Many women are spoken of as house-church leaders in the New Testament (Col 4:15; 1 Cor 1:11; cf. Acts 12:12; 16:14–15, 40, etc.).

But to say this is not enough. In the New Testament we find also many leaders with specific titles, which as I said above usually reflect function. We need to understand who these people were and what they did. We cannot simply ignore them. I give in brief what I explain more fully in my book, *Patterns of Ministry*.

Apostles. In the New Testament we find two kinds of apostles. First, the twelve apostles who were all eyewitnesses of Jesus' ministry and resurrection (Acts 1:21–22). These men obviously could not have successors as eyewitnesses. However, at some point after Pentecost God began raising up other leaders who are recognized and called apostles such as Paul, Barnabas, James the brother of Jesus, Apollos, Timothy, and the couple, Andronicus and Junia. Most, possibly all, of these people did not hear Jesus' teaching and were not eyewitnesses of the resurrection. It seems that those in this larger group of apostles were missionaries who were pioneer church planters (So Paul and Barnabas in their missionary journeys, see also 1 Cor 9:1–3). Paul is a missionary apostle, but of a unique kind. God gives him a special ministry, to lead the mission to the Gentiles.

The Twelve and Paul cannot have successors. They had a unique, time-bound ministry, but the other kind of apostles who are not limited in number are always present in the church. We simply use the Latin transliterated equivalent of the word apostle (one who is sent), "missionary."

Prophets. In the New Testament the most prominent church leaders are the prophets. We should understand this ministry in the light of the Old Testament. The Old Testament prophets spoke in the power of the Spirit as teachers of God's people. They were more "forth-tellers" than "fore-tellers." Paul says the prophet speaks for the "edification, encouragement and consolation" of members of the church (1 Cor 14:3)—what preachers do. In the Old and New Testament, all prophecy, like all preaching, is to be judged as to whether or not it is a human word or a word from God (1 Cor 14:29; 1 Thess 5:21; 1 John 4:1). Paul thinks of prophecy as the second most important ministry in the church (1 Cor 12:28), and with Luke, envisages many forms: teaching, exhortation, words of judgment, and occasionally prediction. Many a sermon today has a prophetic element. When God lays on the preacher's heart a word specifically for the hearers, this is a form of prophecy. Women in the Old

Testament (Exod 15:20–21; Judg 4:4; 2 Kgs 22:14; Neh 6:14) and in the New are called prophets or said to prophesy (Luke 2:38; Acts 2:17–18; 1 Cor 11:5; Rev 2:20).

Teachers. In the New Testament age, some were designated prophets and others teachers (1 Cor 12:28; Eph 4:11), but it is almost impossible to clearly demarcate prophecy and teaching. Once Luke speaks of the leaders of the church at Antioch as "prophetic-teachers" (Acts 13:1). All those given leadership titles are said to teach: apostles, prophets, elders, bishops, deacons, and house-church leaders. To argue that women may prophesy but not teach is fatuous. Not only can prophecy take the form of teaching but why, we ask, would Paul allow women to lead in prophecy, a "word ministry," and yet not teach? To give teaching precedence over prophecy is to reverse Paul's own ordering. He ranks the ministry of the apostle "first," the prophet "second," and the teacher "third" (1 Cor 12:28; cf. Eph 4:11–12).

Elders. In the ancient world, as in much of the two-thirds world today, senior men and women are community leaders. The elders mentioned in the New Testament were older men (Acts 2:17; Titus 2:2; 1 Pet 5:1–5) or women (1 Tim 5:2; Titus 2:3). We may presume therefore that virtually everyone who gave leadership in the early church, whether apostle, prophet, teacher, house-church leader, bishop, or something else, was a respected senior person—an elder. In Paul's first ten epistles he never mentions the *office* of elder or even uses the word. The selection and appointment of specific people to be office-bearers called "elders" seems to have emerged as a second stage in the development of church leadership (Acts 14:23). So we note Paul's directive, near the end of his life, to Titus to *appoint* men as elders in *each town on Crete* (Titus 1:5)—not in each house-church. Apparently the Christian community on Crete had existed for many years without any *office* bearers called "elders." These *appointed* older believers formed a "council" (1 Tim 4:14) and provided general oversight of all the Christians in each town who met in small house-churches. These first elders were not the equivalent of the pastor today.

Bishops and deacons. There are only two explicit references to bishops in the New Testament (Phil 1:1; 1 Tim 3:1–7)—in both cases in association with deacons. The best guess is that these two titles for an office were first used of house-church leaders and their assistants. Presbyterians equate bishops and elders, but neither Phil 1:1 nor 1 Tim 3:1–7 does this and the evidence cited for this claim is doubtful. What is certainly true is all bishops were older men (elders), but this does not mean all elders were bishops.

In the second century, the title "bishop" became the name of the leader of a city-wide Christian community with many house-churches. The bishop's assistants and advisors were called deacons. The elders were older respected men who met in council. They are not depicted as pastors set over congregations.

The argument that those called deacons had a "nonteaching, non-authoritative, servant role" is to be rejected.[141] The title deacon/*diakonos*, is used of those who are clearly significant Christian leaders and thus teachers (Paul, Apollos, Timothy, Phoebe, Tychius, and Epaphras). What this means is that the title *diakonos* characteristically speaks of those who preach and teach. John Collins makes this point very forcefully. He says, "A third of the early instances [of the use of the *diak,* word group] relate to the preaching of the word."[142] So we note in support that in reply to his opponents in Corinth, Paul says he and his coworkers are *diakonoi* of the new covenant. As such, they do not "peddle" or "falsify" the word of God (2 Cor 2:7; 4:2) but rather "preach God's Gospel in order to serve (*diakonia*) the Corinthians (2 Cor 11:7–8). The message proclaimed "is from God, who through Christ reconciled us to himself and gave us the ministry (*diakonia*) of reconciliation." So we are, Paul continues, "ambassadors for Christ, God making his appeal through us" (2 Cor 6:18–20).

Ordination. We only have three possible examples in the New Testament of the laying on of hands and prayer to commission certain people (Acts 6:6; 13:3; 1 Tim 4:14; 2 Tim 1:6—the last two references are probably parallels), but we have no mention of ordination as we know it today. These texts speak of the prayerful commissioning of people for a specific ministry; but in no instance of the public and prayerful legitimizing of pastors for individual churches. In the apostolic age, it was the Spirit who initiated and empowered men and women for servant-leadership.

It cannot therefore be demanded that all church leaders be ordained on the basis of anything said in Scripture. However, the church as an institution in this world, as it is realized today, can demand that its leaders be ordained, that they be legitimized in public by the laying on of hands and prayer.

---

141. Köstenberger and Köstenberger, *God's Design*, 194.
142. Collins, *Diakonia*, 63.

To Sum Up

Those who want to believe the Bible prescribes how the church should be led in every age have great difficulty with what I have just outlined. To establish one form of leadership that could be made prescriptive they need to ignore some ministries, argue that others should be equated, and for complementarians deny that any women had a leadership "role" in the apostolic age.

We see this illustrated in the Köstenbergers' claim that "the Scriptures teach a plurality of local church leadership in the form of a team of pastors or elders and allow for (though it does not demand) a group of deacons.[143] This order is not found anywhere in the New Testament, let alone prescribed. We only find the term "pastors" once in the New Testament and then it is hyphenated with the ministry of teaching and this ministry stands alongside that of the apostles, prophets, and evangelists (Eph 4:11). Certainly elders are called on to be pastors/shepherds of the flock (Acts 20:28; 1 Pet 5:2) but these texts do not equate the ministry of the elder and the pastor. They simply ask the older men who give leadership to be good pastors, something all Christian leaders should do. When it comes to deacons we should carefully observe how this term and ministry develops over time. First of all the term *diakonos* spoke generically of Christian leadership (Matt 20:26; Mark 10:43; 1 Cor 12:5), then of significant leaders (Paul, Apollos, Timothy, Phoebe, Tychius, and Epaphras) and finally of an office associated with the office of the bishop (Phil 1:1; 1 Tim 3:1–7).

If the New Testament *prescribes* how the church today should be led in all ages then we would think the pattern would be apostles, prophets, and teachers (1 Cor 12:28), or possibly with several evangelists and pastor-teachers as well (Eph 4:11), and women in all these ministries.

If this clearly enunciated church order given in 1 Cor 12:28 and Eph 4:11–12 is not going to be made *prescriptive* then I think it would be much more honest to argue that what is said about leaders and leadership in the New Testament is *not prescriptive* for the church of all ages, but rather *descriptive* of the church in the first century. If we agree on this then it means we are free to encourage patterns of leadership that work best in our age and best capture the principles we see implied in the New Testament, most importantly that all leadership is Spirit-given,

---

143. Köstenberger and Köstenberger, *God's Design*, 194.

all Christian leadership is servant-leadership, church leadership is plural, and the leadership of women is endorsed and encouraged.

ADDENDUM 3: THE DISPUTED GREEK WORDS KEPHALĒ AND AUTHENTEIN

The Köstenbergers say that one of the inexcusable hermeneutical errors evangelical egalitarians make is to give "unlikely word meanings" for key Greek terms.[144] The words they have in mind are *authentien* (1 Tim 2:12)[145] and *kephalē* (1 Cor 11:3; Eph 5:23),[146] the two most contested words in the debate over what the Bible actually says on the man-woman relationship that has raged for the last forty years among evangelicals. They say rightly, "It is not good scholarship to propose word meanings that lack supporting linguistic evidence."[147]

Kephalē/Head

Early in the debate among evangelicals about the status and ministry of women in 1985, Wayne Grudem claimed that the Greek noun *kephalē* when used metaphorically *always* carries the sense "head-over" or "authority-over," never "source,"[148] and the Köstenbergers endorse this view in 2014. They dismiss the metaphorical meaning "source," arguing that the *kephalē* "denotes first and foremost the notion of authority ('head')."[149] They give four reasons for this conclusion. First, they say, it is unnecessary "to resort to wide-ranging, extra-biblical lexical analysis" to establish the meaning of this word. Second, in the two key texts where this word is used, 1 Cor 11:3 and Eph 5:24, the meaning "authority" is clearly indicated, "while [the meaning] 'source' seems strangely foreign to the context."[150] Third, in Ephesians, *kephalē* is used throughout the book

144. Köstenberger and Köstenberger, *God's Design*, 350–51.

145. Köstenberger and Köstenberger, *God's Design*, 351.

146. Köstenberger and Köstenberger, *God's Design*, 170–71.

147. Köstenberger and Köstenberger, *God's Design*, 351.

148. They footnote Grudem's 1985 article, "Does *Kephalē* (Head) Mean 'Source,'" in *God's Design*, 170, n. 15. This article with some editing was republished in 1991 as an appendix in Grudem and Piper, *Recovering Biblical Manhood*, 425–68.

149. Köstenberger and Köstenberger, *God's Design*, 171.

150. Köstenberger and Köstenberger, *God's Design*, 171.

to denote authority."[151] And fourth, "logical reason and common sense" imply the meaning "authority over."[152] "On a literal level, the head is the location of the brain," the place where decisions are made. "From this literal referent—the head as the command and control center directing human beings' thoughts and actions—it is a small step to the figurative sense 'head' as denoting authority."[153]

We now critically evaluate these arguments.

1. In opposition to the Köstenbergers I argue that when the meaning of any Greek word is uncertain or disputed, the meaning is best determined by "wide ranging, extra-biblical analysis." I have the weight of scholars on my side. Paradoxically, more than a hundred pages later the Köstenbergers agree with me and say the opposite. "It is not good scholarship to propose word meanings that lack supporting linguistic evidence."[154]

2. To claim that *kephalē* "denotes first and foremost the notion of authority" and that the meaning "source seems strangely foreign to the context" of 1 Cor 11:3 is unconvincing. For an ever-growing number of commentators the meaning "source,"[155] in the sense of "source of life" in verse 3, is suggested by the context and the meaning of "authority" (over) "strangely foreign." Why would Paul say men have authority over women and then endorse men and women *leading* the church in prayer and prophecy (1 Cor 11:3–4)? And why would he speak a few verses later of women having authority over their own head (1 Cor 11:10)?[156] Then there is the problem of speaking of the Father having "authority over" the Son. For some decades, complementarians almost universally paralleled the Father's headship or "authority over" the Son and the man's headship/authority

151. Köstenberger and Köstenberger, *God's Design*, 171.

152. Köstenberger and Köstenberger, *God's Design*, 171.

153. Köstenberger and Köstenberger, *God's Design*, 171.

154. Köstenberger and Köstenberger, *God's Design*, 351.

155. Payne, *Man and Woman*, 117–18, n. 7, lists forty scholarly works that argue that *kephalē* means "source" in 1 Cor 11:3. This book was published in 2009; the list is now far longer.

156. The Köstenbergers imply that here Paul is speaking of the woman's subjection to male authority (*God's Design*, 171), but this is not the case. The word *exousia/* authority always speaks of an authority exercised by someone personally. In this verse Paul is speaking of the authority a woman has over her own head. See further Payne, *Man and Woman*, 181–83.

over the woman, quoting 1 Cor 11:3, but since June 2016 when they realized this led them into a modern form of the Arian heresy they have been abandoning this argument.[157]

3. Third, the Köstenbergers say that "in Ephesians [5:23] *kephalē* cannot mean 'source' because it is used throughout the book to denote authority."[158] It can be used in this epistle in this sense but immediately before Paul uses this word in Eph 5:23, in 4:15–16, he exhorts his readers to grow up into him who is the head (*kephalē*) "from whom" (*ex hou*) the body grows. This wording implies that growth comes from the head. The head is the source of growth. This interpretation is supported by what Paul says in Col 2:18–19, a text that has many parallels with Eph 4:15–16. In the Colossians text Paul exhorts his hearers to hold fast "to the head (*kephalē*), from whom (*ex hou*) the whole body . . . grows." This text certainly implies the meaning "source."

4. Fourth, the Köstenbergers say that "logical reason and common sense"[159] indicate the meaning "authority." We all know, they say, that the head is "the command and control center." In this case, "logical reason and common sense" is a very bad guide. In Greek thinking, some thought the heart was the control center and some the head. Paul seems to have made it the heart (Rom 1:21; 2 Cor 9:7).[160] What is more, as I am about to show, in Greek literature, the word *kephalē* was not used to speak of leaders who had authority over others.

Kephalē Can Mean "Authority Over," "Source," and Other Things

The Greek noun *kephalē* literally refers to the flesh covered cranium, the top part of the human body. It is thus a natural metaphor for the top part of something, what is uppermost, most prominent, preeminent.[161] "Head-over" and "source" are secondary metaphorical meanings of this word, but not the only ones. In Greek literature we find many metaphorical uses

157. Giles, *Rise and Fall*.

158. Köstenberger and Köstenberger, *God's Design*, 171.

159. Köstenberger and Köstenberger, *God's Design*, 171.

160. Cervin, "On the Significance," 12.

161. Cervin, "On the Significance," 10. Thiselton, *First Epistle*, 812, 815, 817.

of this word.[162] The context is always the best indicator of the meaning implied. Significantly, in classical Greek *kephalē* was not used to speak of "authority over" or of leaders. The scholarly consensus is that this word in the Greek language did not imply leadership.[163] In Hebrew in contrast, as in English, the word for head, *rosch*, was used to speak of leaders. We find 171 examples of this usage in the Hebrew Old Testament.[164] What is significant is that when the Hebrew word *rosch* appears speaking of leaders, the Septuagint (LXX) translators in most cases chose another word than *kephalē* to translate it. Payne concedes only one clear instance, but most scholars find more examples.[165] This, of course, does not suggest that a Greek speaking Christian would infer the meaning "leader," let alone a leader with authority over others, when hearing this word. Few of them would have been influenced by usage in the Greek Bible. Professor Murphy-O'Conner says, "There is simply no basis for the assumption that a Hellenized Jew [in the time of Paul] would instinctively give *kephalē* the meaning, 'one having authority over someone.'"[166] I nevertheless concede that *kephalē* can mean "authority over" (Eph 1:22; Col 2:10).

The meaning "source" is also an undeniable meaning of *kephalē*. The evidence for this conclusion is overwhelming.[167] This meaning is listed from the earliest Greek dictionaries to the present. At least seventeen examples from classical Greek writings can be cited. Philo, the Jew, writing roughly at the same time as the New Testament was written uses it in this sense, as do other Jewish writings. The Greek Fathers, including Cyril of Alexandria, Theodore of Mopsuestia, Athanasius, and Eusebius also use *kephalē* in this sense. Finally, I note the competent contemporary linguists Richard Cervin,[168] Cynthia Westfall,[169] Anthony Thiselton,[170] Gordon Fee,[171] and Joseph Fitzmyer,[172] among others, argue that *kephalē* can

---

162. Thiselton, *First Epistle*, 812–20.

163. Payne, "Evidence," 1–2.

164. See on this Payne, "Evidence," 5–10

165. Payne, "Evidence," 5–10.

166. Murphy-O'Connor, "Sex and Logic," 492.

167. In what follows I am dependent on Payne, "Evidence." His extensive citations and evidence should be read first hand.

168. Cervin, "On the Significance."

169. Westfall, *Paul and Gender*, 79–105

170. Thiselton, *First Epistle*, 812–22.

171. Fee, *First Epistle*, 502–5.

172. "Another Look at *Kephalē*."

mean "source." This means, *pace* the Köstenbergers, that "source" is not an "unlikely meaning" of the noun *kephalē* supported *only* by egalitarian evangelicals.

What should be concluded from what I have said above is that among the possible metaphorical meanings of the noun *kephalē*, the meaning "head-over"/"authority over," and "source" are possibilities, but these are not the only possibilities. This means that any claim that this Greek word always means "head-over"/"authority over," when used metaphorically, or that it always means "source," must be rejected. When it comes to the exegesis of the two New Testament texts in which this word is found, 1 Cor 11:3 and Eph 5:24, the context should be the most important indicator of what Paul had in mind when he used this word. The meaning of "source" or "authority over" are both possibilities as are other options.

Authentein

In 1 Tim 2:12, Paul says, "I permit no woman to teach or to have authority over a man" (NRSV). In this translation two things are prohibited to a woman, teaching *or* exercising authority over a man, and the verb, *authentein,* found only this once in the Bible, is rendered "to have authority." The Köstenbergers are perfectly happy with this translation that is paralleled or closely paralleled by most modern translations.

Both of these translation decisions must be disputed. It is most likely that one prohibition is implied, as some complementarians argue,[173] and it is a mistake to translate *authentein* to mean (rightful) "authority'" in the same way as *exousia/exousiadō* do (Paul's usual word for authority). I explore the second matter first.

The Translation of the Verb Authentein

The complementarian argument that *authentein* is a positive word referring to the rightful authority a male pastor exercises, excluded to women, has nothing to commend it. I summarize the evidence to the contrary.

1. The rendering of *authentein* as "authority" in a positive or neutral sense is a modern phenomenon. In arguing for this translation, the

173. See below.

Köstenbergers and other complementarians break with the historic position. "There is virtually unbroken tradition, stemming from the oldest translations down to the twenty-first century, that translates this verb as "to dominate," or sometimes "to usurp authority."[174] In the Authorized Version of 1611 the Greek is translated into English as "to usurp authority," and in the somewhat literal translation, the Revised Version of 1885, it is rendered "to have dominion over." These translations are to be preferred to the neutral word "authority" because they give a distinctive meaning for this distinctive word. The Greek verb *exousiazein* is accurately taken to mean to exercise rightful authority; *authentein* is not.

2. The rendering of the verb *authentein* as "authority" in a positive or neutral sense is not supported by the meaning of the cognate nouns, *authentēs* and *authentia*. Both nouns carry negative overtones, speaking of domination. Albert Wolters, a complementarian linguist, tells us that *authentēs* meant "murderer," "master," or "doer."[175] Cynthia Westfall, building on Wolter's work and in dialogue with him, concludes that these three meanings speak of an "autonomous user or possessor of unrestricted force/power."[176] Marshall concludes, "Ideas such as autocratic or domineering use of power and authority appear to be more naturally with the verb in view of the meanings of the cognate nouns *authentēs* and *authentia*."[177]

3. The rendering of the verb *authentein* as "authority" in a positive or neutral sense is not supported by the etymology of the verb. Etymology never dictates the meaning of a word, but it can help in the determining of the meaning of a word. The first part of the word *authentien* is derived from *autos*, "signifying by one's self, of one's own initiative."[178] The second, from the word *hentēs*, means to achieve or realize.[179] This suggests the word has something to do with achieving one's own way. "Thus it is not surprising," says, Payne, "that

174. Belleville "Teaching and Usurping Authority," 209–10; Belleville, "Exegetical Fallacies."

175. Wolters, "Semantic Study," 145–75; Wolters, "*Authentēs*," 719–29.

176. Westfall, "Meaning of *Authenteō*," 166.

177. Marshall, *Pastoral Epistles*, 457.

178. Payne, *Man and Woman*, 363; Belleville, "Exegetical Fallacies." See also in more detail Belleville's forthcoming article, "Lexical Fallacies."

179. Payne, *Man and Woman*, 163.

many of the uses of the *authent-* root refer to self-initiated activities and, consequently up through Paul's day carry a negative nuance."[180]

4. The rendering of *authentein* as "authority" in a positive or neutral sense has no support at all in literary texts and non-literary material before or around the time of Paul. Unquestionably, usage is the most important indicator of meaning. Following her meticulous study of the use of the verb *authentein*, and the noun and adjective *authentēs* in classical literary works, Belleville concludes these cognate words have to do with murder.[181] In the Hellenistic period, in literary material "the primary meaning was still 'murder,' but the semantic range widened to include 'perpetrator,' 'sponsor,' 'author,' and 'mastermind of a crime or act of violence.'"[182]

In the Papyri, Payne argues, we have only two uncontested uses of the word *authentein* before the end of the first century and one text is corrupted, and two other possibilities,[183] apart from 1 Tim 2:12.[184] For him, the most important pre–New Testament reference is the Papyrus BGU 1208.38, where he argues the verb means "'to assume authority over,' in the sense of taking authority unto oneself that had not been delegated."[185] In the other undisputed pre-Pauline use of this word in the corrupted papyrus fragment, the *Rhetorica* of Philomenus, who lived roughly between 110 and 140 BC, some letters are missing. Payne argues we have here a verbal form of the root *authent-* and in this context it means "murderer"[186]—someone who uses violence against another. Belleville, on the other hand, argues that we find here an adjectival form of the root *authent-* meaning "powerful" that modifies the noun "rulers" or "lords."[187] Another later important use of this verb is found Ptolemy's (AD 127–148) work, *Tetrabiblos,* where the complementarian linguist, Henry Bald-

180. Payne, *Man and Woman,* 363.

181. Belleville, "Exegetical Fallacies," 3–6.

182. Belleville, "Teaching and Usurping Authority," 212; Belleville, "Exegetical Fallacies," 6.

183. Payne, *Man and Woman,* 361–62. Hubner, "Translating *Authetein*," lists five texts before the end of the second century. This article gives an up-to-date account of the debate over this word and makes many significant points.

184. Payne, *Man and Woman,* 373–97.

185. Payne, *Man and Woman,* 370.

186. Payne, *Man and Woman,* 372.

187. Belleville, "Exegetical Fallacies," 5.

win, agrees with Payne that it means "to control, to dominate."[188] What is to be noted is that none of these texts suggest a positive, or even a neutral meaning, of the word *authentein*. Baldwin, it is to be carefully noted, in his article on the meaning of *authentein*, in a book edited by Andreas Köstenberger, cannot find one use of this verb to mean in a positive or neutral sense "to exercise authority over" or "to have authority over,"[189] before or about the time of Paul.

5. The rendering of *authentein* as "authority" in a positive or neutral sense has no support on the basis of "systemic functional linguistics and discourse analysis."[190] This is Cynthia Long Westfall's independent argument. In ascertaining the meaning of any verb, she argues, it is necessary to ask, "Who is doing what to whom?" She concludes that *authentein* speaks consistently of "the autonomous use or possession of unrestricted force."[191] In this sentence, she says, the word "autonomous," speaks of "self-willed, origination, independent and sovereign action without legitimacy or appointment. The actor takes matters into his or her own hands."[192] Early in this essay, she critically evaluates the complementarian linguist Henry Baldwin's study of the word *authentein* (that the Köstenbergers follow)[193] and finds his methodology flawed, and his conclusions unsubstantiated.[194] On his claim that the verb speaks of the rightful authority of a pastor she says, "In the 82 occurrences of the verb that Baldwin uses to support his position, there is not an example of a male doing this to another person . . . or of a group of people . . . with a positive evaluation in a ministry or leadership context."[195]

6. The rendering of *authentein* as "authority" in a positive or neutral sense in 1 Tim 2:12 is not supported by the context. The historical context of this specific usage reflects a situation where heretical teaching is rife (1 Tim 1:3–7, 19–20; 4:1–2, 16; 6:3–5; 2 Tim 2:14–19;

188. Baldwin, "Important Word," 49. Payne, *Man and Woman*, 378; Hubner, "Translating *Authetein*," 17.

189. Baldwin, "Important Word," 49–51.

190. Westfall, "Meaning of *Authenteō*," 147.

191. Westfall, "Meaning of *Authenteō*," 166.

192. Westfall, "Meaning of *Authenteō*," 167.

193. Baldwin, "Important Word," 49.

194. Westfall, "Meaning of *Authenteō*," 141–47.

195. Westfall, "Meaning of *Authenteō*," 165.

3:10–16; Titus 1:10–16; 2:1–2; 3:8–10), and women are active in propagating this false teaching (1 Tim 5:13). The literary context of 1 Tim 2:8–15 indicates something very wrong is happening in house-church gatherings. Virtually everything said in 1 Tim 2:8–15 has no parallels in the rest of the New Testament. This suggests an exceptional situation as does the verb *authentein*. If Paul was simply forbidding women from teaching and exercising authority as male church leaders may do, why does he not use his normal term for rightly exercising authority, *exousia/exousiazō*? As no answer can be given to this question, we must conclude he chose deliberately the verb *authentein* to make it clear that he is prohibiting a kind of teaching not acceptable in a house-church setting.

The evidence is compelling; the verb *authentein* is not a word that speaks positively of authority rightly exercised, certainly not of the rightful authority male pastors exercise. It speaks rather of usurped authority, self-taken authority, of a malevolent kind, specifically of domineering authority.

One or Two Prohibitions?

Now to the question of whether or not Paul is forbidding one or two things in 1 Tim 2:12. In the first few decades of the debate over what the Bible actually says on the status and ministry of women, it was agreed that Paul is addressing one issue. Donald Carson says Paul is simply refusing women the opportunity to "*enjoy* a church-recognized teaching authority over men."[196] Similarly, Thomas Schreiner says, 1 Tim 2:11–15 "prohibits *only* authoritative teaching" by women.[197] Arguing that Paul is forbidding two separate things does not immediately come to mind because Paul often uses two or more words to say much the same thing, especially in the Pastoral Epistles. In 1 Tim 2:8–15 there are examples of this in almost every verse. In verse 1, Paul speaks of "supplications, prayers, intercessions and thanksgivings"; in verse 2a "of kings and all who are in high positions"; in verse 2b of "a quiet and peaceful life"; in verse 2c of "what is right and is acceptable in the sight of God"; and so he continues.[198]

196. Carson, "Silent in the Churches," 152. Italics added.
197. Schreiner, "Valuable Ministries," 223. Italics added.
198. See on this Blomberg, "Complementarian Perspective," in Beck and Blomberg,

Notwithstanding what has just been said, Andreas Köstenberger has put a huge amount of effort into arguing that 1 Tim 2:12 prohibits two things.[199] His reason for doing this is because he wants to prove that *authentein* is a positive word, speaking of the rightful authority a male pastor exercises that is denied to women. Let me explain the point. The lexical evidence for *authentein* being a positive term that speaks of the rightful authority of male pastors is completely missing and there is much evidence to the contrary. To get around this problem Andreas seeks another route to get the conclusion he wants.

It is his argument that the conjunction *oude* that links the words *didaskein* (to teach) and *authentein* (to exercise authority in some sense) in 1 Tim 2:12 always link verbs that are both negative or both positive in content, never negative and positive. In other words, *oude* always correlates synonyms not antonyms.[200] This is simply not true. Both Philip Payne[201] and Linda Belleville[202] have carefully assessed the evidence and found to the contrary. Indeed, Payne shows that "the vast majority of Paul's *oude* clauses combine two elements to express a single idea."[203] To argue that the two ideas must be either synonyms or antonyms, Payne says, is beside the point, because it presupposes that Paul is conveying two ideas, not one, in 1 Tim 2:12.[204] But this is not the only problem with Andreas' thesis. The logic of his argument is flawed. He argues that the verb to teach is always a positive word and therefore the conjunction *oude* demands that the verb *authentein* must be taken also as a positive way. The problem with this argument is that if you begin with the verb *authentein*, which lexical studies indicate is a negative word, you get another answer. The prohibited teaching is a teaching that is not acceptable for some reason. To suggest that teaching is always something viewed positively in the Pastorals is simply not true. The most serious problem facing the churches addressed in these epistles is false teaching (1 Tim 1:3–7; 4:1–2; 5:13;

Two Views, 69.

199. Köstenberger, Schreiner, and Baldwin, *Women in the Church*, 81–104; Köstenberger and Schreiner, *Women in the Church*, 53–84; Köstenberger, "Complex Sentence."

200. Köstenberger, "Complex Sentence," 53–85.

201. Payne, *Man and Woman*, 337–59; and more recently, Payne, "1 Tim 2.12 and the Use of *Oude*."

202. Belleville, "Exegetical Fallacies," 6–7.

203. Payne, "1 Tim 2.12 and the Use of *Oude*," 26.

204. Payne, "1 Tim 2.12 and the Use of *Oude*," 26.

6:3–5; Titus 1:11, etc). Linda Belleville on her part drives a stake into the heart of Andreas' argument. In Rev 2:20, she notes, we have an explicit example where teaching is paired with something negative, deceiving, in a text with close parallels to 1 Tim 2:12. Jezebels' teaching "deceives my servants" (*kai didaskei kai plana tous emous doulous*).

What this means is that this novel argument put by Andreas Köstenberger must be rejected. The linguistic, lexical, and contextual evidence unambiguously indicates that the verb *authentein* in 1 Tim 2:12 speaks of an autonomous exercise of authority in an unacceptable way. Andreas Köstenberger's attempt to counter this fact by arguing that the verb in this context must be positive in meaning because it is paired with teaching, something positive, cannot bear critical evaluation.

How Then Should 1 Timothy 2:12 Be Translated?

This question implies two questions, how are the two prohibitions, not to teach and not to *authentein* a man related, and what does *authentein* mean in this verse? Payne argues that the verb *authentein* in 1 Tim 2:12 is best translated as either "to dominate" or "to assume authority" [205]—or more exactly "to assume authority [to oneself]," [206] and he prefers the latter, [207] and because "the vast majority of Paul's *oude* clauses combine two elements to express a single idea," [208] one forbidden activity makes the most sense of 1 Tim 2:12. On this basis he translates v 12 as follows, "'I am not permitting a woman to teach and assume authority over a man,' namely to take for herself authority to teach without authorization from the church." [209] I am not convinced by this translation. I think Payne fails to bring to attention the negative implications of the Greek verb *authentein* and is mistaken to suggest teachers in the first century needed "the authorization of the church." The church at this time is not an institution that authorizes teachers or other leaders. In the little house churches of the apostolic age every one was free to minister and to teach.

I think Linda Belleville gives a much better translation. She argues that *authentein* is best translated "to dominate" or "to gain the upper

205. Payne, *Man and Woman*, 395.

206. Payne, *Man and Woman*, 385.

207. Payne, *Man and Woman*, 385.

208. Payne, "1 Tim 2.12 and the Use of *Oude*," 26.

209. Payne, *Man and Woman*, 393.

hand."[210] On the question of sentences with the conjunction *oude* in them, she documents six patterns, and argues the one that makes the most sense of 1 Tim 2:12 is where the second part of the sentence defines the purpose of the action. She gives Matt 6:20 as an example: "Where thieves neither break in nor (*oude*) steal, i.e., break in to steal."[211] On the basis of these two well-documented conclusions she argues that 1 Tim 2:12 is best translated either as "I do not permit a woman to teach so as to gain the upper hand over a man," or, "I do not permit a woman to teach with the view of dominating a man."[212]

210. Belleville, "Exegetical Fallacies," 6.

211. Belleville, "Exegetical Fallacies," 7.

212. Belleville, "Exegetical Fallacies," 7.

7

Male "Headship":
The Creation Order or the Fallen Order?

IN MANY EVANGELICAL, PENTECOSTAL, and charismatic churches, the leadership of men in the home and the church, usually referred to as "male headship," is of huge importance. Some years ago, I heard a well-known American New Testament scholar say in a crowded auditorium, "The headship of the man is taught from cover to cover in the Bible; nothing is more important in understanding what the Bible says on the sexes than this principle."[1] The Köstenbergers are of the same opinion. They argue that the Bible throughout "exhibits a male pattern of leadership."[2] The English Baptist theologian David Pawson puts this view eloquently in the title of his book, *Leadership Is Male*.[3]

Before we study what the Bible says specifically on this matter, a few facts should open our minds to consider the possibility that this is not the case.

1. The term "headship" does not appear at all in the Bible.

2. There are only two instances in the whole Bible where the Greek word *kephalē*, translated into English as "head," is used in connection

---

1. Donald Carson said this. It was at a Church Missionary Summer School Conference. I did have his talk on tape but I have since lost the tape.

2. Köstenberger and Köstenberger, *God's Design*, 69, 83, 91–92, 120.

3. Pawson, *Leadership Is Male*.

with the male-female relationship (1 Cor 11:3; Eph 5:23), and scholars are divided as to meaning of the word in each case.

3. Genesis 1–3 explicitly makes the rule of the man over the woman a consequence of the fall (Gen 3:16). It is an expression of sin, not God's ideal. Putting to one side for the moment Eph 5:23, what has to be noted is that no other verse in the Bible can be quoted to say God has appointed men to rule over women, or husbands over wives; not one.

4. In the Gospels, Jesus says not one word about male "headship"/leadership, and much to the contrary.

5. Paul has women leading in prayer and prophecy in church, commends a woman apostle ("first in the church," 1 Cor 12:28; Rom 16:7; cf. Eph 2:20; 4:11), approves of women overseeing house-churches, and says "in Christ" men and women are "one."

6. The idea that men should rule over women (male "headship"/leadership) is *not distinctive Christian teaching.* Until modern times this was universally believed and it is still believed very widely today. What is more, all the great religions of the world teach that the man should be the leader and the more conservative the expression of that religion the more this is emphasized and made oppressive.

PAUL ON THE MALE-FEMALE RELATIONSHIP

In seeking to understand what Paul believed about the man-woman relationship, four passages need to be studied—1 Cor 11:3–16; Eph 5:21–33; 1 Cor 7:1–40; and 1 Tim 5:14. The first two passages use the word *kephalē* /head, but in this chapter I only study in detail the second passage because we have already carefully considered what Paul says in 1 Corinthians 11:3–16, particularly verse 3 where we concluded the word *kephalē* /head, almost certainly carries the meaning of "source"—in the sense of "source of life." The meaning "authority over" in this context makes no sense and is theologically dangerous. Why would Paul say men have authority over women, then allow that men *and* women may *lead* in prayer and prophecy in church, and in verse 10 speak of the "authority" a woman has over her own head? Then there is the problem that if *kephalē* /head in verse 3 is taken to mean "head over/authority over," it results in a hierarchically ordered Trinity, the essence of the Arian error. We should also note that in this passage the ruling on head-coverings is addressed to *all* men and *all* women (1 Cor 11:4–5). The marriage relationship never comes into view in 1 Cor 11:3–16.

EPHESIANS 5:21–33

I have spent a lifetime thinking about what Paul says in Eph 5:21–33 and reading whatever I can on this passage, usually with little satisfaction. My journey of understanding of this profound passage in Scripture parallels my journey of fifty years in coming to understand what makes a marriage wonderfully rewarding for both parties.

In these fifty years I have held three very different views of the headship of the husband, and in each case my change of thinking has been caused by an amalgam of experience and study of the Bible.

1. For about fifteen years I believed strongly that the man should be the head/leader of the home and that women should not be in church leadership or preach. I entered marriage thinking that I would be in charge and I expected Lynley to support me in my important ministry and manage the home. I believed without a doubt that God had appointed me to be the head of my wife. I saw this clearly said in Eph 5:23, "the husband is the head of his wife," and I believed what I had been told, that this teaching is grounded in God's creational ordering of the sexes. This means it is transcultural and weighty theology. It was not easy for me to change. I only began critically thinking about this dogma when I discovered having my own way and doing very little to support my wonderful wife did not make for marital happiness or a rewarding marriage. My bossy and selfish behavior hurt Lynley and because I loved her dearly, I felt awful pain through hurting her. Slowly, step by step, I began doing more around the home, listening more carefully to her, never making important decisions unilaterally, avoiding at all costs going all out to win arguments, putting all our money into one joint account; in brief, I became less selfish. I made these changes while in my mind I still believed I was the head of the home, and this ordering of the marriage was grounded in God's ordering of the sexes in creation before the fall.

2. Then after about ten years of marriage I came to the conclusion that the Bible made the equality of the sexes the creation ideal. I changed

my mind theologically because I could see in Scripture women in leadership in the Christian community, and I found the complementarian interpretation of their proof texts (Gen 1–3; 1 Tim 2:11–14; 1 Cor 11:3–16; and 14:34–35) that I had believed excluded women from leadership unconvincing, indeed mistaken. Ephesians 5:21–33 was another matter. I could not get past the fact that Paul said, "Wives be subject to your husbands . . . for the husband is the head of the wife." I thus continued to believe that in marriage the man was to be the leader, albeit a loving leader. This was the God-given ideal prescribed by Scripture. In practice, this had no consequences. It meant nothing. I did not insist on having the casting vote or claim any special privileges. The result was that for me there was a tension between what I believed on male "headship" and how my marriage worked. The truth was that I had a profoundly equal marriage and it was far more rewarding than when I had acted imperially, yet I still believed the Bible taught that I was the head of my wife in some way.

3. Then after many years, one day it suddenly dawned on me that male headship is not the God-given ideal. I was then able to bring my ecclesiology and theology and practice of marriage into harmony. In that moment I realized that how I had interpreted Eph 5:21–33 was mistaken. I had believed that Paul's words, "the husband is the head of the wife," enunciates a weighty theological principle. It is what Scripture clearly teaches about the "role" of the husband. He is to lead. I guess because I am a man I was slow to see the problems with this view. What forced me to rethink my interpretation of Eph 5:21–33 was again an amalgam of experience and reflection on Scripture. I had clearly seen for a long time that my marriage and other good marriages were the result of accepting our partners as substantial equals and operating on this basis. This was a prerequisite for a happy and mutually rewarding marriage. Men insisting on being the head of the home and making all the major decisions results in conflictual and unhappy marriages. My unease with headship teaching became more acute with the passing of time. Happy marriages tend to become more equal. This discovery made me think even harder on Paul's words, "The husband is head of the wife." I had long recognized that Gen 3:16 unambiguously makes the rule of the man over the woman a consequence of the fall, something not good; Jesus depicted marriage as a profoundly equal

relationship, and in Eph 5 Paul does not ground the subordination of the wife on any theological basis, definitely not in creation before the fall. But still Paul's words, "the husband is the head of the wife," rang in my ears. I continued to think these words were binding on couples, even if they did not "fit" my experience or match up with my basically egalitarian ecclesiology. What allowed a breakthrough for me was the realization that Paul's argument in Eph 5:21–33 is profoundly dialectical in nature. He says things that are seemingly contradictory. For a long time I resisted this insight. It was hard for me as an evangelical with a high view of Scripture to concede that there is no easy way to reconcile Paul's call to mutual subordination (v. 21) and his demand that husbands love their wives to the point of giving their lives for them (v. 25), and asking wives to subordinate themselves "in everything" to their husbands, their head. I found contemporary attempts to get around this seeming contradiction in what Paul says unconvincing. I was not persuaded by the argument that Paul in fact does not ask for mutual subordination in verse 21 and in verses 25–33 he is only asking husbands to rule in a loving way. And I was not persuaded by arguments that Paul is simply speaking of the husband as "the source of life" of the wife. A far better solution I could see was needed, one that matches up with what is said on the man-woman relationship in the weightiest texts on this matter in Scripture. In what follows I outline this interpretation of Eph 5:21–33.

EXEGETICAL PREREQUISITES

Before I outline how I now understand Eph 5:21–33 I need to speak of what is required for a right understanding of this text.

To understand rightly what Paul is arguing in verses 22–24 on the husband as the head of his wife, and the subordination of the wife, the historical context of Paul's words must be fully appreciated. Paul wrote these words in the first-century, Greco-Roman world where husbands had rights, privileges, and freedoms denied to wives, and husbands held most of the power and provided all of the income. The *paterfamilias*, the father of the family, had ultimate authority. In the last chapter, and later in this chapter, I make the point that the wife was the *materfamilias*, the mother of the family, and as such was expected to manage the home.

This, of course, was to the advantage of men. They could leave completely all the responsibilities and cares of the home to their wife. In this world, the vast majority of women were not educated except in home duties, once married were either pregnant or nursing children for most of their life, and in an urban setting were expected to stay within the home. They could not support themselves financially, except in very rare cases such as the wealthy widow. They were dependent on and set under a man— father, husband, guardian—all of their life. In this world, subordination was the lot of children, slaves, and women. Free men were supposed to be assertive, in control, and to manage. They were to look after their own interests. Humility and lowly service were not thought of as virtues in free men. What this means is that the husband-wife relationship in Paul's world is to be contrasted rather than compared with what is the reality today. Thus, to read this text apart from its historical context means the text is not properly understood.

We thus cannot expect Paul to think of the marriage relationship as egalitarian Christians do today. To expect Paul to say outright that a Christian marriage should be a union of two fully equal human beings is to ask too much of him. Women were not equal to men in any way in the ancient world. They were dependent on a man all their life, as I said above. Paul could not have imagined a world where more women than men had higher education, women could live independent lives, were in control of their own fertility, and could financially support themselves. What was possible for Paul was that he lay down the theological groundwork for a fully equal marriage, and I believe this is what he does in this passage and in 1 Cor 7:1–40 where he gives his longest discussion on Christian marriage. This means hearing what Paul says to his first-century audience on the marriage relationship is just the first step in the hermeneutical quest. The second and more important step is to ask, if Paul said this then what would he say to us now in a totally different cultural context? What is the trajectory his words set?

But Paul's words in Eph 5:22–24 must also be understood in their literary context. Paul's exhortation to Christian wives to be subordinate to their husbands because they are their *kephale* (head) is preceded by an exhortation to mutual subordination and followed by one that asks husbands to love their wives to the point of giving their life for them. To interpret verses 22–24 apart from their literary context, as far too many evangelicals do, is bound to lead to a misinterpretation of what Paul is actually arguing in Eph 5:21–33 taken as a whole. Here, as much as anywhere in all the Bible, the rule already mentioned applies, "a text without a context [historical and/or literary] is a pretext for a proof text."

What Paul, the master communicator, is doing in this passage is seeking to get the ears of Christian men who do not want to hear what he says. He knows they want him to endorse their unqualified leadership and privileges in their marriages so he must word his case very carefully to get a hearing. Therefore, we should not expect him to say outright, husbands subordinate yourself to your wife, although this is what he implies in verse 21 and verses 25–33 where he asks for mutual subordination and the love of one's wife that knows no bounds.

To understand rightly Eph 5:22–24, it is also essential to appreciate Paul's distinctive understanding of Christian leadership, which he learned from his master, Jesus Christ. A leader is one who serves. Jesus said, "Whoever wishes to become great among you [a leader] must be your servant, and whoever wishes to be first among must be slave of all" (Mark 10:43–44). And then he says of himself, "The Son of man came not to be served but to serve" (Mark 10:45). In John 13 Jesus illustrates what leadership involves for him and his followers; he took a towel, kneeled, and washed his disciples' feet. This is what a slave characteristically did. In the footsteps of his master, Paul defines all leadership in the Christian community in terms of *diakonia*/service. He uses the *diakon* . . . words about forty times, almost always of lowly service. For him, all Christian leaders, even apostles, are *diakonoi*, "ministers" or "servants."

It is against the backdrop of this distinctive Christian understanding of leadership that we are to understand all of what Paul says to husbands in Eph 5:21–33. He says to them, you are "head of your wife"; therefore, lay aside your privileges, power, and superior status and give yourselves in costly love and service for your wife, even to the point of giving your life for her. The motivation and model for such behavior is Christ himself, the head of the church, his body. He so loved the church that he gave himself in death for her. This is a complete reversal of what the Greco-Roman world said to free men. Thus, to read this text as an endorsement of male privilege, precedence, and power is to miss completely what is basic to what Paul is saying to husbands. What Paul does in this passage is exhort Christian men who within their culture were viewed as the leaders in their marriages, to become servants in the most countercultural way imaginable. In other words, he writes to subvert male leadership, patriarchy, as it was known and practiced in the Greco-Roman home. He asks the husband, the leader, to become a servant to his wife.

In the light of these comments I now turn to a verse-by-verse commentary on what Paul says in this passage.

Ephesians 5:21

Paul begins his discussion of Christian marriage in verse 21 with an exhortation, "Be subordinate to one another." This verse is transitional. It looks back to the string of imperatives that depend on the verb in the exhortation, "Be filled with the Spirit" (5:18).[4] Paul believed that when Christians are filled with the Spirit they will sing and make melody, give thanks *and subordinate themselves to one another*. It looks forward by introducing what Paul goes on to say about the marriage relationship in verses 22–33.

Paul's exhortation, "Be subordinate (*hypotassesthai*) to one another out of fear/reverence for Christ," tells Spirit-filled believers how they are to relate to one another. He exhorts all Christians, men and women, as those set free by the Spirit to defer to and humbly serve one another. This is distinctive Christian teaching. Pope John Paul II says Paul's teaching that "subjection is not one sided but mutual" is "an innovation of the Gospel."[5] It is profoundly countercultural; distinctive Christian teaching. As I said above, the free Greco-Roman man believed that subordination was for women, slaves, and children. The idea that humility and self-denial are virtues is found first in the words and example of Paul's own master, who said of himself, "I am gentle and lowly in heart" (Matt 11:28–29), and that "I came not to be served but to serve" (Mark 10:45). Paul asks Christians to submit to one another "out of reverence for Christ"—in other words, to please Christ, who exemplified such behavior.

The vast majority of commentators accept that verse 21 is an exhortation to mutual submission. There is, however, an idiosyncratic complementarian interpretation of this verse that denies this. It was popularized among complementarians by Wayne Grudem[6] and is taken up by the Köstenbergers. They argue that in this instance "one another" does not speak of mutuality and reciprocity. It cannot, the Köstenbergers say, "if

---

4. The Köstenbergers agree. See Köstenberger and Köstenberger, *God's Design*, 185.

5. John Paul II, *Mulierus Dignitatem*, 88.

6. Grudem, *Evangelical Feminism and Biblical Truth*, 188–200.

the Bible teaches distinct and non-reversible male-female roles."[7] Men do not submit to their wives. In support, they say, forgiving one another does not "necessarily mean that in a given instance the roles of the sinning and the offended party are identical. . . . Forgiving one another in such instances involves the offending party asking for forgiveness and the offended party extending forgiveness to the person who has sinned against them." Then they give what they call "an even more compelling example" in the book of Revelation. In Rev 6:4 the opposing armies are said "to slay one another." The Köstenbergers say, "Clearly these people don't kill each other at exactly the same time."[8]

This argument is not serious scholarship. It is an attempt to give an interpretation of a text to make it conform with prior dogmatic understanding of male headship. The illustrations given by the Köstenbergers in opposition to the reciprocal force of this exhortation are simply clever argumentation. Forgiving one another means we forgive others as we hope they will forgive us, nothing more and nothing less. Killing one another means the two armies were slaughtering each other. Loving one another means to love others as we hope they will love us. To be subordinate to one another means to give ourselves in service to others as they give themselves in service for us.[9] Every occurrence of the Greek reciprocal pronoun *allēlōn*/one another in Paul's epistles speaks of reciprocal action.[10] Paul does not qualify this word in this verse and nor should we.

Many complementarians do not agree with Grudem and the Köstenbergers on this matter. The father of complementarianism, George Knight, argues against this view. He says mutual submission is envisaged in Eph 5:21.[11] Clinton Arnold, a complementarian, has a long section

---

7. Köstenberger and Köstenberger, *God's Design*, 182.

8. Köstenberger and Köstenberger, *God's Design*, 182.

9. Arnold, *Ephesians*, 356, says, "There are four problems with this view." 1) It fails to recognize that the participle in verse 21 is dependent on the main verb in this section in verse 18, "be filled with the Spirit," which is addressed to all believers. 2) It fails to recognize that verse 21 provides a fitting conclusion to the previous exhortations beginning at verse 18 by calling all believers to a radical form of self-denial and love that Christ modelled for the church. 3) It unduly restricts the unqualified reciprocal pronoun, *allēlois*, to wives. 4) It does not take into account the fact that the primary verbal element in the household code moves from submit to obey when Paul moves his focus away from wives to children and slaves.

10. Payne, *Man and Woman*, sets out the evidence for this assertion. For another scholarly rejection of this argument, see Marshall, "Mutual Love," 195–98.

11. Knight, "Husbands and Wives," 166.

in his scholarly commentary on Ephesians where he gives four reasons why Grudem and the Köstenbergers' view cannot be accepted. Calvin definitely endorsed the reciprocal nature of Paul's exhortation. He says,

> God has so bound us to each other, that no man ought to avoid subjection. And where love resigns, there is mutual servitude. . . . Therefore it is very right that he [Paul] should exhort all to be subject to each other.[12]

Verses 22–24

In verses 22–24, Paul specifically addresses Christian wives, telling them what the universal Christian virtue of subordination means for them. In verse 22 he says, "Wives be subject to your husbands as you are to the Lord. For the husband is head of the wife just as Christ is head of the church, the body of which he is the savior."[13] The verb, "be subject," is carried over from verse 21. What Paul asks of all Christians, he now asks exclusively of wives. Like verse 21, verse 22 is an exhortation. Paul exhorts Christian wives, set free by the Spirit, to voluntarily subordinate themselves to their husbands (cf. Col 3:18; Titus 2:5; 1 Pet 3:1). He does not say, "You are a subordinate person," or, "God has assigned to you for all time a subordinate *role*." Rather, Paul exhorts wives to submit freely to their respective husbands; he asks of them "a voluntary yielding in love."[14] Their culture expected them to do this; and as Christians, Paul asks them to do this. He starkly says, "Be subject to your husbands *as you are to the Lord.*" He similarly starkly exhorts slaves to obey their masters "as you obey Christ" (Eph 6:5).

The reason a wife should submit to her husband, Paul says, is because "the husband is *kephalē* /head of the wife" (v. 22). What Paul means by this word in this context has become central to the conflict between complementarians and evangelical egalitarians. The former insist that here the word means "head over"/"authority over," most egalitarians that it means "source," in the sense of "source of life."[15] Payne believes that "Paul defined 'head' in Eph 5:23 as 'savior' in the sense of 'source of love

---

12. Calvin, *Epistle of Paul the Apostle to the Galatians, Ephesians,* 204.

13. My translation. I omit the definite articles not present in the Greek following Payne.

14. Payne, *Man and Woman,* 283.

15. Payne, "Evidence," 5–10; Westfall, *Paul and Gender,* 100–101.

and nourishment,'" because in the second half of verse 22 Paul explains "head" in apposition that "Christ [is] head of the Church, the savior of the body." He goes on to explain what Christ did as savior of the body: "'Christ loved the Church and gave himself up for her' and 'nourishes and cherishes her.'"[16]

These alternatives are suggestions as to what Paul *implied* when he said, "The husband is *kephalē*/head of the wife." We have, however, no external evidence to establish what Paul meant by this metaphorical expression. There are no antecedent uses of the metaphor "the husband is the head of the wife." It seems Paul invented this metaphor; it originated with him.[17] And thirty years of debate over the metaphorical meaning of *kephalē* has established one fact, no one meaning is lexically prescribed. Definitely, "head-over"/"authority-over" or "source" are possibilities.[18] This means that again, as with 1 Cor 11:3, the context is our best guide to what is signified by this word in this verse. The immediate context is the exhortation, "Wives be subject to your husbands" (verse 22a) and, "Wives ought to be, in everything [subject] to their husbands" (verse 24). This suggests that the apostle, in saying that the "husband is head of the wife," is acknowledging the precedence of the husband. People yield to others they regard as having precedence in some way. Certainly Paul's first hearers would have inferred this is what he meant because this was exactly how they understood marriage. In support of this conclusion I note that the Greek word *kephalē* speaks of the top part of the body; the most "prominent" part of the body.[19] It is on this basis that the alternative English metaphorical meanings of this word, "head-over" and "source," are postulated. They both imply *the idea* of precedence, or prominence.

In saying this I am not conceding that the complementarians are right in their understanding of male "headship." To allow that *kephalē* implies in this literary context precedence, or prominence, in some way does not mean this Greek word means "head-over"/"authority-over," or that Paul is teaching that male leadership in marriage is predicated in creation before the fall. In my earlier addendum on the meaning of this word, I point out that the meaning "head-over/"authority-over," for most if not all the Greek-speaking Christians at Corinth would not have been

16. Payne "What About Headship?" 141–61.

17. So Barth, *Ephesians*, 2:617–18.

18. See the addendum on this word at the end of the previous chapter.

19. Cervin, "On the Significance."

known. Furthermore, the idea of precedence, or prominence, does not necessarily indicate authority-over. Someone may be given precedence or prominence in a group without any thought that they have authority over others. What we have in this comment is *a descriptive metaphor* for the husband. Paul acknowledges the prominence and preeminence of the husband in his age and culture. He is not on some profound theological basis *prescribing* the "role" or authority status of the husband for all time and in all cultures.

But this is not my most fundamental disagreement with complementarians on the interpretation of Eph 5:22–24. They take Paul to be speaking of the leadership of the man in marriage on the basis that in creation, before the fall, God set the man over the women. "Male headship" in marriage is thus the God-given, transcultural ideal. It is what is pleasing to God. I think they are wrong. Genesis 1–3 does not teach the pre-fall subordination of woman. Genesis 3:16 makes the rule of the man over the woman entirely a consequence of the fall. Jesus says not one word on male "headship" and much to the contrary, and Paul affirms women, including married women, in leadership positions, as we have seen. In Eph 5:31 Paul does quote Gen 2:24, not to establish woman's subordination, but rather to speak of the mysterious and profound oneness of the man and woman in marriage. Let me say it emphatically, Paul nowhere mentions or alludes to a supposed hierarchical, pre-fall *creation order* where the husband rules over his wife in Eph 5:21–33, or anywhere else in his writings. In Eph 5:22–24, Paul addresses a cultural situation in which women were subordinated to their husbands and exhorts Christian women not only to accept this cultural reality, but to do so "as you would to the Lord." In that context they had no other alternative. In other words, Paul is giving advice to Christian women congruent with *the fallen order* where husbands ruled over their wives. Paul is tacitly accepting *the fallen order* where men ruled over their wives, and asking Christian women to accept this reality. This fallen order is also reflected in Paul's exhortations to masters and slaves. God is not pleased to see those made in his image and likeness subjugated by force and degraded. Nevertheless, the apostles exhorted slaves in the so-called "household rules," of which Eph 5:21—6:9 is the longest (see also Col 3:18—4:1; 1 Pet 2:18—3:7), to accept their subservience. Paul tells slaves to obey "your earthly masters . . . as you obey Christ" (Eph 6:5). If we do not take these exhortations to slaves to obey their masters to be a reflection God's perfect will, then we should not interpret apostolic exhortations to wives to be subordinate as a reflection of God's perfect will. In both cases, we rightly read these parallel exhortations as wise advice to Christians, living in a culture where the subordination of wives and slavery were taken-for-granted realities.

There is, however, a wider context to what is said in verses 22–24; verse 21 and verses 25–33 are like book ends with verses 22–24 in the middle. This wider context says things, as I have already noted, that obviously stand in tension with what is said in verses 22–24. Preceding, in verse 21, Paul asks for mutual subordination, and following in verses 25–33, he asks husbands to give themselves in loving service for their wives even to the point of giving their life for them. These comments cannot be simplistically harmonized with the exhortation, "wives be subject to your husbands as you are to the Lord." The common complementarian solution to this seemingly contradictory teaching is to reject that Paul calls for mutual subordination in verse 21 and argue that in verses 25–33 Paul is *only* asking men who are head-over/have authority over their wife to lead in a loving way. The common egalitarian solution is to argue that *kephalē* does not mean "authority over" and that verses 22–24 must be understood in the light of verse 21. I am not convinced by either attempt to get Paul to speak with one voice. I feel compelled to accept that Paul in fact does say things in verse 21 and verses 25–33 that stand in stark tension to what he says in verses 22–24.

It seems to me obvious that in Eph 5:21–33 we have two contrasting understandings of marriage: one that prevailed in Paul's day that reflects the fallen order where the man rules over the woman (Gen 3:16), and one where Paul outlines a distinctive Christian understanding of marriage in verse 21 and verses 25–33. I think Pope John Paul II, in his binding encyclical on all Catholics, *Mulierus Dignitatem*, accurately captures what Paul is arguing in Eph 5:21–33. The Pope says the idea that the man is the head of the wife and women should be subject is a reflection of what is "old"; it speaks of a way of thinking "profoundly rooted in the customs and religious tradition of the time."[20] What is "new," "an innovation of the Gospel," is that "subjection is not one-sided but mutual."[21]

What this means is that there is no context-free interpretation of Eph 5:22–24, or of the word *kephalē* in verse 22. What Paul says in these verses must be understood in the context of all that he says in verses 21–33. Yes, the wife is to subordinate herself to her husband, her "head,"

20. John Paul II, *Mulieris Dignitatem*, 88.
21. John Paul II, *Mulieris Dignitatem*, 88.

but couples must subordinate themselves to one another and husbands must on their part give themselves in loving, costly service for their wife. In this argument Paul turns upside down this world's understanding of what it means for the husband to be the leader of his wife. The one who has precedence is to become a servant. Paul does not ask husbands to be subordinate; he asks far more. He asks them to give themselves in service and love for their wife to the point of giving their life for her. We therefore should not make anything of the different wording. I agree with the commentator Andrew Lincoln. Paul sees, "submission and love [*agape* love] as two sides of the same coin—selfless service of one's marriage partner."[22]

Now let me make clear what I have just said. I have argued that Paul's exhortation to wives to be subordinate, and his words, "the husband is the head of his wife," speak of marriage in this fallen world where men rule over women (cf. Gen 3:16). In contrast, Eph 5:21 and 5:25–33 speak of Paul's new creation understanding of marriage. This is what we should preach and practice.

In his first-century cultural context, Paul asks women to accept their subordinate status as Christians, just like he asks slaves to accept their servitude. Neither the unilateral subordination of wives nor the slave-master relationship are the creation ideal. We should therefore not support slavery, as many evangelicals of Reformed persuasion did in nineteenth century America, claiming Paul endorsed slavery. And we should not support, let alone teach, the subordination of women, claiming this is what the Bible makes the creation ideal. It does not. This also means we should not support or teach male "headship," understood as men having authority over women, albeit for Christians in a loving way. Male "headship" in this sense is not pleasing to God any more than is slavery. It reflects the fallen world. What we should teach is what is distinctively Christian and new: mutual subordination in marriage and husbands giving themselves in costly love and service for their wives.

Verses 25–33

Having addressed Christian wives in *three verses*, exhorting them to "be subject to your husbands," which I believe added nothing to what their culture expected of wives, Paul then addresses Christian husbands in *seven verses*. What he says to husbands definitely introduces something new

22. Lincoln, *Ephesians*, 393.

and something not expected. What Paul's audience would have expected was for him to go on to tell husbands how they were to make sure their superior status and honor were upheld. A husband in the Greco-Roman world was served by his wife who was supposed to advance his honor. Instead, Paul exhorts husbands to serve and honor their wives. In these seven verses we find teaching that is novel, revolutionary, *and distinctively Christian*. In these verses, Paul subverts what he says in verses 22–24. He asks those who are the head to act like servants. He asks husbands to love their wives "just as Christ loved the church and gave himself for her," and to love them "as they love their own bodies." He does not use the Greek word *eros* (sexual love), or *philia* (brotherly/family love), but *agapē* (self-giving love), which as far as we know, no one before Paul had used for the marriage relationship. *Agapē* is the noblest and loftiest word in the Greek language for love. We understand its meaning through the self-sacrifice of Christ who "loved (*agapaō*) the church and gave himself up for her" (v. 25). This kind of love is not an emotion, but a way of behaving. This is how Christian husbands are to give themselves for their wives. No one, save Christ, had ever suggested anything like this.

Verses 28–29

In verses 28–29, Paul explains more fully what the love of a husband for his wife entails.

> In the same way [as Christ loved the church] husbands should love their wives as their own bodies. He who loves his wife loves himself. For no one ever hates his own flesh, but he nourishes and tenderly cares for it, just as Christ does for the church because we are members of his body.

Christ's love for the church described in verses 25–27 is now given as the model ("in the same way") for how a Christian husband should love his wife. The idea of the husband loving his wife as his own body reflects Christ's love for the church, his body. "He nourishes it and tenderly cares for it." This is how a Christian husband should love his wife. To so love your wife, Paul explains, is to love her as you love yourself.

Let me reiterate; in exhorting husbands to love their wives like Christ loved the church, and to love them like their own body, Paul is not simply asking men who are the *paterfamilias* (the father of the family) to exercise the authority they have in a loving way. He is asking of them far more, he is asking them to give up the precedence and privileges that they have as men and become the loving servant of their wives. What Paul says here subverts patriarchy; it envisages marriage of two people of equal worth and dignity and one in which the husband gives himself in sacrificial, lowly service for his wife, even to the point of giving his life for her.

Verse 31

Paul now moves beyond what he expects of wives and husbands individually, to the most mysterious reality of human existence, the oneness of husband and wife. He quotes Gen 2:24, as Jesus did (Mark 10:8), to explain marriage: "For this reason a man shall leave his father and mother and be joined to his wife, and the two shall become one flesh." At this point any thought of hierarchical ordering in the Christian marriage relationship is excluded. In marriage two people become one. Note carefully: *Paul quotes Gen 2:24 not to ground the subordination of women in creation before the fall, but the exact opposite: to tell his readers that before the fall marriage resulted in a profound oneness of man and woman, and this is now possible in Christ.*

Verse 33

Paul concludes with a summary: "You men love your wives; you women reverence your husbands." To suggest that men are to love their wives and wives are to reverence their husbands as two distinct ways of relating has nothing to commend it. Paul's words are just a rhythmic way to conclude what he has said on Christian marriage. These duties are reciprocal. Men should reverence their wives and women should love their husbands. We definitely know Paul thought wives should love their husbands. In Titus 2:4 he explicitly says this.

The same response must be made to those who, along with the Köstenbergers,[23] say Paul asks women to submit to their husbands, never husbands to wives. Husbands are asked only to love their wives. First, Paul asks all Christians to subordinate themselves one another (v 21). This must include husbands to wives as well as wives to husbands. This primary exhortation is not gender specific. Second, Paul elsewhere asks wives to love their husbands (Titus 2:4). For him, love of one's partner

---

23. Köstenberger and Köstenberger, *God's Design*, 182.

is not gender specific; it is a mutual obligation. And third, Paul is *not* making contrasting demands, one to wives and another to husbands, although as a master communicator addressing men who are anxious about their status, he subtly words his case. He does not ask men specifically to submit to their wives; he asks far more of them in less threatening language. He calls on them to give their life in love for their wives.

The reply that marriages cannot work unless someone has the final say, the so-called "casting vote," is hardly a serious objection, or one with any biblical warrant. Certainly, armies need generals, ships need captains, and businesses need managers; but good marriages are like friendships. To have a friendship does not require that one party make all the major decisions nor have the casting vote. Indeed, such a rule would destroy most friendships. The truth is that most couples find that with lots of talking and much prayer, given time, they can come to a common mind on even the most difficult matters. I speak from fifty years of experience!

The Köstenbergers say the subordination of wives to their husbands "is deeply countercultural and incompatible with deep-seated egalitarianism."[24] It is true that in today's world, arguing for the subordination of wives is deeply countercultural and incompatible with the substantial equality of the sexes. This does not say it is wrong. Much Christian teaching is countercultural. It is, however, not true that "deep-seated egalitarianism," to use their expression, is "incompatible" with what the Bible teaches. The thesis of this book is that, in fact, the Bible makes the substantial or essential equality of the sexes the God-given ideal. On the basis of this conviction I believe that God is pleased to see Christians finding great reward and happiness in their profoundly equal marriages.

To sum up: In Eph 5:21–33 Paul outlines a distinctive Christian understanding of marriage in which the ideal is mutual subordination and mutual unconditional love. It is given against the backdrop of a world where men ruled over women. Today, we Christians live in a world where the substantial equality of the sexes is accepted and affirmed. We are now free to put into practice this ideal in our marriages. Our responsibility is to follow the trajectory Paul set in what he said to the Ephesian Christians on marriage by working to make our marriages a profound equal union of a man and a woman bound together in mutual love and service.

---

24. Köstenberger and Köstenberger, *God's Design*, 184.

1 CORINTHIANS 7:1-40

Well before Paul wrote on marriage in Eph 5:21-33, he had discussed this important matter at some length in his earlier first epistle to the Corinthians in chapter 7. This chapter is of huge importance in any consideration of what Paul taught on the husband-wife relationship; it must not be ignored. Paul begins this chapter by saying, "Now concerning the matters about which you wrote," and then, "It is well for a man not to touch a woman" (i.e., sexual intercourse). Commentators generally take these words to be a slogan used by a group of spiritual elitists at Corinth who were arguing that it is more spiritual to be celibate. From what Paul says in reply we see what they were arguing given their basic premise disclosed in this slogan: if you are married do not have sex, or better still, separate or divorce, and if single, do not marry. Paul has little sympathy with such ideas and he counters them one by one. What is so surprising is that in his reply he considers twelve possibilities, and in each case, he says the same rule applies to men and women, husbands and wives.[25] He implies the principle that the rights and the responsibilities of the man and the woman are exactly the same. In the patriarchal context in which Paul and the Corinthians were situated, this is radically countercultural teaching. It envisages a fully reciprocal view of marriage—a marriage of equals. I now give the evidence for this assertion:

7:2. "Each man should have his own wife and each woman her own husband."

7:3. "The husband should give his wife her conjugal rights, and likewise the wife to her husband."

7:4. "For the wife does not have authority over her own body, but the husband does; likewise, the husband does not have authority over his own body, but the wife does."

7:5. "Do not deprive one another except perhaps by agreement for a set time."

7:10-11. "The wife should not separate from her husband . . . and the husband should not leave his wife."

7:12-13. "If any believer has a wife who is an unbeliever and she consents to live with him, he should not divorce her. And if any woman

25. I follow closely in this section, Payne, *Man and Woman*, 105-8. I thank him for his insightful and important work on this passage

has a husband who is an unbeliever, and he consents to live with her, she should not divorce him."

7:14. "The unbelieving husband is made holy through his wife, and the unbelieving wife is made holy through her husband."

7:15. "But if the unbelieving partner separates, let it be so; in such cases the brother or sister is not bound."

7:16. "Wife, for all you know, you might save your husband. Husband, for all you know, you might save your wife."

7:28. "But if you [a man] marry, you do not sin, and if an unmarried woman marries she does not sin."

7:32, 34b. "The unmarried man is concerned about the affairs of the Lord. . . . An unmarried woman is concerned about the affairs of the Lord."

7:33–34a. "The married man is concerned about the affairs of this world, and how to please his wife. . . .The married woman is concerned about the affairs of the world and how she can please her husband."

Professor Richard B. Hays says that Paul's answers to the questions on sex and marriage put by the Corinthians,

> must have struck many first-century hearers as extraordinary. . . . The marriage partners are neither set in a hierarchical relationship with one over the other, nor set apart as autonomous units each doing what he or she pleases. Instead, the relationship of marriage is one of mutual submission, each partner having authority over the other.[26]

Before leaving this chapter, we should carefully note that not only does Paul not mention male headship in this, by far his most extended discussion on Christian marriage, but the idea that men have precedence in marriage is inimical to everything he says. Paul excludes the patriarchal understanding of marriage where the man has rights that the woman does not have, advocating instead a fully symmetrical and equal marriage relationship.

---

26. Hays, *First Corinthians*, 116.

The Köstenbergers have no discussion of this passage. They ignore Paul's longest treatment of the marriage relationship that counters their primary thesis.

1 TIMOTHY 5:14

Nowhere in the Bible do we find the idea or expression, "the husband is the head of the home." This turn of phrase and concept comes late in human history. When people use this expression today, they reflect their own cultural presuppositions, not those of the biblical writers and their contemporaries. In the ancient world, a sharp distinction was made between the public sphere (*polis*), which was the domain of men, and the home (*oikos*), which was the domain of women.[27] In the Greco-Roman world, the husband was called the *paterfamilias*, the father of the family, and his wife the *materfamilias*, the mother of the family. The *materfamilias* had the responsibility of managing the home, educating the children, directing and disciplining slaves, and paying the bills. She was "the head of the home." Against this backdrop, Paul's advice to young widows to marry and *manage or rule* their households (1 Tim 5:14) makes sense. This is what all wives were supposed to do. The Greek verb translated by the NRSV as "manage" is *oikodespotein,* literally means "to be house despot."

Yet again the Köstenbergers have no discussion at all on this important text.

HEADSHIP THEN AND NOW

Now to the twenty-first century.

There are at least four understandings of male "headship" among Christians today, each with its variants. The Köstenbergers do not note this.

1. Paul is teaching, and the whole Bible implies, that men are the leaders in the home and the church, and ideally in society as well. "Leadership is male." In the home the finances, the discipline of the children, and all major decisions are the father's final responsibility.

---

27. In the last chapter I outlined the basis for this assertion. On the separation of the public and private domains see also, Westfall, *Paul and Gender,* 22–24.

Those who take this position insist that headship means "authority over" and this authority must be complete because Paul told wives to "be subject to your husbands in all things" (Eph 5:24). Some advocates of this view name it "Christian or Biblical Patriarchy";[28] others, "strong patriarchy." This point of view has many supporters, mainly in the United States. It is basically what the Köstenbergers advocate. Men inclined to be controlling are very attracted to this understanding of headship. This is the historic position, almost universally held by theologians until about 1960.

2. Far more common today is what is called "soft patriarchy." On this view, the husband is the servant leader in the home, but his headship/leadership takes a sharp edge when a couple cannot come to a common mind; then he has the casting vote. Almost always this view, like "strong patriarchy," involves the idea that women should not lead or preach in church. This would set women over male heads of homes. On the question of women leaders in society, what is said is very muffled. When pressed, "soft-patriarchy" theologians have to admit that because they ground women's subordination in creation before the fall, women's subordination must be the God-given ideal for all of creation, the home, the church, and society.

3. Some who would call themselves "egalitarians" have a very similar view to the position just enunciated in reference to the home. With "soft patriarchalists" they feel bound to endorse Paul's words, "the husband is the head/leader of the wife." They have been told this so many times that they have lost sight of the context in which these words are set. They miss the fact that what Paul says before and after these words subverts the idea that the husband rules over his wife. Their belief is that Paul does make the husband the leader but softens this by insisting that he leads as a servant even to the point of giving his life for his wife. Rightly, however, they see nothing in the text at all about who makes decisions, even difficult ones, or anything excluding women from leading in church or preaching. In reply, other egalitarians ask if this is a consistent egalitarian position. They say, "Does not this view of marriage suggest that men

---

28. "Biblical Patriarchy," *Wikipedia*. One well-known complementarian theologian argues that the complementarian movement can only be saved if all complementarians endorse biblical patriarchy. See Moore, "After Patriarchy."

have some vague and undefined leadership in the marriage that the wife does not share?"

4. Finally, there is the view that I hold and advocate, namely that "male headship" reflects *the fallen order*. The distinctive Christian vision of marriage is one characterized by mutual subordination, mutual responsibility, and mutual *agape*-love; a marriage of equals. The Köstenbergers call this "the consensus model" of marriage and reject it as contrary to the Bible.[29] Evangelicals and Pentecostals who understand Eph 5:21–33 to be the foreshadowing of the "consensus model" of marriage see Paul in his cultural context as working to transform patriarchy. They thus reason that given an egalitarian cultural context, as is known today, the trajectory Paul set should be followed. Selfless, loving service for one's spouse is what is distinctive and primary in Christian marriage for the man and the woman. This is the ideal to which Eph 5:21–33 points. This they argue is also the model of marriage Jesus endorsed. Contemporary Christians who seek to make mutual subordination, mutual responsibility, and mutual love the guiding norms for their marriage find this model of marriage very challenging but hugely rewarding.

QUESTIONS FOR DISCUSSION

1. What would you say to someone who said, "Every ship needs a captain, every army a general, every business a manager, and so, in every marriage someone has to be in charge?" How do you make big decisions in your home?

2. What does a fully equal marriage look like? Is it hard to realize? If so why?

3. How might teaching that the husband is the head of his wife (her manager/boss) encourage men to leave all the hard work in a family up to the wife?

4. In looking at how Christian couples actually relate, I outline three often-seen options: 1) Sometimes one or both partners insist that the man is the head/leader, and this is true; he does run the show. 2) Sometimes one or both partners insist that the man is the head/

29. Köstenberger and Köstenberger, *God's Design*, 278.

leader, but in reality, it seems that the wife is in charge. 3) Sometimes one or both partners insist that theirs is a fully equal marriage, but in reality it seems either the husband or the wife is dominant. Why is it that often what people say about "headship" in their marriage is not grounded in reality?

5. Could headship teaching in church encourage some men who are prone to be controlling and angry to be abusive in their homes?

ADDENDUM: THE COMPLEMENTARIAN POSITION IS NOVEL

Conservative evangelicals committed to "male headship" as the creation ideal claim that what they teach is what the church has always believed. Their understanding of the relationship of the sexes is the "traditional" one. The 1989 Danvers Statement, which enunciates the complementarian position, goes further. The complementarian position, it says, "is the teaching of Scripture."[30] This is what every complementarian I have read or heard claims explicitly or implicitly. "What we teach is what the church has always taught and it is what the Bible teaches." They will not concede that what they teach has no historical antecedents or that this debate is entirely about how we should rightly interpret the Scriptures. They want to make it a debate about who accepts what the Bible says, and people like Kevin Giles who cannot accept what the Bible teaches. This argument makes dialogue between complementarians and egalitarian evangelicals impossible. Before the Bible is opened and what it actually says can be discussed, the complementarians rule out of court the egalitarian voice as the voice of liberalism and feminism.

In what has been said so far I have argued that the complementarians are in fact the ones that have misinterpreted the Bible and got it all wrong. In this addendum I make the point that what they are teaching is novel. It stands in contrast with the historical position articulated by the great theologians of the past.

---

30. This statement is given as an appendix in Grudem and Piper, *Recovering Biblical Manhood*, 469–71, and can be found online.

The Historical Interpretation of What the Bible Says
on the Sexes, 200 AD to 1960: Tertullian, Chrysostom, Augustine,
Aquinas, Luther, Calvin, the Puritans, Hodge, etc.

For long centuries, Christian theologians interpreted the Bible to be
teaching that God had made men "superior," women "inferior."[31] These
two words are used consistently. All the theologians were agreed, men
and women are not "equal" in any substantive sense. I find no dissenting
voices. These men developed their doctrine of the sexes by reading the
Bible presupposing the cultural norms of their day. They understood the
key texts in this way.

1. Man was created first to show he is first in rank. Chrysostom said
   God made man first to show "male superiority" and to teach that
   "the male sex enjoyed the higher honor . . . having preeminence in
   every way."[32] Writing as late as 1957, the evangelical Donald Guthrie
   in his Tyndale commentary on the Pastorals says, "The priority of
   man's creation places him in a position of *superiority* over women."[33]
   From the time of Augustine it was generally thought that women do
   not fully bear the image of God (key text 1 Cor 11:7).[34] Calvin says,
   woman was created to be "a kind of appendage to man."[35]

2. Woman is responsible for the fall and sin. The historic interpretation
   of 1 Tim 2:14 is that here Paul blames the woman for the fall, she
   should suffer for this, and the lesson to be learned is that women are
   more prone to sin and error. Tertullian said woman is the "devil's
   gateway."[36] Calvin said that because the woman "seduced the man
   from God's commandment, it is fitting that she be deprived of all
   freedom and placed under a yoke." To woman, he adds, "is to be

---

31. The following is a summary of my chapter on women in the Christian tradition
in my book, *Trinity and Subordinationism*, 145–55. A parallel account of women in the
Christian tradition given is by the complementarian theologian Daniel Doriani in his
appendix "History of the Interpretation of 1 Timothy 2," in Köstenberger, Schreiner,
and Baldwin, *Women in the Church*, 213–68. Not surprisingly, this appendix that gave
away so much was omitted from the 2005 edition of this book.

32. Quoted and referenced in Giles, *Trinity and Subordinationism*, 151.

33. Guthrie, *Pastoral Epistles*, 77. Italics added.

34. Giles, *Trinity and Subordinationism*, 150–51. See also Borresen, *Image of God*.

35. Calvin, *Paul's Second Epistle*, 219.

36. Quoted more fully and referenced in Giles, *Trinity and Subordinationism*, 153.

imputed the sin of the whole human race."[37] Again, I note the evangelical Donald Guthrie's *interpretation* of this verse in 1957. He says that Paul has in mind "the greater aptitude of the weaker sex to be led astray."[38]

3. In the historical understanding of what the Bible teaches it was universally agreed that women should not hold authority in the home, the church, and the state. Commenting on 1 Tim 2:12 Calvin says, "The rule of women is an unnatural monstrosity."[39] Charles Hodge says, "[Mans'] superiority . . . enables and entitles him to command. . . . The superiority of the man is . . . taught in Scripture, founded in nature and proved by all experience." For this reason, he added, "The general good requires us to deprive the whole female sex the rights of self-government."[40]

4. Lastly, I mention that in the historic understanding of what the Bible teaches on women it is argued that women should keep silent in *all* public settings, not just the church. Calvin, commenting on 1 Tim 2:11 says, "Quietness means silence, they [women] should not presume to speak in public."[41] Charles Hodge says the Scriptures forbid women from "speaking in public, especially in the church."[42]

The complementarian theologian Daniel Doriani says until modern times theologians presumed the "ontological inferiority of women."[43] Aquinas eloquently expresses this opinion. He asks, is the woman a deficient and defective male? He answers in the affirmative. He says woman "by nature [are] of lower capacity and quality than man."[44]

In the twenty-first century we all find these interpretations of what the Bible says about women very confronting, if not abhorrent. I have not sought to give a list of misogynistic comments from theologian writing before the 1960s, but from the quotations that I have given, the often harsh misogyny of theologians from the past cannot be missed.

37. Calvin, *Paul's Second Epistle,* 218–219.

38. Guthrie, *Pastoral Epistles,* 77.

39. Calvin, *Paul's Second Epistle,* 219.

40. Hodge, *Commentary on the Epistle to the Ephesians,* 312.

41. Calvin, *Paul's Second Epistle,* 216, 217.

42. Hodge, *Commentary on the First Epistle to the Corinthians,* 305.

43. Doriani, "History of the Interpretation," 257.

44. Quoted and referenced in Giles, *Trinity and Subordinationism,* 152.

The Novel Elements in Complementarian "Exegesis"

What I have just outlined makes it undeniable that the post-1970s complementarian arguments for the subordination of women, or in their words the "role" differences between men and women, are novel. They are certainly not how theologians interpreted the Bible until 1960. I highlight some of the elements that are entirely novel in the contemporary complementarian position.

The idea of "role" subordination is entirely novel. This must be the case because the word "role" only came into the English language in the late nineteenth century. But more importantly, the historic position holds that the Bible teaches, as the complementarian theologian Daniel Doriani admits, "the ontological inferiority of women." Women *are* inferior to men. They are not merely permanently "role" subordinated or differentiated.

In contrast to the historic position, complementarians consistently say that they reject the idea that men are "superior," women "inferior." They insist the sexes are "equal." This is a strange "equality" when women are permanently subordinated to men but this is what they say.

Then we have the novel interpretation of key texts. Junia, mentioned in Rom 16:7, cannot be an apostle like James, Apollos, and Timothy, despite the fact this is what Paul seems to say. She cannot be an apostle exercising authority and teaching because she is a woman. For the Köstenbergers, she is merely the wife of a missionary apostle whose "ministry was with other women."[45] Before the thirteenth century virtually every theologian accepted that Junia was an outstanding woman apostle. Complementarians agree, women were prophets and prophesied, but prophecy, they tell us, is not an authoritative word ministry like teaching and so it must not be seen as a form of preaching.[46] In contrast, most Protestant theologians and commentators before the complementarians came on the scene argued that prophecy is a form of preaching, if not expository preaching, and it was one of the most important ministries in the early church. John Calvin says prophecy is "the interpretation of Scripture applied to the present need."[47] In other words, it is expository preaching. Charles Hodge, commenting on 1 Cor 11:4–5, says prayer and

45. Köstenberger and Köstenberger, *God's Design*, 155.

46. Köstenberger and Köstenberger, *God's Design*, 141–42, 179–80, and most complementarian books.

47. Calvin, *Epistle of Paul to the Romans and Thessalonians*, 377.

prophecy were "the two principal exercises in the public life of the early Christians."[48] In 1 Corinthians, the Köstenbergers insist, Paul is only saying "that women may participate in praying and prophesying in church under male spiritual leadership."[49] In 1 Cor 14:33b–36, they say, following other complementarians, that here Paul specifically forbids women from judging prophecies.[50] I cannot find this interpretation of these verses in any commentary or theological book before 1960. Furthermore, it is novel to take the commands to women to keep silent (1 Cor 14:34; 1 Tim 2:11) as only applying in the church and that "male headship" only applies in the home and the church. When it comes to the most important texts for complementarians, 1 Tim 2:11–14, the changes from how this text has been historically interpreted are far reaching and profound. On this passage the complementarian theologian Daniel Doriani says the complementarian exegesis is a "reinterpretation." Contemporary complementarian theologians reject that in this passage Paul grounds the subordination of women in "ontological arguments." They argue instead that women's subordination is grounded in the "creation order" before the fall. They deny that Paul's phrase, "Adam was not deceived but the woman was deceived," means that "women are liable to deception."[51] On this verse, they opt rather for their own novel interpretation; here Paul speaks of the dire consequences of "role reversal." When it comes to the translation of the highly disputed verb *authentein* in verse 12, complementarians reject the translation given by Authorized Version of 1611, "to usurp authority," and the somewhat literal Revised Version of 1884, "to have dominion" (over a man). They argue instead for the neutral modern translation, "authority," which as I have shown has no historical or semantic support. Lastly, I mention 1 Tim 2:15, women "will be saved through child bearing." This text has had a number of interpretations over the centuries but never the characteristic complementarian "exegesis" given by the Köstenbergers, "women will be spiritually preserved if they devote themselves to their God-given role in the domestic and familial sphere."[52]

Finally, I note that the misogynist comments, many very stark, characteristic of the historic position are missing in complementarian books.

---

48. Hodge, *Commentary on the First Epistle to the Corinthians*, 208.

49. Köstenberger and Köstenberger, *God's Design*, 160.

50. Köstenberger and Köstenberger, *God's Design*, 179–80.

51. Doriani, "History of the Interpretation," 258–59.

52. Doriani, "History of the Interpretation," 216.

What is characteristic of the complementarian position today is euphemistic and obfuscating language. We believe in the "complementarity"
of the sexes; men and women are "equal" yet "role differentiated," and to
quote the Köstenbergers, "the man is ultimately responsible for leading in
the marriage . . . while the woman is his partner."[53]

---

53. Köstenberger and Köstenberger, *God's Design*, 24. What they believe is, of
course, that the man leads and the woman obeys. She is his subordinate.

8

The Bible and Human Liberation: Slavery and Women

IN THE BIBLE, SLAVERY is often mentioned and never directly condemned. For centuries, most Christians believed the Bible endorsed both
the subordination of women and the institution of slavery. In the late
eighteenth century, for the first time, Christians began arguing that slavery is an evil to be opposed and abolished. Not all Christians agreed. In
the nineteenth century both the strongest opponents and the strongest
supporters of slavery were evangelicals. The evangelical and Reformed
supporters of slavery appealed to the Bible and were able to develop an
impressive "biblical theology" to make their case.

Today we see the same in regard to the subordination of women.
Some evangelicals argue that women are a subordinate class, while others argue for the substantial equality of the two differentiated sexes. The
evangelical and Reformed supporters of the subordination of women,
like the pro-slavery theologians, have developed an impressive "biblical
theology" to make their case that the subordination of women is taught
in Scripture.

Those who argue for the permanent subordination of women today
("complementarians"), do not want to discuss, and generally ignore, the
bitter intramural evangelical debate over slavery in the nineteenth century, in which appeal to the Bible was so central. The Köstenbergers, with
whom I am in dialogue in this book, side step this issue completely. They
say nothing on it. They do so when Andreas is fully cognizant of what

follows on slavery, which is just a summary and update of work I have published earlier, and he has read.[1]

How the Bible speaks of slavery and women, and how previous Christians have understood these two matters, can't be ignored or dismissed as unimportant. This issue is one of the most significant in this debate over the man-woman relationship, and the most difficult for the complementarian position.

Most Christians have heard many a sermon and read many an article telling how evangelicals led the great fight to abolish slavery in the late eighteenth and the nineteenth centuries. The evangelicals who fought for the emancipation of slaves and the abolition of slavery are well-known: William Wilberforce, John Wesley, John Newton, Charles Finney, the Grimke sisters, and Harriet Beecher Stowe—all white people—and black people like Oloudah Equiano, Frederick Douglass, and Sojourner Truth. The story of these people is inspiring.

What most Christians have not heard in sermons and not read in Christian literature is that other Christians, most of whom were evangelicals of Reformed conviction, *led* the opposition to the emancipation of slaves. They wrote numerous books arguing that slavery was endorsed by the Bible and acceptable to God. This is a well-kept secret because it is so embarrassing to evangelicals, especially to those who today teach that the Bible permanently subordinates women to men. William Wilberforce in England had his strident opponents among the clergy and bishops. In the United States the Christian opposition to the emancipation of slaves was far more extensive and bitter. Almost all the clergy in the "Old South" supported slavery by appeal to the Bible and the leading evangelical and Reformed theologians of the day (Charles Hodge,[2] Robert Dabney,[3] and J. Henry Thornwell[4]) wrote substantial works arguing that the Bible unequivocally endorsed slavery. It was in this context that

1. He has read my book, *Trinity and Subordinationism,* which has forty pages on the slavery argument. He quotes me in a book he edited and wrote a chapter for, Köstenberger and Schreiner, *Women in the Church,* a book in which Robert W. Yarborough gives four pages to opposing what I say about slavery. What is more, Andreas and I have corresponded on this matter.

2. Hodge first set out his biblical case for slavery in his commentary on *Ephesians,* 365–66. His definitive essay, "Biblical Argument for Slavery," is found in Cartwright, *Cotton Is King.*

3. See Dabney, *Discussions,* 3:33–38.

4. See Thornwell, *Collected Writings,* 4:387–436.

in 1845 the Southern Baptists broke from the Northern Baptists to form a separate proslavery denomination. Thornwell, who wrote the most impressive "biblical" case for slavery was a Southern Baptist. Evangelicals in the South were so convinced that the Bible endorsed slavery that they gladly took up arms in the Civil War to kill or be killed to maintain the institution of slavery.[5] Charles Hodge was the greatest Reformed theologian of his day. His essay, "The Biblical Case for Slavery," was hugely influential. Gutjar says, "Hodges' biblical defense of the institution . . . made him "immensely popular among Southern Presbyterians."[6] Because he was convinced that slavery was endorsed by the Bible he bought slaves to run his home.[7]

In summary, the so-called "biblical" case for slavery that these evangelical and Reformed theologians developed is as follows:[8]

1. *God established slavery.* In cursing Noah's son, Ham, to be a slave (Gen 9:20–27), God himself instituted slavery.

2. *God approved of slavery.* Most of the significant leaders God raised up in the Old Testament period had slaves. Abraham (Gen 12:5; 14:14; 24:35), Isaac (Gen 25:5), Joshua (Josh 9:23), David (2 Sam 8:2, 6), Solomon (1 Kgs 9:20–21), and Job (Job 1:15–16; 3:19; etc.) are all said to have owned slaves. If these men that God blessed owned slaves and saw no issue with this, then slavery cannot be displeasing to God.

3. *The Mosaic Law sanctioned slavery.* Twice in the Ten Commandments it is assumed that God's people will own slaves (the fourth and tenth commandments). It thus cannot be a sin to own slaves. What God regulates he must approve. Furthermore, in the Law the Israelites are told that they may make destitute Jews slaves for six years (Lev 25:39–41; Deut 15:12–18), and when they go to war they

5. For scholarly support and more information on what follows see Giles, *Trinity and Subordinationism,* 215–68. On slavery in the Old South and appeals to the Bible in support by evangelicals see also Noll, *Civil War;* and Wilson-Hartgrove, *Reconstructing the Gospel.*

6. Gutjar, *Charles Hodge,* 296.

7. Gutjar, *Charles Hodge,* 156, 174. For an account of Hodges' views on slavery see, Gutjar, *Charles Hodge,* 171–75.

8. This summary of the biblical case for slavery I compiled from the writings of the pro-slavery theologians. See further Giles, *Trinity and Subordinationism,* 215–33. For a later account very close to mine see Noll, *Civil War,* 33–36.

should make slaves of those defeated (Lev 25:44–46), which they usually did (Gen 14:21; Deut 20:14; 21:10–14; 1 Sam 4:9; 2 Chr 28:8).

4. *Jesus accepted slavery.* The Gospels tell us Jesus often encountered slaves (Luke 7:2–10; 22: 50, etc.) and he mentions slaves in many of his parables (Matt 13:24–30; 18:23–35; 22: 1–14; etc.), yet he uttered not one word of criticism of slavery. What he did not condemn he must have condoned.

5. *The apostles endorsed slavery.* They commanded slaves to obey their masters (Eph 6:5–8; Col 3:22—4:1; 1 Pet 2:18–25; 1 Tim 6:1–3; Titus 2:9–10) and Paul sent Onesimus the Christian slave back to his Christian master Philemon not asking him to set Onesimus free.[9]

6. *God has ordered society hierarchically.* In creation, the man was set over the woman and this implies hierarchical rule is pleasing to God. This is how he wants society ordered. Some are born to be rulers, some subjects. (It was assumed as self-evident by white men that God had given to them the ruling position.)

7. *God regulated and thus approved of slavery.* In both Old and New Testaments slave masters are instructed on how to behave toward their slaves (Deut 5:12–15; Exod 21:21; Eph 5:9; Col 4:1; etc.). If God regulated and legislated on slavery, he must approve.

8. *The apostolic exhortations to wives, slaves, and children to be subordinate or obedient, given sequentially and in parallel, reflect the mind of God. They don't differ and are alike permanently binding* (Eph 5:21—6:9; Col 3:18—4:1; 1 Pet 2:18—3:7). In an age when male leadership/headship was assumed in the state, the church, and the home, the pro-slavery evangelical theologians argued that to reject the apostolic teaching on the master-slave relationship called into question the authority of husbands and parents.

It was obvious, they said, that the apostles held these matters to be of equal force.[10] In commenting on the related exhortations in Ephesians, Hodge wrote,

9. See the epistle of Philemon.

10. Modern-day supporters of the permanent subordination of women claim the exhortations to slaves are profoundly different to those to wives/women, an argument we will explore in due course. This claim was opposed by the pro-slavery theologians. They were united in seeing these exhortations as of one kind. For example Bledsoe,

> What the Scriptures teach, is not peculiar to the obedience of
> the slave to his master, but applies to all the other cases in which
> obedience is regulated. . . . It applies to children in relation to
> their parents and wives to their husbands. Those invested with
> lawful authority are the representatives of God. The powers (i.e.,
> those invested with authority) are ordained by God.[11]

Masters and slaves are spiritually equal as Gal 3:28 and Col 3:11
teach, but in this world difference prevails. To be in Christ does not negate that we are Jew or Gentile, man or woman, and thus it does not
negate the fact that some are masters and some slaves.

The defenders of slavery were convinced that they had a watertight
biblical case. The argument they made countless times, they believed, was
the plain and unambiguous teaching of Scripture. Mark Noll writes that
they said to doubters and to their opponents,

> First, open the Scriptures and read, at say Leviticus 25:45, or,
> even better, at 1 Corinthians 7:20–21. Second, decide for your-
> self what these passages mean. Don't wait for a bishop or king
> or president or meddling Yankee to tell you what the passage
> means, but decide for yourself. Third, if anyone tries to convince
> you that you are not interpreting such passages in the natural,
> commonsensical, ordinary meaning of the words, look hard at
> what such a one believes with respect to other biblical doctrines.
> If you find in what he or she says about such doctrines the least
> hint of unorthodoxy, as inevitably as you will, then you must
> rest assured that you are being asked to give up on the plain
> meaning of Scripture.[12]

In nineteenth century America this comprehensive *biblical case* in
support of slavery seemed compelling, especially to those who benefited
from being part of the Southern slave economy. To argue that slavery
was displeasing to God and sinful was for the Southern theologians and
most of the Southern clergy proof that those who spoke and worked for
abolition had rejected biblical authority. They accused them of being
"liberals," of embracing the radical secular egalitarianism of the French
Revolution, and of denying undeniable differences among people.

"Liberty and Slavery," 354; Stringfellow, "Biblical Argument," 480–81; Hodge, "Biblical
Argument," 848–49; and Thornwell, *Collected Writings*, 4, 386.

11. Hodge, *Commentary on the Epistle to the Ephesians*, 366.

12. Noll, *Civil War*, 50.

THE CASE AGAINST SLAVERY AND FOR EMANCIPATION

The change of thinking on slavery was evoked by a change in thought about society, particularly how it should be ordered. Beginning in the late eighteenth century, intellectuals began postulating about how society could be better ordered and governed to guarantee the dignity and worth of everyone. Egalitarian and democratic ideals flowered, and the first voices in opposition to slavery appeared.[13]

These revolutionary ideas were introduced by the Enlightenment thinkers, Montesquieu (1689–1755) and Rousseau (1712–1778), the first to oppose slavery. However, it was Christians who stepped forward first to do something about slavery and who led the opposition at a political level. The first Christian to openly oppose slavery and denounce the institution was Benjamin Lay, a Quaker. He published a tract in 1736 condemning slavery as "a hellish practice . . . the greatest sin in the world." In 1774, after reading another Quaker tract denouncing slavery, John Wesley took up the cause of the abolition of slavery and the emancipation of the slaves. Soon after, other evangelicals in England followed him and began working for the abolition of slavery.

These first Christian emancipationists were primarily opposed to slavery because of its awful consequences, cruelty, and injustice. They did not seek texts to prove that the Bible condemned slavery, but rather appealed to basic biblical principles such as that all human beings are made in the image and likeness of God, that God loves all human beings, and that we should treat others as we ourselves would like to be treated. These foundational biblical principles, they believed, excluded slavery.

In nineteenth century America, the emancipationists had a much harder road to travel.[14] They were confronted by learned evangelical and Reformed theologians of the highest calibre who, as we have just seen, had constructed an impressive "biblical theology" in support of slavery. Like the English emancipationists, in reply, they appealed to the foundational biblical principles mentioned above, often adding to these republican ideals.[15] In the American Declaration of Independence, the

---

13. I tell this story in much more detail with documentation in Giles, *Trinity and Subordination*, 234–37.

14. With this paragraph I draw on Noll, *Civil War*, 46–54.

15. Noll, *Civil War*, 40–41.

assertion is made that all men have "natural and inalienable rights." The abolitionist took this principle as something implied in Scripture.

In a significant public debate over slavery that lasted for four days, the abolitionist Jonathan Blanchard returned repeatedly to "the broad principles of the Bible" and to "the whole scope of Scripture," where to him it was obvious that "the principles of the Bible are justice and righteousness."[16] His view was that you could quote texts in support of almost anything and end up opposing the most fundamental truths revealed in Scripture.

For the pro-slavery evangelical theologians, only one thing mattered (what the Bible said), and they were convinced the Bible endorsed slavery. They ignored what slavery involved for the slaves, arguing no example of abuse could negate what the Bible clearly taught. The appeal by abolitionists to the great liberating themes in the Bible fell on deaf ears. What proved to be the most effective counter to pro-slavery theology were the descriptions of what slavery actually involved for the enslaved, the very matter the Southern theologians did not want to discuss. The most significant accounts of the reality were John Newton's 1787 book, *Thoughts on the African Slave Trade*; Theodore Weldt's 1839 book, *American Slavery As It Is: Testimony of a Thousand Witnesses*; and Harriet Beecher Stowe's *Uncle Tom's Cabin: Life Among the Lowly*, the best-selling novel of the nineteenth century. These books convinced many people that there must be something wrong with the "biblical" case for slavery. Slavery, with all its cruelty and injustice, simply could not be endorsed by the loving and just God revealed in the Bible.

Tragically, the debate about slavery was ended not by winning the biblical argument, or by convincing people of the awful cruelty and injustice of slavery, but by military might. The pro-slavery Southern Christians lost the civil war at the cost of a million lives and slavery was abolished.

The civil war did not spell the end of "America's deeply ingrained racism,"[17] says Noll, but it did spell the eventual end of evangelical and Reformed appeals to the Bible in support of slavery. Virtually every evangelical and Reformed theologian today argues that the Bible does not support slavery, and it is sinful. In 1995, on its 150th anniversary, the Southern Baptist Convention passed a motion reflecting this conclusion. It apologized for its biblical defense of slavery.

16. Noll, *Civil War*, 41–42.
17. Noll, *Civil War*, 160.

WHAT DO WE LEARN FROM THIS TRAGIC STORY?

1. Evangelical and Reformed Christians with the highest view of the Bible can come to the wrong conclusions. They can appeal to the Bible to prove something that is contrary to the mind of God.

2. There's a great danger in basing one's theology on a series of texts and selected biblical stories. A more theological reading of Scripture is demanded in *doing theology*. A doctrine or theological position should be based on what is revealed in the whole scope of Scripture and on truths that are foundational to the biblical witness.

3. Culture, collective opinion, and self-interest corrupt the human mind. The Southern pro-slavery theologians lived in a society that benefitted from slavery, and as white men they were privileged and exercised rule. Human beings find it hard to think independently of their cultural context and often read their cultural presuppositions into the Bible, resisting at all cost the giving up of power. They think of reasons why they should rule and be privileged.

4. When Christians are trying to validate their privileges and power they often forget how, on other matters, they understand/interpret the Bible. All the pro-slavery theologians accepted that the Bible is an historical document, and as such reflects the world in which it was written; but when they came to comment about slavery, this insight was ignored.

5. In arguments to preserve privilege and power, almost invariably those arguing for the *status quo* to be maintained, never admit this is the issue. For the pro-slavery theologians it was the authority of the Bible, or the proper ordering of society, or state rights, or the right to own property—the pro-slavery theologians argued a slave was purchased property.

6. It is never wise to ignore your fellow evangelical and Reformed critics. The pro-slavery theologians were so convinced that slavery was endorsed by the Bible that they categorically refused to even consider what their critics were saying. They dismissed them as liberals.

HOW SHOULD WE UNDERSTAND THE TEXTS THAT SEEM TO ALLOW SLAVERY?

To rightly understand what the Bible says on slavery we need to know that in the ancient world there were only two options available to the victors in war: kill their captives or enslave them. The latter was thought to be the better option. Prisoner-of-war camps were unknown. When destitute, a man had only two options. He could starve along with his family, or sell himself into slavery. There were no social welfare benefits available. In both cases slavery was better than death. In this setting, slavery was a relative good. In the ancient world, slavery was not related to race or color, as it was in the Americas. Some slave owners were black, some white, and the same was true of slaves. The pro-slavery theologians ignored this fact. They would not concede that their theology in support of slavery was in fact a theology of white supremacy. It was racist.

The Bible is set in this world. Contemporary scholarship on slavery in the Old Testament agrees slavery was taken for granted in every period in Israel's history, even though Israel was never a slave-based economy.[18] Two kinds were recognized: Jewish "debt slavery," where bondage was supposed to be temporary, and foreign "chattel slavery," where bondage was permanent.[19] What was distinctive about Israel's laws governing slavery was the concern that slaves should be treated well and be included in the religious life of Israel, particularly so if they were Jewish slaves in bondage to Jewish masters. The Israelites were to rest their male and female slaves on the Sabbath (Deut 5:14) and set Jewish slaves free after six years (Lev 25:39–41; Deut 15:12–18).[20] They were to recall that they too had once been slaves in Egypt (Deut 5:12–15). Laws and exhortations do not mirror reality. We should not make the mistake of thinking that because there are humane laws in the Old Testament, that slaves were always treated humanely in Israel, or that the minority who were Jewish slaves were always set free after six years.[21] Once men are given absolute

---

18. See Chirichigo, *Debt-Slavery in Israel.* An excellent article on Old Testament slavery is Kitchen, "Slavery," 1121–24. See also De Vaux, *Ancient Israel,* 80–90.

19. I note, however, that Callender, "Servants of God(s)," 73–77, lists three forms: chattel slavery, debt slavery, and forced labor. On the latter, see Kitchen, "Slavery," section "e" of his essay, 1123.

20. It is to be noted that the legislation that allows a Jewish man to sell his daughter as a slave does not allow her master to sell her later to a foreigner. See Exod 21:7–11.

21. See Jer 34:8–14. See also Patterson, *Slavery and Social Death,* 275.

power over others, laws and exhortations seldom, if ever, eradicate the abuses of power that follow. The conservative evangelical Old Testament scholar K. A. Kitchen says,

> The treatment accorded to slaves [in Israel] depended directly on the personality of their masters. It could be a relationship of trust (Gen 39:1–6) and affection (Deut 15:16), but discipline might be harsh, even fatal (Exod 21:21).[22]

In the Old Testament there are innumerable references to slavery and the taking or making of slaves. In the Pentateuch, legislation on slavery is invariably depicted as given directly by God. To suggest that these laws and instructions only "regulate" an institution of which God disapproves is disingenuous (e.g. Exod 21:10, 17, 20–21, 26–27, 32; Lev 25:2–7; 47–55; Deut 15:12–18; 20:10–14; etc.). In these passages God legislates on slavery without making one negative comment. What is more, in Lev 25:44–46 and Deut 20:10–14, God commands the Israelites to take slaves from the nations round about. Nowhere in the Old Testament is it ever suggested that God viewed the institution of slavery as an evil, or that he desired that all slaves be set free.

In openly acknowledging that the Bible reflects a cultural setting that took slavery for granted, we are affirming that the Bible is a historical document. It describes the world and thought of its authors, as well as being an inspired reflection of the mind of God that transcends this world and its thinking. The human element in Scripture is illustrated in its comments about cosmology and farming. We do not take these as God-inspired inerrant teaching on the movement of the sun, the shape of the earth, or on agriculture, and we should not take comments on slavery in the ancient world this way either. The primary error the nineteenth century pro-slavery theologians made was to conclude that comments on slavery in the Bible, which simply reflected the world of the writers, endorsed slavery. To discover what God is trying to say to us on historically conditioned issues demands careful thought and a keen eye for what is fundamental and primary in Scripture.

When it comes to the apostolic exhortations to masters and slaves, given in parallel to those to husbands and wives, and parents of adult

---

22. Kitchen, "Slavery," 1123. In Prov 29:19–21 the advice seems to be that masters should treat their slaves very firmly, possibly harshly. Because slaves were often treated poorly by Jewish masters, runaway slaves were a problem (see 1 Sam 25:10; 30:15; 1 Kgs 2:39, 40; cf. Sir 33:33).

children (Eph 5:21—6:9; Col 3:18—4:1; 1 Pet 2:18—3:7), they are rightly read as good practical advice to those living in a cultural world that assumed male leadership, slavery, and that (adult) "children" would respect, obey, and care for their parents as long as they lived. These exhortations cannot be applied woodenly, if at all, in a very different cultural context.

ARE THE COMMENTS IN THE BIBLE ON WOMEN AND SLAVES TO BE COMPARED OR CONTRASTED?

The parallel apostolic exhortations to wives and slaves to be subordinate or obedient, just mention above, complementarians insist should be contrasted, not compared. The two issues, Knight says, are like "apples and oranges."[23] The subordination of women is grounded in creation, the institution of slavery is not. The Köstenbergers uncritically adopt this argument.[24]

The *only evidence* complementarians offer for this principled distinction between the parallel exhortations to wives and slaves is, to repeat myself, that the former are predicated on the created ordering of the sexes, the ones to slaves are not. There are seven passages in the New Testament where either women alone or both women and slaves are exhorted by an apostle to be subordinate or obedient (1 Cor 14:33–34; Eph 5:21—6:9; Col 3:18—4:1; 1 Pet 2:18—3:7; 1 Tim 2:11–14; 6:1–3; Titus 2:3–10). Complementarians assert that all the exhortations to women are grounded in creation. We now examine this claim.

In three of these six passages the reason given for the exhortation to women to be subordinate is one of expediency or appropriateness: "as is fitting in the Lord" (Col 3:18); "that the word of God may not be discredited" (Titus 2:5); so that unbelieving husbands may be won for Christ (1 Pet 3:1). In each of these cases, the apostle is simply giving practical advice to women living in a first-century culture. *None of these three exhortations are grounded in creation.*

In Eph 5:21–33 Paul exhorts wives to be subordinate to their husband as their head/*kephalē* (v. 23). If *kephalē* here carries the sense of "boss" it reflects the prevailing *fallen order.* Genesis 3:16 makes the rule of the man over the woman a consequence of sin. In drawing his discussion

---

23. Knight, "Husbands and Wives," 177.
24. Köstenberger and Köstenberger, *God's Design*, 92n13.

about Christian marriage to a conclusion, Paul comes to the "mystery" of the oneness of the husband and wife and quotes Gen 2:24: "For this reason a man will leave his father and mother and be joined to his wife and the two will become one flesh." He takes the Genesis text to speak of marital oneness *not* the subordination of the wife. *In Eph 5:21–33 there is no appeal to the creation order as the basis for women's subordination.* In this discussion of Christian marriage, Paul subverts the patriarchy of his day by turning "headship" on its head and defining it in terms of sacrificial loving service.

In 1 Cor 14:34 the reason given as to why women should be "silent" in church, asking their questions at home, is because "the law says." This is a very perplexing comment because there is no Old Testament passage that commands women to be silent. Almost every commentator lists possibilities, but to assert Paul has in mind the creation order is a guess with little merit and is special pleading. What is more, as I have already noted, it now seems very unlikely that Paul wrote these words.[25] They are a later scribal addition.

In 1 Cor 11:3–16, Paul appeals more than once to the creation stories to bolster his argument that when women lead in prayer and prophecy in church, they should do so with heads covered, and men with heads uncovered. He appeals to the creation stories, not as the ground and reason for the subordination of women, but for the ground and reason why women should cover their heads when leading in prayer and prophecy in church. No one lists this passage among the household rules and there is no mention of the husband-wife relationship. Paul speaks of "every man" and "every woman" in verses 3–5.[26] There is, however, a bigger problem that this passage raises for complementarians. As far as I can see no "complementarian" argues that Paul's teaching on head coverings, despite his appeals to creation, is universally binding. All agree that Paul's ruling on head coverings, even though he appeals to the creation narratives for support, is not binding in our cultural setting.

---

25. See Payne, *Man and Woman*, 217–70, and more recently with added evidence, Payne, "Vaticanus Distigme-Obelos Symbols," 604–25.

26. Most of the discussions of this passage by "complementarians" argue that Paul has in mind only husbands and wives. This is a modern interpretation that makes the case for the permanent subordination of women more consistent and palatable, but it is exegetically untenable. In reply, see Knight, *New Testament Teaching*, 35n13. Here he gives seven reasons why Paul must be understood to be speaking of men and women in general—not specifically of husbands and wives.

This leaves only 1 Tim 2:13–14 as a possible appeal to the created order as the ground for women's subordination. In this case, Paul refers to what took place in the garden of Eden to back up his prohibition on women teaching and usurping authority or being domineering. The prohibition is supported first by saying man was created chronologically "first" and because "Adam was not deceived, but the woman was deceived." In chapter 4 we outlined the most likely interpretation of this exceptional prohibition on women teaching and of the two reasons given for it. I argued that in verses 13 and 14 Paul is not quoting from the text of Genesis or giving his interpretation of what is said there, but rather making an analogy, pointing to a parallel between the Genesis story and what has happened in Ephesus in the first century. Adam was created first, implying that these domineering women should not put themselves first, because, like Eve, they have been deceived. This passage alludes to *disorder* in the first century Ephesian church, not to a supposed ideal *creation-given, hierarchical social order* in the past.

What this means is that none of the seven exhortations to women in general or wives in particular make any appeal to a supposed creation-given, pre-fall subordination of women. We should not expect this because as we have seen in chapter 3 of this book, Gen 1–3 does not teach the pre-fall subordination of the woman; the rule of the man over the woman is entirely seen as a consequence of the fall. Jesus is of the same opinion.

One significant difference between what the Bible says on slavery and the subordination of women is nevertheless to be recognized. The Bible says far more on slavery than it does on the subordination of women. For this reason, the pro-slavery theologians could find more texts in support of their position than complementarian theologians can who want to subordinate women. The reasons given by the apostles to slaves to accept their lot in life are more developed and weightier than those to women. The exhortations to slaves to be subordinate and obedient are consistently grounded in an appeal to the example of Christ (Eph 6:5; Col 3:22; 1 Pet 2:18–25). The apostles could make no higher appeal.

Notwithstanding what has just been said, the truth is biblical comments about slavery and the subordination of women are basically the same in nature and force. They simply reflect the world of the biblical writers where these two things were taken for granted. They are not *prescriptive* for all time and all places. They are *descriptive* of life in the first century. When it comes to the apostolic directives to wives and slaves to be subordinate or obedient, what we have are *exhortations*—words addressed to men and women set free by Christ and filled with the Holy Spirit, asking them to follow the example and teaching of their master and submit themselves to those set over them in the historical context in which they find themselves. In a different cultural setting like ours today, the exhortations to slaves should not be read as endorsing slavery or those to wives as endorsing the unilateral and permanent subordination of women.

THE QUESTIONS THIS STORY RAISES

What we have just outlined on slavery raises acutely three questions for those supporting the permanent subordination of women today on "biblical" grounds.

1. If now virtually all Christians agree that the comments on slavery in the Bible should *not* be interpreted to endorse slavery, should we now agree that the comments on the subordination of women in the Scriptures should *not* be interpreted to justify and endorse the subordination of women?

2. If possibly the worst error the nineteenth century pro-slavery evangelical theologians made was to completely ignore the practical outworking of their "biblical case" for slavery, should not the practical outworking of teaching the subordination of women, not only in the Western world but also in the developing world, be considered as very important evidence in evaluating any appeal to the Bible in support of the subordination of women?

3. If now we all agree that the evangelicals with the highest view of Scripture who devised and supported the "biblical" case for slavery 150 years ago got it wrong because self-interest blinded them, should we not suspect that present-day appeals to the Bible to justify the permanent subordination of women also reflect self-interest?

CONCLUSION

The great cause to abolish slavery suddenly erupted in the late eighteenth century and evangelicals more than anyone else pursued this noble crusade. Sadly, however, many evangelicals of Reformed persuasion were the most strident opponents of emancipation. It took more than a hundred years for all evangelicals to come to a common mind on this matter. Thankfully today we are agreed that the Bible reflects a cultural setting where slavery was taken for granted, but never endorses such an evil. The universal Christian opinion is that slavery demeans and devalues human beings and as such cannot be pleasing to God.

At this point we should now see why this study is one of the most important in this book. The unhappy story about the sharp divide among evangelicals over slavery explains more than anything else the present-day sharp divide among evangelicals over the subordination of women. From the slavery debate we learn that privileged Christian men can appeal to the Bible to support what is clearly unjust, unfair, and demeaning. They can loudly claim to hold to the authority of Scripture and quote many texts, yet can be wrong on what they conclude the Bible is teaching. Self-interest and power can blind Christians, even evangelical Christians. We cannot avoid the question this observation puts to us. Are we to see in the present-day division among evangelicals over the subordination of women an almost one-for-one reenactment of history?

QUESTIONS FOR DISCUSSION

1. What would you say to a Christian who said the Gospel only bestows *spiritual equality*; it has no social consequences?

2. Why do some Christian women today support the idea that they are subordinated by God to men?

3. How is it that with the emancipation of slaves and women, Christians with Bible in hand have been so divided? What is the way forward in such disputes over what the Bible teaches?

4. Today, there are more true slaves in the world than at any other time (probably more than 20 million). Many are women forced into prostitution in this way. What should we think about this and what should we do as Christians?

5. What have you learned from this study?

ADDENDUM: THE "BIBLICAL" ENDORSEMENT OF APARTHEID

Just as evangelical and Reformed theologians in the nineteenth century appealed to the Bible in support of slavery, evangelical and Reformed theologians in South Africa in the twentieth century appealed to the Bible in support of apartheid. Like the pro-slavery theologians, they too devised an impressive "biblical theology" in support of their position. This was developed by learned and evangelistically minded Reformed theologians. These men, like the pro-slave theologians, were convinced that the Bible endorsed the separation of the races. Any suggestion that apartheid was unjust and self-serving and excluded by anything said in Scripture was angrily rejected.

In the twentieth century South Africa was a church-going nation. Dr. H. Verwoerd, a theologian who became prime minister in 1958, said his goal was "to establish Christian civilization in South Africa."[27] The largest and by far the most influential denomination was the white Dutch Reformed Church.[28] This church had a number of large and well-supported theological seminaries with very high standards. All their professors had doctorates, mainly from Dutch universities. What is more, this church was evangelistically committed. Their missionaries worked tirelessly to see black South Africans, Indians, and "coloreds" converted and worshipping in their own churches

In the face of external attacks on apartheid, Dutch Reformed theologians gave their able minds to developing a biblical case for separate development (apartheid). Numerous books were written by Reformed theologians who argued that the Bible undeniably endorsed apartheid. They insisted that apartheid was pleasing to God because it reflected the mind of God revealed in Scripture. I outline the "biblical" case they developed in support of apartheid.[29]

1. The world is predicated on a number of unchanging creation orders (i.e., God-given institutions, structures, relationship), namely, the family, the state, work, and race. Racial differentiation was based in the creation order.

27. Quote taken from Loubser, *Apartheid Bible*, 86.

28. I speak of the white Dutch Reformed Church of South Africa (NGK). They had also established churches for black Africans, Indians, and "coloreds."

29. See in more detail, Loubser, *Apartheid Bible*, 92–97.

2. The Bible teaches that God has created different races. The story of Babel tells us that the separation of people into different races with different languages is God's will. In Acts 2:5–11; Rev 5:9; 7:9; 14:6; and other passages, the Bible states that God recognizes people are divided and identified by race. For the apartheid theologians, difference between races trumped any similarities.

3. Possibly the most important text for the apartheid theologians was Acts 17:26: "From our one ancestor God made all nations (Greek *ethnoi*) to inhabit the whole earth, and he allotted the time of their existence and the boundaries of the places where they would live." This text was taken to say that God had divided all the people of the world into different nations or races and allocated a region for each. This they saw as unambiguous endorsement of the policy of separating the different races of South Africa and allotting an area to each.

4. In Rom 13:1–7, Paul teaches that the governing authorities have been "instituted by God" and thus these Reformed theologians concluded an elected government has the right to create laws that citizens must obey.

5. People are different and thus treating them differently is the right approach. What Paul says on oneness in Christ in Gal 3:28 and Col 3:11 does not deny God-given differences and identity in the church or the world. To read these texts as a mandate for treating everyone alike is invalid. In the report to the 1974 Dutch Reformed annual synod, entitled, "Human Relations and the South African Scene in the Light of Scripture," we read, "The church should avoid the modern tendency to erase all distinctions among peoples."[30]

6. Thus, it must be concluded there can be no rational, moral, or biblical objection to the idea of the different races each having their own geographical area and being encouraged to develop separately at their own pace.

The Dutch Reformed theologians, like the pro-slavery theologians, were convinced that what they believed was the clear teaching of Scripture. One of their most respected theologians, F. J. Potgeiter, put this point eloquently:

---

30. Loubser, *Apartheid Bible*, 95.

> It is quite clear that no one can ever be a proponent of integra-
> tion on the basis of the Scriptures. It would be in a direct contra-
> diction of the revealed will of God to plead for a commonality
> between whites, coloured, and Blacks.[31]

Similarly, the Dutch Reformed New Testament scholar Evert P. Groenewald concluded in his book in support of apartheid that "the principle of apartheid between races and peoples, also separate missions and churches, is well supported by Scripture."[32]

Over the years, a number of commissions were set up by the white Reformed church, with theologians from several disciplines, and they all came to the same conclusion, that the Bible supports the doctrine of apartheid.

What they all established in fact was that the Bible accepts that people of different races may live in different areas, not that white people should rule over other races, which was in fact the essence of apartheid theology. These weighty theological documents, we should also note, did not discuss the practical outcome of the apartheid system. In this system, white people were advantaged and colored people were disadvantaged in many profound and damaging ways.

In July 2018, Lynley and I traveled to South Africa, stopping first in Johannesburg to speak to the Christians for Biblical Equality chapter. Afterward we visited Capetown, where we went to the Apartheid Museum. It was a very moving and informative experience. What I found most confronting were the historic film clips where visitors can hear and see the most significant leaders of the National Party, all Reformed Christians, defending white rule in euphemistic and obfuscating language in an attempt to make it sound completely innocuous and noble. These Christian men emphatically rejected the accusation that apartheid was all about white privilege and white men holding onto power, as it obviously and undeniably was. Apartheid, they consistently argued, affirmed the equality of the races; it simply stood for separate development. Each race should develop at its own pace and in its own way. Rather than bestowing privilege on the white men, these politicians with straight faces said it placed a huge burden of responsibility on them.

31. Quote taken from Corrado, "Godliness of Apartheid Planning."
32. Corrado, "Godliness of Apartheid Planning."

DISSENT WAS COSTLY

Those who opposed apartheid were severely dealt with by their "Christian" rulers. Many opponents were summarily murdered by special units of the police force, something openly admitted in the Truth and Reconciliation Commission chaired by Archbishop Desmond Tutu, following the end of apartheid. More were imprisoned, often indefinitely. Nelson Mandella spent twenty-seven years in prison. Others were "banned." This was an important tool in the repression of dissent. Someone "banned" had their movements restricted and was virtually silenced.

Dissident Christian ministers were not exempt from any of these punishments but ministers of the dominant Reformed church were mainly punished by exclusion and shunning. I give two examples.

In 1960, following the Sharpeville massacre, ten Reformed Afrikaner theologians published a series of essays condemning apartheid and the claim that the Bible endorsed racial separation. They were put on trial in 1961 for heresy, found guilty, removed from office, and denounced by the prime minister, Dr. H. Verwoerd.

In 1963, 280 white church leaders from various churches established the Christian Institute to give a Christian voice to opposition to apartheid and the claim that it was supported by the Bible. The first director was Dr. Beyers Naudé, a Dutch Reformed theologian. For openly opposing apartheid, he and his family were completely ostracized by their fellow Afrikaners. He was forced to resign as a minister and was put out of his home without a salary.[33]

THE FALL OF APARTHEID "BIBLICAL" THEOLOGY

In South Africa today, it would be hard to find a Reformed theologian who supports apartheid, or says that it is justified by Scripture. Reluctantly, step by step, beginning in the 1980s, the Dutch Reformed Church conceded that it had been wrong. Apartheid was an oppressive and unjust regime and it can in no way be supported by appeal to the Bible.

Opposition to apartheid came mainly from those outside the Dutch Reformed Church; but what was the most threatening and most difficult for the Dutch church were the voices of protest and rebuttal that came

---

33. His story is well-worth reading. See, "Reverend Beyers Naudé," South African History Online, at http://www.sahistory.org.za/people/reverend-beyers-naude.

from within. I have just given two examples of this.[34] I now give a third. In 1982 the most serious and damaging offensive from within came when Dr. Allan Boesak, a "colored" minister of the colored Dutch Reformed Church, gave a paper at a meeting of the World Alliance of Reformed Churches, meeting in Ottawa, in which he argued apartheid is a "heresy." The next day those present concluded his argument was right, voted to suspend the membership of the white South African Church and elected Dr. Boesak the president of the Alliance.

This caused a tremendous amount of anger and hostility toward him in South Africa, but it was the beginning of the end. The church appointed yet again another working party to consider the issue, and in 1986 produced a report, called "Church and Society." This document bears witness to an ongoing conflict within the church over apartheid; but at the synod that received this report, the decision was made to open membership to all races in all their churches and to condemn "the scriptural justification of apartheid."[35]

The next major step came in 1989 when at another General Synod it was agreed,

> The Dutch Reformed Church acknowledges that for too long it has adjudged the policy of apartheid . . . too abstractly and theoretically, and therefore too uncritically. While the Dutch Reformed Church, over the years, seriously and persistently sought the will of God and his Word for our society, the church made the error of allowing forced separation and division of peoples in its own circle, to be considered a biblical narrative. The Dutch Reformed Church should have distanced itself much earlier from this view and admits and confesses its neglect. Any system which in practice functions in this way is unacceptable in the Light of Scripture and the Christian conscience and must be rejected as sinful. Any attempt by the church to defend such a system biblically and ethically, must be seen as a serious fallacy, that is to say it is in conflict with the Bible.

The first of these clauses needs highlighting. Just as the pro-slavery theologians ignored the awful degradation, cruelty, and injustice of slavery, so too did the pro-apartheid theologians ignore the awful consequences of the apartheid system. J. A. Loubser, in his important book *The Apartheid Bible*, says,

34. This story is told in detail in Plaatjies and Voslool, *Reformed Churches*.

35. Loubser, *Apartheid Bible*, 1.

> Apartheid theology was conducted almost in complete oblivion
> to the vested material interests involved: the entrenchment of
> white economic privileges was never reflected upon and was
> covered by paternalistic altruism towards other (presumably
> lesser) ethnic groups, diversity was preached but total segrega-
> tion was meant. . . . An analysis of apartheid theology can be
> seen as an uncovering of the accompanying political agenda
> which was sometimes openly stately and more often mystified.[36]

The concrete application of this abstract theology had terrible consequences for non-whites. Apartheid legislation impacted on almost every aspect of daily life. Mixed marriages were prohibited, churches were
segregated, public facilities were segregated, certain areas were reserved
for white people, the level of education available to non-whites was restricted, all the better jobs were reserved for whites, non-whites were
excluded from the national government, and much more. To peacefully
protest against apartheid could get you shot, as the 1960 Sharpeville massacre illustrates.

In South Africa today, there are no Dutch Reformed ministers or
theologians who openly support apartheid, let alone hold that it is sanctioned by Scripture. With one voice they acknowledge their appeal to
Scripture was self-serving and mistaken. The tragedy is that the white
Dutch church has suffered terribly as a consequence of its support of
apartheid by appeal to the Bible. Confidence in the church and membership has plummeted. The church has been shamed and disgraced by its
theologians.

WHAT WE LEARN FROM THIS SAD STORY

The lessons we learn from this sad story are much the same as those we
learned from the sad story of how evangelical and Reformed theologians,
by appeal to the Bible, supported slavery.

1. Those holding power are the ones who devise these oppressive "theologies" that privilege them. This reminds us of Lord Acton's dictum,
   "Power tends to corrupt and absolute power corrupts absolutely."

2. Christians can find verses that seem to say what they already believe,
   and yet somehow miss what the Bible taken as a whole is saying.

36. Loubser, *Apartheid Bible*, 132.

3. Refusing to listen to your critics and marginalizing them is never wise. Theology is a communal exercise.

4. No theological position can be correct if it results in injustice and unfair discrimination. A doctrine that has social implications must, if it is to reflect the mind of God, be just, fair, and equitable.

5. Emphasizing the difference between people is theologically mistaken. In arguments for slavery, apartheid, and the subordination of women, difference is to the fore and equality eclipsed. Differences exist between people, especially between men and women who have different bodies and chromosomes; but we are first and foremost all made in the image and likeness of God, all sinners, all offered salvation, and all loved by God—and in Christ we are "one" (Gal 3:28). By placing all emphasis on differences in color, which is only skin deep, the Reformed apartheid theologians eclipsed oneness in Christ.

6. Obfuscating the issue in contention is disingenuous and unhelpful. Granted that in the world, some rule and some obey. But why should blacks (and women) distinctively be the ones to obey? The Bible allows that different races *may* live apart, but why should one race determine where other races live, especially when they choose for themselves what is theirs? We may speak of the "differing roles" of men and women, but why not speak in plain English of men commanding and a woman obeying, when this is what is in mind?

THE PROBLEM WHEN JESUS IS LEFT OUT

In his important book, *Imitating Jesus: An Inclusive Approach to New Testament Ethics*, Richard A. Burridge argues the ultimate test of any attempt to apply the Bible to concrete issues facing human beings must be the example and teaching of Jesus. Theologians too often think otherwise. Apartheid theology, he argues, shows how disastrous the consequences of ignoring this rule can be. A "biblical theology" was devised to the advantage of white people and many texts were found supposedly in support; but the result was a theology that denied what Christ exemplified in his most important ethical rules, "Love your neighbor as yourself" (Matt 19:19), and, "In everything do to others as you would like them do to you" (Matt 7:12).

The parallel should be carefully noted. Complementarian theology likewise generally ignores the teaching and example of Jesus in regard to women, except for highlighting the fact that the twelve apostles were all men.

9

"I, the Lord, Love Justice" (Isaiah 61:8)

WHAT MOST PROFOUNDLY DIVIDED the evangelicals who wanted slavery abolished and those who wanted to preserve slavery were their contrasting understandings of the Gospel, the good news revealed in Jesus Christ. Those who appealed to the Bible in support of slavery quoted numerous texts that they thought legitimated slavery and they largely ignored what slavery actually involved for the thousands of black people they "owned." For them, the Gospel was about salvation in Christ and the hope of heaven; it had no social implications. In contrast, those committed to the emancipation of the slaves and the abolition of the institution of slavery believed the Gospel had profound social implications. Most New Testament scholars today think the abolitionists were right.[1] The Gospel always involves two things: individual salvation and an imperative to work for a better, more just, and more equitable world. Or, to put it another way, the mission Jesus gave his disciples always comprises two things that cannot be separated: preaching salvation in Christ and social concern and action. How do we know this? We learn this from the Gospels where Jesus exemplifies a ministry in word and deed. He preaches the Gospel and heals the sick, identifies with the poor and the oppressed, and gives his life in costly service. This holistic understanding of the Gospel is the basis for what is called today *Christian social justice*.

---

1. I commend two books written by well-known evangelicals making just this point. De Young and Gilbert, *What Is the Mission*; and Keller, *Generous Justice*.

CHRISTIAN SOCIAL JUSTICE

In speaking of *Christian social justice* we need to define our terms.

- First, we are speaking of something distinctively *Christian* because it is informed by biblical teaching and as such has distinctively Christian elements.

- *Social* because it focuses on how human beings interact with one another.

- *Justice* because it is concerned with upholding and pursuing what is right and just and fair. It is opposed to injustice. Justice is never something abstract, never simply theory or theology. Justice is concrete, this-worldly, practical. Its goal is to have people relate to one another equitably and to do to others what they would like done to them.

Basic to Christian social justice teaching is the belief that the God revealed in the Bible is just and he wants justice done on earth. So we pray, "Your will be done on earth as in heaven." On this premise anything unjust, unfairly discriminatory, or inequitable is not pleasing to God. One distinctive element in Christian social justice teaching is the belief that God is biased toward the oppressed and the downtrodden, because the Bible says this. Thus, in the Old Testament Law Israel is frequently told to care for the poor, the widows, the orphans, and the sojourners— who today we would call "refugees" (Exod 22:21–27; Deut 10:17–19; 24:17–18; 24:21–22; Lev 19:9–10). In the prophetic writings justice for the disempowered and the oppressed is a major theme (Isa 1:17; 61:1, 8; Amos 5:11–15, 23–24; 8:4, 13; Mic 6:8). Jesus, standing in this prophetic tradition, says that he has come "to bring good news to the poor . . . to proclaim release for the captives" (Luke 4:18) and he commands his disciples to love their "neighbor as themselves" (Matt 22:39). Mary in her song of praise on hearing that she will bear the promised Messiah sees him bringing down the powerful and lifting up the lowly (Luke 1:52). In his ministry Jesus shows special concern for the marginalized and the disempowered, widows, lepers, and women.

ONE-SIDED EVANGELICALISM

Sadly, this holistic understanding of the Gospel assumed by the nineteenth century evangelical emancipationists was lost in the first part of the twentieth century. It was eclipsed as evangelical leaders became preoccupied with battling the growing impact of liberal views of the Bible, opposing evolution and debating among themselves when and what would happen on Christ's return (the millennial controversy). For them, the Gospel was entirely about the forgiveness of the sins of individuals and the promise of a home in heaven in the future; it was something "spiritual," without social implications for this present world.

They argued that if Christians concentrated on evangelism the world would become a more just and loving place. No evangelical disputes the importance of evangelism but evangelism alone does not make more just societies. Christians individually and collectively can be very uncaring and act unjustly, if they are allowed or even encouraged to believe that the Gospel is solely about the forgiveness of my sins and the promise of a place in heaven. What we must recognize is that sin corrupts both individuals and communities. The United States and South Africa well illustrate this point. There are, percentage-wise, more who claim to be "born again" Christians in America than in any other nation but social injustice, corporate vice, political corruption, racism, and sexism are endemic. What is more, in the nineteenth century it was in the profoundly evangelical Southern states that the most articulate and fiercest opponents of the abolition of slavery and later racial integration were found. The Southern Baptists broke away from the Northern Baptists in 1845 to form a new denomination on the issue of slavery, which the Southern Baptists supported unanimously. In South Africa, in the twentieth century, the praying, Bible believing members of the Reformed Church fully supported the apartheid system with all its injustices and unfairness. Why did this happen, you ask? It seems that once the Gospel is reduced solely to a message about "my" personal salvation and right doctrine, Christians become blind to injustice and oppression.

Thankfully, the fact that the Gospel is not just "pie in the sky when you die" but also a message of hope for the oppressed, the marginalized, and the poor, surfaced again in the late 1960s, but it only gained the attention of a fraction of evangelicals. In the twenty-first century it is gaining more support not only among evangelicals but also among Pentecostals and charismatics. In growing numbers, theologically conservative Christians are coming to recognize that the Gospel has two sides to it, the forgiveness of sins for the individual and social concern and action.[2] The Gospel announces that God wants to transform individuals and society.

2. See the books referenced above by De Young and Gilbert, *What Is the Mission*, and Keller, *Generous Justice*.

WOMEN'S SUBORDINATION AND THE GOSPEL

Unfortunately when it comes to women, too many evangelicals simply cannot see that subordinating women to men is unjust and a denial of the teaching and example of Jesus or that it can have harmful consequences for them. Complementarian evangelicals, Pentecostals, and charismatics angrily reply that "male headship" cannot be contrary to the Gospel or unjust nor have sinful consequences (if practiced properly) because it is taught in the Bible.

In the late nineteenth century, the best Reformed theologians and most clergy in the "Old South" said exactly the same about slavery and they had a most impressive list of texts that seemed to support their "theology of slavery," yet it had dire consequences for the slaves. In the twentieth century, Reformed theologians in South Africa who quoted the Bible in support of apartheid similarly rejected the charge that apartheid was unjust and contrary to the Gospel and its practical consequences. It could not be, they insisted, because it is sanctioned by Scripture. A visit to the Apartheid Museum in Cape Town soon dispels such claims. The apartheid system was unjust, cruel, and degrading to non-whites. Virtually all Christians are now agreed that slavery and apartheid are expressions of human sin, not pleasing to God, and those who quoted the Bible in support of these two forms of oppression were appealing to Scripture to maintain their own privileges and power. Only slowly is it dawning on *some* evangelicals and Reformed Christians that despite the fact that they can quote texts to convince themselves that the Bible teaches the subordination of women, this teaching can have awful consequence for women.

WOMEN'S SUBORDINATION IN PRACTICE

Women's subordination does not necessarily result in their exploitation, let alone abuse. In cultures where women cannot support themselves and are thus dependent on their father, brother, or husband, they can be highly respected and play a significant part in the life of their communities. In such cultural contexts, the subordination of women may be a relative good and the only option available to women. The problem is that when one section of a community has unquestioned power over another, abuse of this power has few constraints. Another problem is that in the last forty or so years the world has radically changed. In the Western world women have gained an equality hitherto never imagined and this revolution is now impacting in ever increasing ways on the Third World. In this new context what may have been a relative good has become problematic at best and unjust at worst as better options are seen and become possible.

POWER CORRUPTS

In the modern world there is absolutely nothing that can be said in support of "male headship," understood in terms of men leading, women obeying. When men are privileged and women disadvantaged, women fare badly. In societies where men have precedence and women are subordinated to them we find:

- a preference for boys that leads to tens of millions of aborted female fetuses
- inequality in education for women
- inequality in health for women
- inequality in ownership of property and work for women
- inequality in income for women
- widespread and accepted violence against women
- the trafficking of women, primarily for prostitution[3]

The statistics on all these matters are not getting better, but worse. According to 2016 United Nations, Center for Disease Control report:[4]

> Evidence of physical, sexual and psychological harm—ranging from sexual harassment and assault to trafficking and rape as a weapon of war—is on the rise. Globally, 1 out of every 3 women have experienced physical and/or sexual violence and 200 million girls are missing.[5]

I, for one, cannot believe God is pleased to see female fetuses in the millions aborted, girls excluded from education, women underpaid for their work and going hungry, suffering for lack of medical care, physically abused by their husbands, and in danger of being sold into prostitution. If this is the result of believing that women are a subordinate class, then we should examine our beliefs. To reply "but all your examples are from

3. Sider, "Gender and Justice Today."
4. Basile et al., "Stop SV."
5. "#silenceisnotspiritual: Breaking the Silence."

the third world" is not an answer. It does not matter where these things happen; we need to agree that devaluing women and marginalizing them is not just and has dire consequences for them.

The devaluing and disempowerment of women today is not just a problem for women but a problem for the whole world. It speaks of the loss of the full contribution of half of the world's population. It results in us all being poorer socially and economically. On the economic side, this is an objective fact. Recently, the economies that have grown the most are those Asian countries that have welcomed the full participation of women.[6]

THE ABUSE OF WOMEN IN THE WESTERN WORLD

Teaching that God has subordinated women to men has awful consequences for women in the third world, as we have just seen, but it also has awful outcomes in our modern egalitarian Western culture. It makes many women feel demeaned in their home and church, it results in able, Spirit-gifted women being excluded from significant leadership in their church, it limits our evangelistic opportunities to secular women who think gender equality is a noble ideal, and worst of all it encourages needy, controlling Christian men to be abusive of or violent to their wives.

The extent of abuse must be noted. It is mind blowing. The statistics are these: both in Australia and in the United States, one in four women will experience violent abuse from an intimate partner in their lifetime.[7] For indigenous women in Australia, three in five women will experience abuse. If you are a woman of color in the USA the figures are far higher: 43.7 percent of African American/black women, 37.1 percent of Hispanic/Latina women, and 19.6 percent of Asian and Pacific Islander women have experienced rape, physical violence, and/or stalking by an intimate partner.[8] In Australia, with a population of about 25 million, one woman a week is killed by an intimate partner. In the United States, three women *per day* are killed by an intimate partner.[9]

6. On this see Kristof and WuDunn, *Half the Sky*.

7. Besides numerous web articles on the incidence of abuse and violence in the home see Tracy, "Patriarchy and Domestic Violence." Stephen Tracy is a confessed evangelical complementarian.

8. "#silenceisnotspiritual: Breaking the Silence."

9. Vagianos, "30 Shocking Domestic Violence Statistics."

As hard as I find it to admit, when it comes to the abuse of women in the home by an intimate partner, and this often involves sexual violence, all the evidence indicates that what happens in the world happens in the church, particularly evangelical and Reformed churches. The churches have not wanted to face this issue, so few studies have been done by churches, but the evidence we have indicates the percentages on the abuse of women in the churches is much the same as in society at large. In 1989 the Christian Reformed Church in North America conducted a random study of one thousand members; 28 percent said they had experienced at least one form of abuse.[10] In Great Britain, the United Methodist Church did research on domestic violence within their churches and reports were produced in 2006 and 2016 that said percentages among their members closely matched those in the wider community.[11] In one American study of one thousand abused women, 67 percent indicated that they attended church regularly.[12]

Complementarians until very recently have strenuously argued that any abuse in their homes is exceptional and that complementarian teaching tends to minimize abuse.[13] In 2017 this argument collapsed in the wake of the Harvey Weinstein revelations. First on the hashtag #metoo, and then on the hashtag #churchtoo,[14] large numbers of women came forward to speak of their abuse, in many cases by evangelical men. Following this in December 2017, 140 leading evangelical women from diverse political and church backgrounds began an online petition, #silenceisnotspiritual.[15] Here those who felt the issue of abuse of women in evangelical churches needed to be addressed and things needed to change could sign. When I signed the petition early in January 2018, six thousand Christian leaders had signed.

Later in 2018, the widespread condoning of marital abuse by complementarian leaders came to American national attention in the Paige Patterson scandal. He was one of the most powerful and influential leaders of the Southern Baptist denomination, and a leading complementarian, as I mentioned earlier in this book. Then a transcript of a recording

10. Annis and Rice, "Survey of Abuse."

11. "Domestic Abuse," Methodist Church.

12. Bowker, "Religious Victims."

13. I have been told this innumerable times. For this view in writing see Moore, "After Patriarchy," 576.

14. Gleeson, "#ChurchToo."

15. Shellnut, "Women Speak Up."

of an address he gave in 2000 was published. In this he tells a battered wife with two black eyes to stay with her husband "even if he gets a little more violent," pray for him, and at home "be as submissive in every way you can and elevate him." It was his view that abuse of one's wife was not a valid reason for divorce. When hundreds of Baptist women cried out in dismay he at first refused to modify his words or recant them but later, under huge pressure, he made some ameliorating comments. This women's protest became an open letter to the trustees of the Southwest Baptist Theological Seminary, of which Patterson was the president. Their initial response was to ask him to resign but when it came out that he had behaved improperly to women in other ways and lied to the trustees he was dismissed on May 30, 2018.[16]

Patterson's views were not idiosyncratic. Such advice to women was characteristic complementarian teaching until this present outcry by women.

John Piper, another hugely influential complementarian theologian, has until very recently taught much the same things.[17]

AUSTRALIA

I studied for ordination at Moore Theological College in Sydney and I have served in the Sydney Anglican diocese, one of the largest and wealthiest dioceses in the world. It has many large parishes and is growing through evangelism and church planting. Moore College and the diocese are dogmatically complementarian. Michael Jensen, writing in 2012 as an insider, says, "If there is a single issue with which Sydney Anglicans have found themselves identified, it is surely the matter of the ordination of women."[18] He then says that this can never be accepted in the Sydney diocese because the Bible clearly teaches the headship of men.[19] This is a "line in the sand," he says, that Sydney Anglican theologians can never cross.

Sydney Anglican theologians and bishops have long resisted the idea that teaching on male "headship," a constant theme in their churches, could in any way encourage men to be abusive of or violent to their

16. I tell this story more fully and document it in chapter 2 of this book.

17. Piper, "Does a Woman Submit to Abuse?"; Moon, "Some Humans."

18. Jensen, *Sydney Anglicanism*, 126.

19. Jensen, *Sydney Anglicanism*, 127.

wives. They insist that it is a benevolent doctrine, bringing only blessing to Christian families.[20] In 2017 this argument fell apart; first one clergy wife of a Moore trained clergyman bravely came forward to say he had been repeatedly violent to her and as a result she had left the marriage in fear of her life. Then other clergy wives stepped forward and said the same and soon after women married to lay leaders stood up to say the same.[21] In the annual Synod of 2017, Archbishop Glen Davies, a dogmatic complementarian, had no other option; he had to make an apology to the hundreds of women who had been abused in the diocese, and ignored or criticized by the clergy they looked to for support. The Synod then passed a resolution making an apology to all the women involved, and for the way they had been treated.[22] This has not made the matter go away. As I write, the papers and TV are still airing stories on this matter.

I find writing about this issue very painful. I wish it were all not true. I am compelled to write because I need to press upon my readers the fact that male headship teaching can and often does have adverse consequences for women. Headship teaching does not make Christian men abusive of their wives, let alone violent; the problem is that it encourages and legitimizes abuse and violence in needy, controlling men who are found in all churches and among the clergy. Cynthia Ezel explains the situation well. She says headship teaching,

> Is not responsible for an individual husband's violent action toward his wife. It does, however, create an environment ripe for abuse. A weakened immune system does not create the virus that leads to a deadly infection, but it provides the environment in which the virus can thrive and do its killing. Patriarchal beliefs weaken the marital system so that the deadly virus of violence can gain a stronghold.[23]

Because of these terrible outcomes of male headship teaching, evangelical and Reformed Christians must question if in fact the Bible makes the subordination of women the God-given ideal established in creation before the fall. Rather than just quoting texts in support of their view they need to look again at what the Bible actually teaches on the man-woman

20. On this see Young, "Abuse Inside Christian Marriages."

21. See Young, "Abuse Inside Christian Marriages."

22. Gleeson, "Anglican Diocese of Sydney"; Gleeson, "Sydney Anglican Church Confesses"; "Australian Churches Risk."

23. Ezell, "Power, Patriarchy."

relationship and look for the first time at the consequences of their doctrine that says men should lead in the home, the church, and wherever
possible in society.

Wife abuse and violence have long been an issue in the church, especially in evangelical and Reformed churches, even if there has been
a reluctance to admit this. In my forty years as a pastor I encountered
numerous cases among couples who attended church regularly. When a
woman came to me to tell me of her problems I would presume she was
telling me the truth. I would always meet with the husband to hear his
side of the story but invariably the man said something like, "I only get
angry when she doesn't do as I ask, and at worst I only give her a push. I
am the head of the home, you know, and she should obey me. This is what
the Bible teaches." I have *never* advised a wife who told me her husband
was abusing her, emotionally, financially, sexually, or violently, to endure
this treatment because God wanted her to learn to be submissive. I always
explored with them the options available to them, including going to the
police. Most of them continued in their dysfunctional marriage, believing as Christian women that their love and prayers would change their
husband. I admired them greatly for their perseverance and because they
freely chose to suffer as Christians. Sadly, most of them discovered, as the
scientific literature tells us, controlling and abusive men seldom change.[24]

THE CHANGE THAT IS NEEDED

What we learned from our study of the Reformed theologians who wrote
prolifically in support of slavery and apartheid is that to think that biblical texts and our interpretation of them can settle a dispute over what
is pleasing to God in regard to social ordering, without taking note of
its consequences, is an unforgivable mistake. It allows people with Bible
in hand to justify the unjustifiable. God always wants us to consider the
consequences of our teaching. Headship teaching has bad consequences
for women. It must be rejected as a misreading of what the Bible teaches.

We evangelical and Reformed Christians should not only work
and strive to see justice done in the church, in this instance in regard to
women, we should also work and strive to see justice done in the world,
in regard to women who make up fifty percent of the human race. Sadly,

---

24. My wife Lynley, who is a marriage counsellor, thinks the best book on marital
abuse is Bancroft, *Why Does He Do That?*

this has not been the case, especially among evangelical and Reformed complementarians. They have insisted, as the Köstenbergers do, that patriarchy is always "benevolent and beneficial," a "blessing" for women and children.[25] This is simply not true. Patriarchy can have awful consequences for women and children, as we have shown. What is obvious is that we evangelical and Reformed Christians cannot make a clear and strong stand against all forms of violence and mistreatment of women until we get our theology of the sexes sorted out. What is demanded is that we agree that the Bible makes the substantial equality of the sexes the creation ideal and agree that to treat women any differently than how we men would like to be treated is an offence to God.

There is one notable exception to the silence on the abuse of women by complementarians who must be mentioned and commended: Steven Tracy, professor of theology and ethics at Phoenix Seminary, who identifies himself as a complementarian. He has bravely called on his complementarian friends to stand up and denounce the abuse of women and warned them of the huge dangers of their headship teaching.[26]

THE KÖSTENBERGERS

It is not altogether clear what the Köstenbergers believe about women and justice and the abuse of wives. Speaking on feminism in one exceptionally positive paragraph on this movement they say it

> has had many positive results since its inception almost two centuries ago. Women' status and experience in the Western world, in particular, have been altered for better in many ways, ending discrimination in various spheres of life. . . . In this way *justice* has been served, and women have been lifted from second class status to genuine equality with men in many ways.[27]

In these words they say women should be *justly* treated and be accorded "genuine equality with men." However, when they come to discuss the practicalities of marriage they teach that a wife must always be submissive and obedient "even when it involves suffering." They are emphatic, wives "ought to submit to their husbands," even unbelieving

25. Köstenberger and Köstenberger, *God's Design*, 61–62, 345.

26. See his articles, and he has written others, Tracy, "Patriarchy and Domestic Violence"; and "What Does 'Submit in Everything' Really Mean?"

27. Köstenberger and Köstenberger, *God's Design*, 294.

husbands.[28] They mention marital abuse just once in a footnote where they say, "there are obviously limits" to "the physical" abuse a wife must endure.[29] What these "limits" are we are not told, and the implication is that emotional, financial, and verbal abuse do not count.

What they say reflects what is very common in complementarian teaching. Women should obey their husband and if they evoke his anger or abuse because they do not do as he tells them they need to change their ways, or if it is not entirely their fault, endure their suffering as Peter advises women in such situations (1 Pet 3:1–6, 16–18).

I suspect the Köstenbergers would be in complete agreement with Mary Kassian, the distinguished professor of women's studies at the Southern Baptist Theological Seminary, Kentucky, who says, writing on male headship in the home:

> Practically, there may be situations in which submission to authority is limited. However, these situations are few and far between. Our focus [as women] should be on humility and obedience in *all* circumstances. Submission may indeed have its limits but these limits are the exception rather than the rule. Obedience to God generally means obedience to those in authority over us.[30]

On reading these words I could imagine the pro-slavery and pro-apartheid theologians saying exactly the same thing.

When it comes to abuse and violence in the home, I and other evangelical egalitarians sharply part company with the Köstenbergers and most complementarians. We egalitarians believe to abuse one's wife or be violent toward her *in any way* is sinful. Pushing, shoving, slapping, raising one's voice, the "silent treatment," saying cutting and horrible things to one's wife are all forms of violence. Such behavior directly contradicts Paul's teaching that a man should "love his wife like Christ loved the church and gave himself up for her" (Eph 5:25). To argue that women should submit to their husbands in all but the most extreme situations because the apostles exhort wives to be submissive is simply bad theology and bad ethics. The apostolic exhortations to wives and slaves to be subordinate or obedient are to be understood in *exactly the same way*. They are practical advice to women and slaves living in a world where

---

28. Köstenberger and Köstenberger, *God's Design*, 245.

29. Köstenberger and Köstenberger, *God's Design*, 245, n. 7.

30. Kassian, *Women in Creation*, 38. The italics are hers.

the subordination of women and slavery were taken-for-granted realities. They are not endorsing the subordination of women or slavery as God-given social ordering for all times in all places. They cannot be because in creation all men and women are given the same status, dignity, and authority. The rule of the man over the woman reflects the fall just as does slavery. The Christian husband should give himself in costly loving service for his wife, never abuse or hurt her.

AND TO CONCLUDE

In this chapter we began by talking about God and justice in broad terms, coming last to the specific question of women's subordination and justice. To conclude, I want to go back to the big picture. Christian social justice teaching not only demands that men *and* women be treated fairly, justly, and humanely, it also demands that all people be treated justly, fairly, and humanely, young and old, black, white, and yellow, rich and poor. What is demanded is that we treat others as we would like them to treat us. This is not a left wing secular agenda; it is the Bible's agenda. Treating people as we would like to be treated ourselves is what God expects of all of us. Thus, the primary questions we must ask those who teach the subordination of women and its counterpart, male "headship" as the creation-given ideal, pleasing to God, are these: *Is this teaching and its outcomes just and equitable? Can this teaching be reconciled with the equal dignity, status, and authority given to man and woman alike by God in creation before the fall* (Gen 1:27–28)? *What would Jesus, who said not one word on "male headship" and much to the contrary, say about this teaching?*

QUESTIONS FOR DISCUSSION

1. What would you say to someone who insisted that the Gospel is about the forgiveness of sins and the hope of heaven and no more?

2. Two thirds of the world's hungry, two thirds of the world's illiterate, and two thirds of the world's poor are women, why do you think this is so?

3. Books speak of both the *emancipation* of slaves and the *emancipation* of women. In what ways are these two expressions of liberation similar and different?

4. Why do so many church women passively accept teaching by their pastor/minister on their subordination and make no protest? Even women who are leaders in the community often do this.

5. Look up and read in your group Exod 22:21–27; Lev 19:9–10; Isa 1:17; 61:1, 8; Mic 6:8; Luke 1:52; 4:18. What do these texts say about God's care for the oppressed and downtrodden?

6. "Micro financing" in the third world today is seen as one of the most important ways of helping people escape poverty, especially women. In micro financing, small loans are granted to finance a new business or buy something like a sewing machine. Do you think Christians should promote and get involved in such ventures? If so, why?

ADDENDUM: ELAINE STORKEY, *SCARS ACROSS HUMANITY*

I have read nothing quite like Elaine Storkey's book, *Scars Across Humanity*. It tells the story of violence against women in today's world. The book is very well researched and accessible—and spine-chilling. As I sat with the book in hand I felt both pleased that someone had so powerfully told this awful story and depressed by what I was reading.

After an introductory chapter, the following eight chapters deal with specific forms of violence against women in the chronological order that they are most likely to occur in a woman's life: the abortion of female fetuses and infanticide, genital mutilation, early enforced marriage, honor killing, domestic violence, trafficking and prostitution, rape, and the abuse of women in war. Then follow four chapters exploring the various explanations that have been given for this inexcusable abuse of women. First, Storkey gives a good hearing to evolutionary biology as the root cause, but in the end finds it wanting. It fails to acknowledge that human beings are free agents who can decide how they behave. Second, patriarchy, the belief that men should rule over women, as the root cause is considered. She agrees this is a pernicious idea but again concludes that as free moral agents human beings are not bound to perpetuate patriarchy and its abuses. Third, in two chapters she considers the argument that religion is to blame; the first on religion in general and Islam in particular, and the second specifically on Christianity. She concedes that most religions are conservative and teach the subordination of women, although often at the same time they speak of the worth and dignity of women. What is more, she points out in today's world, most religions include voices advocating for more freedoms for women. Islam is no exception; there are indeed Muslim feminists. For them, she admits, this is a hard path to take because the Qur'an and the *Sunnah* (the record of the life, teachings, and deeds of Muhammad) explicitly give men authority over women and allow polygamy. What is more, they can be read to give permission to men to beat their wives, to condone rape in certain circumstances, to permit the marriage of prepubescent girls, and to encourage honor killings.

Storkey says that, as an evangelical Christian, she found the chapter on Christianity the hardest to write. She has to acknowledge that across the ages Christian theologians have taught the superiority of men and the inferiority of women and often spoken in misogynistic ways. Even today, many evangelicals dogmatically assert that the Bible teaches the permanent subordination of women, usually in euphemistic and obfuscating terminology. Nevertheless, Storkey points out, Christianity has never endorsed any of the appalling abuses of women she speaks about in her book, and the voices for change are growing louder. A pressing issue for those many evangelicals who teach the subordination of women, she says, is partner violence. Telling men that the Bible gives them leadership in the home encourages and legitimates controlling and abusive behavior in needy and insecure men. When women find themselves in this situation, they seldom find support when they turn to a male pastor. Holding to the belief that the man is the head of the home, some pastors place women in dangerous circumstances.

What I found staggering in Storkey's book was the extent of the abuse and suffering of women. One in three women in the world experience violence in their lifetime. Possibly two million female fetuses are aborted a year; one hundred and forty million women have been genitally mutilated; over twenty million people are trafficked each year, the vast majority women; one hundred and forty million women alive today have been forced into marriage in adolescence; it is estimated that one in four women in Western countries will experience domestic violence, and the figures are much higher in other parts of the world. About thirty million women were raped in 2012. In the US one in five women will be raped in her lifetime. Honor killing of women is endemic on the Indian sub-continent and in Middle Eastern Islamic countries, but dependable numeric estimates are elusive. An estimated ten thousand honor killings a year take place in Pakistan alone, and the vast majority go unpunished.

These figures are breath-taking and awful. How can women be so appallingly treated, we cry out!

The extent of the violence and injustices perpetuated against women is hard to comprehend, but even harder to comprehend is that women themselves often acquiesce to or are perpetrators of this violence. For example, it is almost always women who mutilate young girls and carry out abortions on female fetuses. Women are often involved in trafficking and running brothels. And most surprisingly, the majority of women in countries that accept honor killings endorse this practice. This complicity of women is an example of how, in all entrenched social hierarchies, invariably sanctioned by religion, the oppressed internalize their own unworthiness and subordinate status.

Elaine Storkey is an English evangelical academic, writer, and broadcaster. She was once the Director of the London Institute for Contemporary Christianity, founded by John Stott. She was the president of Tearfund, the evangelical aid and development agency, for seventeen years.

Conclusion: Where to Now?

IT IS ALL VERY simple and straightforward for me. The world is not flat and women are not the subordinate sex. The modern world has forced on us all the realization that women make excellent leaders in society and the church, and the happiest and most rewarding marriages are profoundly equal. It is also clearly evident to me that appeals to the Bible to oppose what is empirically observed have not convinced most Christians. The complementarian position is a minority opinion. Let me give the evidence for this assertion. The Roman Catholic Church, the largest church in the world, teaches the "essential" and "fundamental" equality of the sexes, attributing the subordination of women entirely to the fall (Gen 3:16). Pope John Paul II says, "The overcoming of this evil inheritance," spoken of in Gen 3:16, is the task of every Christian.[1] In the mainline Protestant churches, including my own Anglican Church, the majority opinion view is that men and women are essentially equal and thus women may be ordained to lead congregations. The Pentecostals, with an estimated 279 million following, do not exclude women from leadership in the church or from preaching. Their charismatic understanding of ministry and leadership allows that the Spirit can raise up men or women to plant churches, to preach and lead congregations. What percentage of evangelicals are egalitarians and complementarians is disputed. One thing that cannot be disputed is that very large numbers of highly respected and able evangelicals are convinced egalitarians: F. F. Bruce, Leon Morris, Kenneth Kanzer, Ben Witherington, Tom Wright, Millard Erickson, Cynthia Long Westfall, Howard Marshall, Roger Nicole, Lynn Cohick, Craig Keener, Gordon Fee, Mimi Haddad—need I continue? You definitely can be a convinced evangelical, with the highest view of the

1. John Paul II, *Mulieris Dignitatem*, 36–41.

Bible and be convinced without a shadow of a doubt that the Bible makes the substantial equality of the two sexes the creation ideal.

CHANGING ONE'S MIND

For me, my conversion from the complementarian position to the egalitarian position was easy and quick. When asked in 1975 by my bishop to give a scholarly paper on what the Bible actually taught on women I changed my mind over a few days. I concluded Gen 1–2 teaches the substantial equality of the sexes, making the rule of the man over the woman entirely a consequence of the fall. Jesus could not have been more positive about the status, dignity, and leadership potential of women. Paul had a charismatic understanding of church leadership; ministry was given by the Spirit and had nothing to do with gender. In 1 Cor 11:5 Paul endorses women leading in church in prayer and prophecy. In Eph 5:21–33 Paul is subverting patriarchy, turning male headship on its head. Only 1 Tim 2:11–14 is difficult and this passage seems to be addressing an exceptional situation, which is implied by the use of the exceptional verb *authentein*. It is a difficult text but to *interpre*t it so that is contradicts all else in Scripture cannot be an option for an evangelical. These conclusions reached over forty years ago, I still hold.

Large numbers of committed evangelicals have had the same "second conversion" experience. I am not alone. In chapter 2, I gave a long list of well-known evangelicals who have also changed their minds; once they were complementarians and then they became egalitarians. Personally I know hundreds of others who have converted, some of these from far off places who have read articles or books by me and then written to me.

I also know, however, many evangelical brothers and sisters who are "hard-wired" complementarians. They cannot even read a book or article by an evangelical egalitarian, let alone discuss what the Bible actually says on the status and ministry of women. For them, there is one answer on this issue, and one answer only, the Bible clearly teaches God has appointed men to lead. Why, we must ask, do many evangelicals find even thinking about the issue so painful and threatening? This is all the more puzzling a question because most complementarians have profoundly equal marriages[2] and they are pleased to see women in leadership positions in the world.

2. As the complementarian theologian Russell Moore says. See his "After Patriarchy."

WHY COMPLEMENTARIANS REJECT THE
EVANGELICAL EGALITARIAN POSITION

After listening carefully to complementarians for most of my life I know why they say that they cannot become egalitarians and why, without admitting it, they find change almost impossible.

First, why *they say* they cannot change. They give two reasons.

1. The first reason always given is, "I cannot become an egalitarian because I am convinced that the Scriptures make the leadership of men an abiding principle. To argue otherwise is a denial of biblical authority." This is asserted repeatedly by the Köstenbergers.[3] Wayne Grudem subtitles his book, *Evangelical Feminism, A New Path to Liberalism.* In his preface he says that this book is an expression of his "deep concern about the widespread undermining of the authority of Scripture in the arguments that are frequently used to support evangelical feminism,"[4] by which he means "evangelical egalitarianism." No matter how often and how loudly this argument is given it is fallacious. *Not one informed evangelical egalitarian* even questions the authority of Scripture, let alone denies it. The international organization Christians for Biblical Equality (CBE) says in the first clause of its statement of faith, "We believe the Bible is the inspired word of God, is reliable, and the final authority for faith and practice." This incessant accusation made by complementarians is very uncharitable, unfair, and nasty. It necessarily implies that F. F. Bruce, Leon Morris, Rebecca Groothuis, Kenneth Kanzer, Mimi Haddad, Millard Erickson, Tom Wright, Craig Keener, Cynthia Long Westfall, Philip Payne, Kevin Giles and all evangelical egalitarians are liberals who reject the authority of Scripture. For this argument to be taken seriously complementarians need to come forth with examples where egalitarian evangelicals in the last thirty years have in any way denied the authority of Scripture. I certainly have not done so in this book. *The truth is this debate is entirely about the interpretation of Scripture, not about the authority of Scripture.*

   Why, we must ask, do complementarians make this argument basic to their position? The answer is it is a very effective debating ploy. It rules out of court evangelical egalitarians before they are allowed to open their Bibles. You do not have to listen to them.

3. Köstenberger and Köstenberger, *God's Design,* 33–35, 50, 61, 64, 74, etc.

4. Grudem, *Evangelical Feminism,* 11.

Being absolutely convinced that what we say the Bible says is what God says is of course no guarantee that what we teach is what the Bible teaches. The learned Reformed theologians who quoted the Bible in support of slavery and apartheid claimed what they were teaching was what the Bible teaches, but we all agree now that they were mistaken. They were appealing to the Bible to support their own privileges and power.

If we are convinced that our *interpretation* of the Bible is what the Bible says and yet other evangelical and Reformed Christians with exactly the same high view of Scripture are crying out, "You are wrong," we need to listen to them. This is what complementarians refuse to do. They will not under any circumstances enter into a dialogue with egalitarians. To deny this is the situation today is impossible. To disprove what I have just said, complementarians would need to come forward with examples in the last thirty years where they have sat down with informed evangelical egalitarian theologians for an open dialogue on how rightly to interpret the key texts on which their case rests. Be assured I am ready and open for such dialogue in person or in writing and all the well-informed egalitarian theologians I know would love to have such a dialogue. The fact that complementarians refuse absolutely to enter into such a discussion speaks of the weakness of their position not its strength.

I will only believe that appeal to biblical authority is an honest objection to considering what egalitarian evangelicals are arguing the Bible actually teaches when complementarian theologians agree to openly and honestly discuss the egalitarian exegesis of the disputed texts—as I have set it out in this book in my own words.

2. Second, complementarian theologians say they cannot consider the egalitarian position because it is a denial of male-female differentiation. The Köstenbergers make this claim repeatedly in their book. Egalitarians, they say, teach "undifferentiated male-female equality";[5] "they have abolished all male-female role distinctions";[6] "they deny that Scripture teaches distinct and non-reversible male-female roles";[7] and like secular feminists, they "start out with a

---

5. Köstenberger and Köstenberger, *God's Design*, 196, 165.

6. Köstenberger and Köstenberger, *God's Design*, 165.

7. Köstenberger and Köstenberger, *God's Design*, 182.

presupposition of undifferentiated male-female equality."[8] If this is what evangelical egalitarians are teaching, they should be condemned, and we can understand why egalitarian teaching is so threatening to men and women who are told by their leaders this is what egalitarians are teaching—but it is not. We egalitarians believe without any caveats that male-female distinctions are God-given and good. No egalitarian I have ever heard or read denies male-female differentiation. We unequivocally affirm it. No evidence from the pen of an evangelical egalitarian for this complementarian charge can be given. What we deny is that the subordination of women is the creation ideal, that men are to lead, women obey. In saying this the picture comes into focus. When evangelical egalitarians *deny male leadership and female subordination* is the God-given ideal, complementarians *hear* male-female differentiation itself being denied. For them, what makes a man a man is that he is a leader; what makes a woman a woman is that she submits to male leadership. This is a very unsound way to primarily differentiate men and women. Surely a woman is still a woman if she is the president or prime mister of her country? Surely a man is a man even when set under a woman at work? To primarily ground male-female differentiation on "role" differences is even more problematic. Do not the roles of men and women differ from culture to culture and change over time? A far sounder way to indelibly differentiate men and women is to predicate difference on our different bodies and our different chromosomes. This is how I primarily differentiate men and women, and I argue this is how we should all primarily differentiate men and women.

These two arguments are "sound-good" ones. They are very useful politically. The problem is they have no factual basis. Now I mention two reasons why complementarians find it virtually impossible to become egalitarians that they never mention, they vehemently deny, and yet are factual.

1. Complementarians cannot and will not consider changing their mind on male headship and female subordination because it involves men relinquishing power. To question men's God-given leadership of women is to overthrow how they believe the world should

8. Köstenberger and Köstenberger, *God's Design*, 349.

be ordered. For them, as we have just noted, what makes a man a man is that he is a leader; what makes a woman a woman is that she submits to male leadership.

To deny that men should be in charge is thus to deny that men in all cultures in all times should be the leaders. In other words, it is to reject what is passionately believed to be the "biblical principle": God has appointed men to lead.

At this point the ultimate and basic reason why complementarians cannot consider the egalitarian position becomes crystal clear. They recognize it to be a call to men to give up power and as such it is resisted vehemently. Complementarians will never admit this, but it is the truth. Biblical authority and gender difference *sound* like good reasons and can be openly stated but a determination to hold onto power and privilege doesn't sound good and thus cannot be openly admitted. We will never understand why the debate over the male-female relationship is such a divisive and emotional matter for evangelicals unless we recognize that at root it is a conflict over power—who exercises it and who is to submit. Egalitarians are calling on men to relinquish power and complementarians are strenuously holding onto power, using their most effective weapon in any intramural evangelical conflict, the Bible. They cry out, "The Bible teaches male headship from cover to cover."

Human beings resist at all cost giving up power, including most Christians. This fact is illustrated in the conflict over slavery and apartheid. White Christian men, quoting the Bible in support, bitterly opposed relinquishing their power. They insisted God had given them power over others and developed a seemingly weighty "biblical theology" as their defense. In America it cost a million lives to abolish slavery and in South Africa the breakdown of a society and bloodshed to abolish apartheid.

2. There is, however, a second, never spoken about reason why complementarians cannot consider the evangelical egalitarian understanding of the Bible, which is just as powerful as the one just mentioned, but in this case it is more mundane. Most complementarians live in a complementarian world; the Southern Baptist Convention and the Anglican Diocese of Sydney are two good examples, and the academic staff room in a Christian college or university where virtually everyone is a complementarian is a third. In these circles

you gain kudos by speaking in support of male headship. In fact, a very strong stand on this matter will rocket you into stardom. Conversely, to speak against male headship, and its counterpart, the permanent subordination of women, will result in you being marginalized and denigrated. You soon find you have no "friends" in the "tribe" to which you thought you belonged. It is very costly to differ on any issue that gives identity to the group. It is not tolerated. This is a huge barrier to complementarians changing their mind. We all want acceptance and we all want friends.

THE WAY FORWARD

The prospect of complementarian theology being defeated any time soon is unlikely. Those holding power over others never give up their power unless forced to. We are not going to have a civil war over this and complementarians are not going to be brought to their knees because of political or economic pressure. Women have risen up in opposition in our churches and church assemblies and written powerful refutations of complementarian theology, but they are not united in opposition. In any ruling ideology a percentage of those disempowered always support the status quo. In the Hindu caste system and in classic aristocracies, for example, some of the strongest advocates for the prevailing hierarchical social order are those at the bottom. What happens is that they internalize this order; they believe those above them rightfully rule over them and their lowly status is God-given. This support of the existing status quo wins them many accolades from those who benefit most from this ordering, the ruling elite. This is also what we see in the church. Some of the most ardent supporters of the hierarchical ordering of the sexes are able, powerful, articulate women. In every cohort of complementarians there is at least one well-armed and able female warrior who is a great asset to the men and they reward her (them) by bestowing honorary male status. They invite her to teach the Bible to large gatherings of men, often in a church building. Other women will not support the biblical case for equality because they are married to a committed complementarian, even if they in some cases give most of the leadership in their marriage. They understand that to threaten their husband's belief that God has appointed him to be the head of the home would make for a very unhappy marriage.

How, then, can change come? I suggest the following.

1. We evangelical egalitarians must constantly, strongly, and publicly deny the charges that we reject biblical authority and male-female differentiation. We must win on this matter because this accusation is blatantly false.

2. We evangelical egalitarians must continue putting and polishing *the biblical case* for gender equality as the God-given ideal. This argument is very strong. Complementarians cannot make an answer that is open to scholarly scrutiny. I am not expecting any open dialogue with complementarians on what I have written. They do not have an answer to what I have said, nor what other well-informed egalitarians have written, especially the work of Philip Payne and Linda Belleville. Here I need to commend the work of Christians for Biblical Equality International (CBE). This organization unites egalitarian evangelicals and produces an unending flow of helpful material. You should join, if have not already done so

3. We evangelical egalitarians must hope and pray that it will become ever more evident to complementarians that male headship teaching can have awful consequences for women. It is not a "benevolent" doctrine that brings "blessing" to women. Evangelicals have become aware that the subordination of women in the Third World has awful consequences for them but this they have explained away as a cultural distortion of headship teaching. What they have not been able to explain away is the large numbers of women in Western countries who stood up in 2017 and bravely said, "I was abused by my Christian husband," or "I have been raped by a Christian leader." They have had to admit that headship teaching can have tragic consequences for women, and this is something that they had been denying for too long.

   In the case of slavery in nineteenth century America, we noted, it was not counter biblical teaching that caused most problems for the pro-slavery theologians, but the realities of what slavery involved for slaves. People came to see that slavery was grossly unjust and a denial of the law of Christ to "do unto others as you would like them to do to you." Complementarians are now faced with exactly the same problem. It is now undeniable that headship teaching is not good news for women. It can have negative consequences. Complementarians have to face this fact.

CONCLUSION: WHERE TO NOW?   227

4. We evangelical egalitarians need to encourage men to show the supposedly male virtue of bravery. So many men in communities domi-
   nated by complementarians fear saying anything that would upset
   complementarians and so they keep silent. They know to come out
   as an egalitarian would be very costly; they would be marginalized
   and punished. I have spoken at many Christian colleges and universities in the United States on women in leadership or the orthodox
   doctrine of the Trinity, and in almost every case one or two faculty
   members have quietly said to me afterwards, "I agree with everything you said, but I do not come out as an egalitarian because the
   complementarians would punish me." I never forget one experience.
   I was invited to take part in a public debate on the ordination of
   women in Sydney. One of the Moore College lecturers who took the
   opposing position to mine agreed to drive me to where I was staying
   after the event. In the car he said to me, "Kevin, I basically agree
   with you but I cannot say this publicly because this would exclude
   me from teaching at Moore Theological College."

   The time has come: if complementarians cannot answer me
   or other informed egalitarian scholars in an open debate then they
   need to in all honesty concede and admit they were wrong. Continuing to vehemently reject what evangelical egalitarians are saying
   the Bible says by accusing them of denying biblical authority and
   male-female differentiation is becoming very tiresome. It is simply
   not true.[9]

5. What is now needed is what happened in the Trinity debate in
   2016.[10] We need a few complementarian leaders to stand up and
   say we have been wrong. The Bible does not make the subordination
   of women the creation ideal; it is not pleasing to Christ; it demeans
   all women, and results all too often in the abuse of women. Again,
   it seems a woman, Beth Moore, has been the first to cry out, this
   teaching is wrong. Are there any brave male complementarians who
   will now follow her?

6. We evangelical egalitarians, I think most importantly, need to tell
   complementarians loud and clear and often that Jesus opposes all
   claims that some should rule over others in the church and the

9. See further on this and on the women who precipitated the abandonment of the
complementarian doctrine of the Trinity in Giles, *Rise and Fall*, particularly chapter 2.

10. For the full story see Giles, *Rise and Fall*.

home. In word and action Jesus points to a radical alternative to seeking power for ourselves over others. In six passages in the Gospels, Jesus lays down the principle that *those who would lead in his community are to be servants, not rulers* (Matt 20:26–28; 23:11; Mark 9:35; 10:43–45; Luke 9:48; 22:24–27), and once in action he exemplified his teaching (John 13:1–20). He said, unbelievers like to "lord it over others . . . but it is not to be so among you." A leader in my community is "one who serves" (Luke 22:25–26).

Nowhere is this radical, distinctly Christian idea that the powerful should relinquish power more profoundly taught than in Phil 2:4–11. Here Paul says,

> *Let the same mind be in you* that was in Christ Jesus, who though he was in the form of God, did not regard equality with God something to be exploited, but emptied himself, taking the form of a slave, being born in human likeness. And being found in human form humbled himself and became obedient to the point of death, even death on a cross.

As God, Jesus had all might, majesty, and power but he laid this aside for our salvation. In the foot-washing, recounted in John 13, Jesus does something similar in his incarnate ministry. He takes a towel and stoops to wash his disciple's feet.

Paul specifically applies this distinctive and radical understanding of leadership to marriage. In Eph 5:21–33 he exhorts husbands, who the fall and the culture of the day made the "head of the wife," to lay aside their privileges and authority and give themselves in loving, costly service for their wife like Christ gave his life for the church.

At this most basic level complementarian teaching is flawed. It baptizes into the Christian community an understanding of leadership characteristic of this fallen world, an understanding of leadership Jesus rejects.

Far too many Christians cannot comprehend or accept this teaching. Roman Catholics, evangelicals, particularly those of Reformed conviction, are convinced that hierarchical ordering where some have authority over others is what is pleasing to God. The idea that within the Christian family we should lead by becoming servants of others falls on deaf ears or is domesticated. Radical Protestants and liberal Christians have been much better at "hearing" Jesus' countercultural message; leadership in his community is not about exercising authority over others but of humbly serving others.

LASTLY, THE ORDINATION OF WOMEN

In this book, I have only mentioned the ordination of women in passing. I have not written to advocate the ordination of women but to oppose their subordination, which is why complementarians exclude women from ordination. I have always spoken in support of their ordination, but as I am about to explain, I have never been happy with how the mainline churches have included women in church leadership.

The way many of the churches have responded, including my own Anglican Church, to the pressing demands to give equality to women in church leadership, has been unhelpful and unbiblical. The model of church leadership of one man in charge of each church, possibly with one or more assistants, was invented by men for men more than a thousand years ago. It has no biblical support and it is a model of church leadership that does not work well for many men today nor for most women. Nowhere in the New Testament do we find an example of one person in charge of a congregation who does most of the ministry, and nowhere in the Bible do we find mono-ministry prescribed. If we want women to flourish in church leadership we need to invent a model of ministry that will be conducive to this happening. The Bible, read apart from ecclesiastical dogma, offers possibilities to do this.

Paul's theology of leadership in the church is this: every believer on receiving the Spirit is given a *charisma*, a manifestation of the Spirit, a ministry, yet some are leaders, such as the apostles, prophets, and teachers. In the giving of all ministry gender is not a consideration. Those who lead, he makes clear, are to be servants (deacons). Peter says they should not "lord it over the flock" (1 Pet 5:3). The titles of the leaders differ from place to place and from time to time, but they are always plural. I thus agree with the Köstenbergers that the Scriptures envisage a "plurality of local church leadership in the form of a team of pastors."[11] I only differ in that I do not think church leaders must necessarily be called "pastors" or that women be excluded from church leadership. I think women should *necessarily* be included. The church is made up of men and women; men

11. Köstenberger and Köstenberger, *God's Design*, 194.

and women receive the Spirit in like manner, and Paul, as we have seen, affirmed women in leadership.

It is my experience as a pastor of forty years that when women's leadership in the life of the church is affirmed, everything is better. There is more harmony, more spiritual growth, the men and women enjoy church more, and the teaching improves as men and women teach/preach, each from their own gender perspective. For evangelical egalitarians, the leader of a ministry team can be a man or a woman. For Paul, spiritual gifting is what should determine who undertakes each ministry.

Team leadership in a church can take many forms. In a small church, a paid pastor, a part-time paid youth worker and an unpaid parish pastoral assistant may make a team. In a bigger church there may be several paid staff, some ordained, some not. In Paul's understanding of team leadership, the primary work of church leaders is to equip and empower all the church for their ministry (Eph 4:11–12).[12]

I CONCLUDE

The substantial equality of the sexes is the creation ideal and it is what Jesus endorsed. Women's liberation is good news for men and women. I hope and pray that you may, on reading this book, join with me in working to see this God-given ideal realized more and more in our time.

---

12. On this see Giles, *Making Good Churches Better*, chapter 12, 209–28.

Recommended Reading

AT THE END OF their book, *God's Design*, Andreas and Margaret Kostenberger give an annotated list of twenty-one "helpful" books or articles. All but one were written by a complementarian, and fourteen of them I have on my shelves. They provide no works setting out the evangelical egalitarian position and in their book they virtually ignore counter exegetical opinion or ridicule it by misrepresenting the views of their opponents. Complementarians need to read and engage what evangelical egalitarians actually say, never accepting what critics claim egalitarians say or teach.

I list and briefly comment on what I consider to be the best books articulating the evangelical egalitarian case, all written by those holding the highest view of the authority of Scripture, who endorse male-female differentiation, and believe the creation ideal is the substantial equality of the sexes; the subordination of women being entirely a consequence of the fall. I list them in three categories: scholarly books, intermediate books, and easier-to-read books, but in several cases it is not clear whether or not a book should be in category 2 or 3.

1. ACADEMIC BOOKS

Payne, Philip. *Man and Woman: One in Christ: An Exegetical and Theological Study of Paul's Letters*. Grand Rapids: Zondervan, 2009.

Payne's work of over 500 pages is in a league of its own. Payne has a PhD from Cambridge and is a world class linguist, textual critic, and exegete. He begins his book affirming in strong terms his commitment to the doctrine of inerrancy. Often in this book he interacts with Andreas

Köstenberger. No one who wants to be informed on what the Bible actually teaches on women can ignore this book.

Belleville, Linda A. *Woman Leaders and the Church: Three Crucial Questions.* Grand Rapids: Baker, 2000.

Belleville is also a first-class New Testament scholar who, like Payne, has broken new exegetical and linguistic ground. Much of her best work is in chapters in books such as *Discovering Biblical Equality* (which I list next) and in journal articles listed in my bibliography. Her writings are always clear and easy to understand.

Pierce, Ronald W., and Rebecca M. Groothius, eds. *Discovering Biblical Equality: Complementarity without Hierarchy.* Downers Grove, IL: InterVarsity, 2005.

This is a collection of twenty-nine essays by evangelical egalitarian scholars. It comprehensively covers all the key issues. Some essays are stronger than others. It is to be republished with new work in 2019.

Keener, Craig S. *Paul, Women and Wives: Marriage and Women's Ministry in the Letters of Paul.* Peabody, MA: Hendrickson, 1992.

Keener is a top-drawer New Testament scholar and president of the Evangelical Theological Society, 2017–18. This book is a mine of information.

Witherington, Ben. *Women in the Ministry of Jesus.* Cambridge: Cambridge University Press, 1984.
———. *Women in the Earliest Churches.* Cambridge: Cambridge University Press, 1988.
———. *Women and the Genesis of Christianity.* Cambridge: Cambridge University Press, 1990.

Witherington is one of the most published evangelical scholars. In these books we find the best of exegetical work informed by the best of historical information.

Long Westfall, Cynthia. *Paul and Gender: Reclaiming the Apostle's Vision for Men and Women in Christ.* Grand Rapids: Baker, 2016.

This is a very informative book which, after forty years of debate about what Paul teaches on women, breaks new ground—a must read.

Forbes, Greg W., and Scott D. Harrower. *Raised from Obscurity: A Narratival and Theological Study of the Characterization of Women in Luke-Acts.* Eugene, OR: Pickwick, 2015.

It has long been noted that Luke is particularly affirming of women. In this book all the positive things Luke says about women are shown to be part of Luke's narrative and are theologically developed. This book breaks new ground and cannot be ignored. Almost a third of the New Testament is written by Luke.

Giles, Kevin. *The Trinity and Subordinationism: The Doctrine of God and the Contemporary Gender Debate.* Downers Grove, IL: InterVarsity, 2002.

The title of this book, which was chosen by the publisher, is unhelpful. The book is in three sections. The first considers the complementarian argument that just as the Son of God is supposedly eternally subordinated to the Father, so women are permanently subordinated to men. The second explains how the complementarian position emerged and developed and contrasts it with the historic understanding of what the Bible teaches on women. The third section is on the parallels between complementarian appeals to the Bible in support of the subordination of women and the appeals to the Bible by evangelical and Reformed theologians in the nineteenth century in support of slavery.

Giles, Kevin. *The Rise and Fall of the Complementarian Doctrine of the Trinity.* Eugene, OR: Cascade, 2017.

This book tells how the complementarians found that they had to abandon their appeal to the Trinity in support of the subordination of women because it led them into the Arian heresy.

This list of books is selective and I could, and probably should, mention other scholarly books putting the biblical case for gender equality.

2. INTERMEDIATE BOOKS

Bilezikian, Gilbert. *Beyond Sex Roles: What the Bible Says About a Woman's Place in Church and Family.* Grand Rapids: Baker, 1985.

This book, I suspect, has been the most widely read exposition of the biblical case for the substantial equality of the sexes. It is accessible, well-informed, and easy to read.

Besancon Spencer, Aida. *Beyond the Curse: Women Called to Ministry.* Grand Rapids: Baker, 1985 (republished 2010).

In this book, Dr. Spencer very helpfully examines what the Bible actually says on women, and whether or not it excludes women from ordination.

Merrill Groothuis, Rebecca. *Good News for Women: A Biblical Picture of Gender Equality.* Grand Rapids: Baker 1997.

This is a beautifully written, clearly argued, reader-friendly book on women in the Bible. This is the first book I would give to a member of my church who asked me for something to read on this question.

McHaffie, Barbara J. *Her Story: Women in Christian Tradition*. 2nd ed. Minneapolis: Fortress, 2006.

This book is not focused on the Bible but on the oft-ignored or submerged stories of women in Christian history, from biblical times to now.

3. EASIER BOOKS TO READ

I now add a list of a few books that I think are very good and are written for informed church members. These books are easier to digest than the books listed above. But as I said above, my categories are subjective. Popular and usually very helpful books are constantly being published. They are often not stocked in Christian bookshops. I cannot recommend too highly Christians for Biblical Equality online bookshop (http://cbe-booksonline.com), which keeps abreast of what is available and usually provides excellent reviews.

Tidball, Derek, and Dianne Tidball. *The Message of Women: Creation, Grace and Gender*. Downers Grove, IL: InterVarsity, 2012.

The Tidballs have been in Baptist ministry in England for many years. Derek was the principal of the London School of theology for twelve years. In this book, the Tidballs study all the key texts on women, and what they say reflects their deep involvement in the life of the church.

Pierce, Ronald W. *Partners in Marriage and Ministry: A Biblical Picture of Gender Equality*. Minneapolis: Christians for Biblical Equality, 2011.

Drawing on thirty years of teaching classes on gender my friend Ron Pierce examines what Scripture says on gender equality in both marriage and ministry.

George, Janet. *Still Side by Side: A Concise Explanation of Biblical Equality*. Minneapolis: Christians for Biblical Equality, 2009.

This book is an introduction to biblical equality. Each chapter is introduced with a question and brief answer, followed by a more in-depth explanation. It is a valuable resource for individuals or groups who are seeking answers to the questions surrounding gender and the church.

Johnson, Alan F. ed. *How I Changed My Mind About Women in Leadership: Compelling Stories from Prominent Evangelicals*. Grand Rapids: Zondervan, 2010.

This book gives the testimonies of twenty-one well-known evangelicals, some couples, who were once complementarians but after careful study of the Bible became egalitarians.

CHRISTIANS FOR BIBLICAL EQUALITY[1]

CBE International (CBE) is a nonprofit organization of Christian men and women who believe that the Bible, properly interpreted, teaches the fundamental equality of men and women of all ethnic groups, all economic classes, and all age groups, based on the teachings of Scriptures such as Gal 3:28: "There is neither Jew nor Gentile, neither slave nor free, nor is there male and female, for you are all one in Christ Jesus" (NIV 2011).

CBE affirms and promotes the biblical truth that all believers—without regard to gender, ethnicity, or class—must exercise their God-given gifts with equal authority and equal responsibility in church, home, and world.

CBE is supported primarily by donations from individuals who share our vision of a future where all believers are freed to exercise their gifts for God's glory and purposes, with the full support of their Christian communities.

Who We Are

We are Christians, committed to the Bible. We believe that the Bible is the inspired Word of God, is reliable, and is the final authority for Christian faith and practice. We believe that our mission is a result of faithful interpretation and application of the Bible.

We are a global community. CBE partners, supporters, and organizational members come from over sixty countries and every corner of the United States. They advocate for the shared authority of men and women in their families, churches, workplaces, and cultures all over the world. Together, we make this mission a reality.

1. Permission to publish these CBE documents given by Mimi Haddad, president of CBE.

We are lifelong learners. We believe that there is always more to learn about God and God's purposes in the world, and God's Word. We provide educational resources on issues pertaining to gender and the Bible for a variety of audiences. We seek to engage with believers of all backgrounds and together sharpen our understanding.

What We Do

CBE's ministry revolves around several core components.

Publications. We publish an academic journal, *Priscilla Papers*, and a popular magazine, *Mutuality*, quarterly. These award-winning publications are available by mail with a paid subscription or for free on CBE's website. In addition, we publish a blog with a weekly e-newsletter, *Arise*.

Bookstore. CBE Bookstore is the place to find the best resources on the biblical perspective on the equal service and authority of men and women. Each book we carry or recommend has been reviewed for quality and relevance to CBE's mission. Our bookstore also carries exclusive resources including CBE-produced journals and audio and video recordings.

Conferences. Each year, we host an international conference with some of the top scholars and speakers in the world. Our conferences educate, encourage, and equip our community to share about the biblical basis for the shared authority of men and women in their homes, churches, and cultures.

Church and Organization Membership. CBE church and organization membership provides resources and support for organizations eager to build egalitarian momentum. CBE organizational members receive free subscriptions to our publications, conference registration discounts, and other benefits.

Chapters. Chapters are CBE's hands and feet in communities around the world. Chapters are a way for local CBE members and supporters to connect and minister together. They often host lectures, meet for mutual encouragement, represent CBE at regional conferences, and serve their communities together.

Men, Women and Biblical Equality

The Bible teaches the full equality of men and women in Creation and in Redemption (Gen 1:26–28, 2:23, 5:1–2; I Cor 11:11–12; Gal 3:13, 28, 5:1).

The Bible teaches that God has revealed Himself in the totality of Scripture, the authoritative Word of God (Matt 5:18; John 10:35; 2 Tim 3:16; 2 Peter 1:20–21). We believe that Scripture is to be interpreted holistically and thematically. We also recognize the necessity of making a distinction between inspiration and interpretation: inspiration relates to the divine impulse and control whereby the whole canonical Scripture is the Word of God; interpretation relates to the human activity whereby we seek to apprehend revealed truth in harmony with the totality of Scripture and under the guidance of the Holy Spirit. To be truly biblical, Christians must continually examine their faith and practice under the searchlight of Scripture.

Biblical Truths

Creation

1. The Bible teaches that both man and woman were created in God's image, had a direct relationship with God, and shared jointly the responsibilities of bearing and rearing children and having dominion over the created order (Gen 1:26–28).

2. The Bible teaches that woman and man were created for full and equal partnership. The word "helper" (ezer) used to designate woman in Genesis 2:18 refers to God in most instances of Old Testament usage (e.g. I Sam 7:12; Ps 121:1–2). Consequently the word conveys no implication whatsoever of female subordination or inferiority.

3. The Bible teaches that the forming of woman from man demonstrates the fundamental unity and equality of human beings (Gen 2:21–23). In Genesis 2:18, 20 the word "suitable" (kenegdo) denotes equality and adequacy.

4. The Bible teaches that man and woman were co-participants in the Fall: Adam was no less culpable than Eve (Gen 3:6; Rom 5:12–21; I Cor 15:21–22).

5. The Bible teaches that the rulership of Adam over Eve resulted from the Fall and was therefore not a part of the original created order. Genesis 3:16 is a prediction of the effects of the Fall rather than a prescription of God's ideal order.

Redemption

6. The Bible teaches that Jesus Christ came to redeem women as well as men. Through faith in Christ we all become children of God, one in Christ, and heirs to the blessings of salvation without reference to racial, social, or gender distinctives (John 1:12–13; Rom 8:14–17; 2 Cor 5:17; Gal 3:26–28).

Community

7. The Bible teaches that at Pentecost the Holy Spirit came on men and women alike. Without distinction, the Holy Spirit indwells women and men, and sovereignly distributes gifts without

preference as to gender (Acts 2:1–21; 1 Cor 12:7, 11, 14:31).

8. The Bible teaches that both women and men are called to develop their spiritual gift s and to use them as stewards of the grace of God (1 Peter 4:10–11). Both men and women are divinely gifted and empowered to minister to the whole Body of Christ, under His authority (Acts 1:14, 18:26, 21:9; Rom 16:1–7, 12–13, 15; Phil 4:2–3; Col 4:15; see also Mark 15:40–41, 16:1–7; Luke 8:1–3; John 20:17–18; compare also Old Testament examples: Judges 4:4–14, 5:7; 2 Chron 34:22–28; Prov 31:30–31; Micah 6:4).

9. The Bible teaches that, in the New Testament economy, women as well as men exercise the prophetic, priestly and royal functions (Acts 2:17–18, 21:9; 1 Cor 11:5; 1 Peter 2:9–10; Rev 1:6, 5:10). Therefore, the few isolated texts that appear to restrict the full redemptive freedom of women must not be interpreted simplistically and in contradiction to the rest of Scripture, but their interpretation must take into account their relation to the broader teaching of Scripture and their total context (1 Cor 11:2–16, 14:33–36; 1 Tim 2:9–15).

10. The Bible defines the function of leadership as the empowerment of others for service rather than as the exercise of power over them (Matt 20:25–28, 23:8; Mark 10:42–45; John 13:13–17; Gal 5:13; 1 Peter 5:2–3).

Family

11. The Bible teaches that husbands and wives are heirs together of the grace of life and that they are bound together in a relationship of mutual submission and responsibility (1 Cor 7:3–5; Eph 5:21; 1 Peter 3:1–7; Gen 21:12). The husband's function as "head" (kephale) is to be understood as self-giving love and service within this relationship of mutual submission (Eph 5:21–33; Col 3:19; 1 Peter 3:7).

12. The Bible teaches that both mothers and fathers are to exercise leadership in the nurture, training, discipline and teaching of their children (Ex 20:12; Lev 19:3; Deut 6:6–9, 21:18–21, 27:16; Prov 1:8, 6:20; Eph 6:1–4; Col 3:20; 2 Tim 1:5; see also Luke 2:51).

Application

Community

1. In the church, spiritual gifts of women and men are to be recognized, developed and used in serving and teaching ministries at all levels of involvement: as small group leaders, counselors, facilitators, administrators, ushers, communion servers, and board members, and in pastoral care, teaching, preaching, and worship.

In so doing, the church will honor God as the source of spiritual gifts. The church will also fulfill God's mandate of stewardship without the appalling loss to God's kingdom that results when half of the church's members are excluded from positions of responsibility.

2. In the church, public recognition is to be given to both women and men who exercise ministries of service and leadership.

In so doing, the church will model the unity and harmony that should characterize the community of believers. In a world fractured by discrimination and segregation, the church will dissociate itself from worldly or pagan devices designed to make women feel inferior for being female. It will help prevent their departure from the church or their rejection of the Christian faith.

Family

3. In the Christian home, husband and wife are to defer to each other in seeking to fulfill each other's preferences,

desires and aspirations. Neither spouse is to seek to dominate the other but each is to act as servant of the other, in humility considering the other as better than oneself. In case of decisional deadlock they should seek resolution through biblical methods of conflict resolution rather than by one spouse imposing a decision upon the other.

In so doing, husband and wife will help the Christian home stand against improper use of power and authority by spouses and will protect the home from wife and child abuse that sometimes tragically follows a hierarchical interpretation of the husband's "headship."

4. In the Christian home, spouses are to learn to share the responsibilities of leadership on the basis of gifts, expertise, and availability, with due regard for the partner most affected by the decision under consideration.

In so doing, spouses will learn to respect t heir competencies and their complementarity. This will prevent one spouse from becoming the perennial loser, often forced to practice ingratiating or deceitful manipulation to protect self-esteem. By establishing their marriage on a partnership basis, the couple will protect it from joining the tide of dead or broken marriages resulting from marital inequities.

5. In the Christian home, couples who share a lifestyle characterized by the freedom they find in Christ will do so without experiencing feelings of guilt or resorting to hypocrisy. They are freed to emerge from an unbiblical "traditionalism" and can rejoice in their mutual accountability in Christ. In so doing, they will openly express their obedience to Scripture, will model an example for other couples in quest of freedom in Christ, and will stand against patterns of domination and inequality sometimes imposed upon church and family.

We believe that biblical equality as reflected in this document is true to Scripture.

We stand united in our conviction that the Bible, in its totality, is the liberating Word that provides the most effective way for women and men to exercise their gifts distributed by the Holy Spirit and thus to serve God.

Gilbert Bilezikian, W. Ward Gasque, Stanley N. Gundry, Gretchen Gaebelein Hull, Catherine Clark Kroeger, Jo Anne Lyon, Roger Nicole

Endorsed by: Miriam Adeney, Astri T. Anfindsen, Timothy Paul Allen, James Alsdurf, Phyllis Alsdurf, John E. Anderson, P atricia W. Anderson, Carl E. Armerding, Myron S. Augsburger, Raymond Bakke, Sandra Bauer, James Beck, Virginia L. Beck, Elizabeth Bell, Roy D. Bell, David G. Benner, Gordon C. Bennett, Joyce R. Berggren, Char Binkley, Sandra Bostian, Mark A. Brewer, Bettie Ann Brigham, D. Stuart Briscoe, Kathleen K. Brogan, James A. Brooks, Beth E. Brown, H. Marie Brown, F. F. Bruce, Cheever C. Buckbee, David H. Burr, Donald P. Buteyn, Anthony Campolo, Linda Cannell, Daniel R. Chamberlain, Caroline L. Cherry, Jack M. Chisholm, Gerald Christmas, Rosemary Christmas, David K. Clark, Shirley Close, Bonnidell Clouse, Robert G. Clouse, David W. Clowney, Naomi C. Cole, Mark O. Coleman, Jim Conway, Sally Conway, Kaye V. Cook- Kollars, C. S. Cowles, R. Byron Crozier, Peter H. Davids, Edward R. Dayton, Paul H. De Vries, Sidney De Waal, J. Jey Deifell, Jr., John R. Dellenback, Mary Jane Dellenback, Gary W. Demarest, Dolores Dunnett, Walter Dunnett, Charlotte Dyck, James F. Engel, C. Stephen Evans, Colleen Townsend Evans, Louis Evans, Gabriel Fackre, Gordon D. Fee, John Fischer, Patrice Fischer, David B. Fletcher, Joan D. Flikkema, David A. Fraser, Nils C. Friberg, Donn M. Gaebelein, Kevin Giles, Alfred A. Glenn, Barbara R. Glenn, Arthur A. Goetze, Tita V. Gordovez, Lillian V. Grissen, H. James Groen, Vernon Grounds, Darrell L. Guder, Lee M. Haines, Robin Haines, Richard C. Halverson, Sandra Hart, Stephen A. Hayner, Jo Ellen Heil, Betty C. Henderson, Robert T. Henderson, John J. Herzog, Bartlett L. Hess, I. John Hesselink, Roberta Hestenes,

Janet S. Hickman, Marvin D. Hoff, Colleen Holby, Arthur F. Holmes, Beverly Holt, Carol D. C. Howard, David Allan Hubbard, M. Gay Hubbard, Anne Huffman, John Huffman, Philip G. Hull, Sanford D. Hull, Richard G. Hutcheson, Jr., William J. Hybels, Vida S. Icenogle, Dorothy Irvin, Evelyn Jensen, Alan F. Johnson, David W. Johnson, Robert K. Johnston, Rufus Jones, Kenneth S. Kantzer, Robert D. Kettering, John F. Kilner, Herbert V. Klem, Richard C. Kroeger, Harold E. Kurtz, Pauline H. Kurtz, Bruce Larson, Michael R. Leming, William H. Leslie, Arthur H. Lewis, Walter L. Liefeld, Zondra Lindblade, Helen W. Loeb, Richard N. Longenecker, Richard F. Lovelace, Deborah Olsoe Lunde, Kenneth H. Maahs, Faith M. Martin, James R. Mason, Alice P. Mathews, Dolores E. McCabe, Te rry McGonigal, David L. McKenna, Lois McKinney, William A. Meyer, Hazel M. Michelson, A. Berkeley Mickelsen, Alvera Mickelsen, Eileen F. Moffett, Samuel H. Moffett, C. Sue Moore, Edward Moore, Graham Morbey, Mary Leigh Morbey, Elizabeth Morgan, Stephen C. Mott, Richard J. Mouw, Jeana Nieporte, William M. Nieporte, Alvaro L. Nieves, Arnold T. Olson, Daisy M. Washburn Osborn, LaDonna Osborn, T. L. Osborn, Grant R. Osborne, Grace Paddon, John Paddon, Elizabeth L. Patterson, Virginia Patterson, Richard Patterson, Jr., Philip Barton Payne, Robert W. Pazmino, Janet M. Peifer, William J. Petersen, Richard V. Pierard, Paul E. Pierson, Carolyn Goodman Plampin, Cornelius Plantinga, Jr., Christiane Posselt, Quah Cheng Hock, Robert V. Rakestraw, Sara Robertson, Lianne Roembke, Lydia M. Sarandan, Alvin J. Schmidt, Richard C. Schoenert, David M. Scholer, Jeannette F. Scholer, Robert A. Seiple, Ronald J. Sider, Lewis B. Smedes, James D. Smith III, Paul R. Smith, P. Paul Snezek, Jr., Klyne Snodgrass, Howard A. Snyder, Aida B. Spencer, William D. Spencer, Adele O. Sullivan, W. Nelson Thomson, Ruth A. Tucker, Mary Stewart Van Leeuwen, Joseph W. Viola, Virginia G. Viola, Emily Walther, George H. Walther, Patricia A. Ward, Timothy Weber, Van B. Weigel, Bruce Wilson, Earle L. Wilson, H. C. Wilson, Nicholas Wolterstorff, Linda R. Wright, Walter C. Wright, Jr., Louis H. Zbinden. (9/95)

CBE International

122 West Franklin Avenue, Suite 218, Minneapolis, MN 5404-2451
Phone: (612) 872-6898 Fax: (612) 872-6891
E-mail: cbe@cbeinternational.org
www.cbeinternational.org

Bibliography

Adam, Edward. *The Earliest Christian Meeting Place: Almost Exclusively Houses?* London: Bloomsbury, 2013.

Alikin, Valeriy A. *The Earliest History of the Christian Gathering.* Leiden: Brill, 2010.

Amos, Clare. *The Book of Genesis.* Peterborough, UK: Epworth, 2004.

Annis, W., and Roger E. Rice. "A Survey of Abuse Prevalence in the Christian Reformed Church." *Journal of Religion and Abuse* 3 (2001) 7–14.

Arnold, Bill T. *Genesis.* New Cambridge Bible Commentary. Cambridge: Chicago University Press, 2009.

Arnold, Clinton E. *Ephesians.* Zondervan Exegetical Commentary on the New Testament 10. Grand Rapids: Zondervan, 2010.

Athanasius. "Discourses Against the Arians." In vol. 4 of *The Ante-Nicene Fathers,* edited by A. Roberts and J. Donaldson. Grand Rapids: Eerdmans, 1985.

"Australian Churches Risk Becoming a 'Haven' for Abusers." *ABC News,* July 28, 2017. http://www.abc.net.au/news/2017-07-21/australia-church-risks-becoming-haven-for-abusers/8651318.

Bailey, Kenneth L. *Through Middle Eastern Eyes.* Downers Grove, IL: InterVarsity, 2008.

Baldwin, Henry Scott. "An Important Word." In *Women in the Church: A Fresh Analysis of 1 Timothy 2:9–15,* edited by Andreas J. Köstenberger and Thomas R. Schreiner, 39–52. 2nd ed. Grand Rapids: Baker, 2005.

Bancroft, Lundy. *Why Does He Do That? Inside the Minds of Angry and Controlling Men.* New York: Berkley, 2002.

Banks, Robert. *Going to Church in the First Century: An Eyewitness Account.* Chipping Norton, Australia: Hexagon, 1980.

Banks, Robert, and Julia Banks. *The Church Comes Home.* Peabody, MA: Hendrickson, 1998.

Barth, Markus. *Ephesians.* 2 vols. Anchor Bible 34. New York: Doubleday, 1974.

Basile, Kathleen C., et al. "Stop SV: A Technical Package to Prevent Sexual Violence." National Center for Injury Prevention and Control, 2016. https://www.cdc.gov/violenceprevention/pdf/SV-Prevention-Technical-Package.pdf.

Bauckham, Richard. *Gospel Women: Studies of the Named Women in the Gospels.* Grand Rapids: Eerdmans, 2002.

Bauer, W., W. F. Arndt, F. W. Gingrich, and F. W. Danker. *Greek-English Lexicon of the New Testament and other Early Christian Writings.* 3rd ed. Chicago: University of Chicago Press, 1999.

Beavis, Mary A. "Christian Origins, Egalitarianism, and Utopia." *Journal of Feminist Studies in Religion* 23.2 (2007) 27–29.

Beck, James R., and Craig L. Blomberg. *Two Views on Women in Ministry.* Grand Rapids: Zondervan, 2001.

Belleville, Linda L. "Exegetical Fallacies in Interpreting 1 Timothy 2:11–15." *Priscilla Papers* 17.3 (Summer 2003) 3–11.

———. "Lexical Fallacies in Rendering *authentein* in 1 Timothy 2:12: BDAG in Light of Greek Literary and Non-Literary Usage." Forthcoming in Bulletin for Biblical Research.

———. "Teaching and Usurping Authority: 1 Timothy 2:11–15." In *Discovering Biblical Equality: Complementarity without Hierarchy,* edited by Ronald W. Pierce and Rebecca M. Groothuis, 205–24. Downers Grove, IL: InterVarsity, 2005.

———. "Women Leaders in the Bible." In *Discovering Biblical Equality: Complementarity without Hierarchy,* edited by Ronald W. Pierce and Rebecca M. Groothuis, 110–25. Downers Grove, IL: InterVarsity, 2005.

"Biblical Patriarchy." *Wikipedia.* https://en.wikipedia.org/wiki/Biblical_patriarchy.

Bedsloe, Albert. "Liberty and Slavery." In *Cotton is King: And Pro-Slavery Arguments,* edited by David Cristy and Albert T. Bedsloe, 354. Google Books, 2014; originally published 1860.

Blocher, Henri. "The Analogy of Faith in the Study of Scripture." In *The Challenge of Evangelical Theology: Essays in Approach and Method,* edited by Nigel M. de S. Cameron, 17–38. Edinburgh: Rutherford, 1987.

Block, Daniel L. *Judges and Ruth.* The New Bible Commentary. Nashville: B&H, 1999.

Boorstein, Michelle, and Sarah Pulliam Bailey. "How Women Led to the Dramatic Rise and Fall of Southern Baptist Leader Paige Patterson." *Washington Post,* June 10, 2018. https://www.washingtonpost.com/local/social-issues/how-women-led-to-the-dramatic-rise-and-fall-of-southern-baptist-leader-paige-patterson/2018/06/10/eacae5a4-6a61-11e8-9e38-24e693b38637_story.html?noredirect=on&utm_term=.3d06aca28b06.

Booth, Catherine. *Female Ministry: Or, the Right of Women to Preach the Gospel.* London: Morgan and Chase, 1859.

Borresen, Kari E. *The Image of God: Gender Models in Judaeo-Christian Tradition.* Minneapolis: Fortress, 1995.

Bowker, Lee H. "Religious Victims and Their Religious Leaders: Services Delivered to One Thousand Battered Women by the Clergy." In *Abuse and Religion: When Praying is Not Enough,* edited by Anne L. Horton and Judith A. Williamson, 229–34. Lexington, MA: Lexington, 1988.

Brauch, Manfred. "Genesis: A Very Good Place to Start, Back to the Beginning: Man and Woman in the Image of God." In *Mutual by Design: A Better Model for Christian Marriage,* edited by Elizabeth Beyer, 9–24. Minneapolis: Christians for Biblical Equality, 2017.

Briscoe, D. Stuart. *The Communicator's Commentary on Genesis.* Waco, TX: Word, 1987.

Brodie, Thomas L. *Genesis as Dialogue.* Oxford: Oxford University Press, 2001.

Brueggemann, Walter. *Genesis: A Bible Commentary for Teachers and Preachers.* Atlanta: John Knox, 1982.

Bure, Michael. "*Episemoi en tois Apostolos* in Rom 16:7 as 'Well Known to the Apostles': Further Defense and New Evidence." *Journal of the Evangelical Theological Society* 58.4 (2015) 731–56.

Burk, Denny. "My Take-Aways from the Trinity Debate." Denny Burk, August 10, 2016. http://www.dennyburk.com/my-take-aways-from-the-trinity-debate/.

———. "Why the Trinity Must Inform Our Views on Gender." Denny Burk, August 13, 2013. http://www.dennyburk.com/why-the-trinity-must-inform-our-views-on-gender-roles-ctmagazine.

Burridge, Richard A. *Imitating Jesus: An Inclusive Approach to New Testament Ethics.* Grand Rapids: Eerdmans, 2007.

Byrd, Aimee. "John Piper's Advice to Women in the Workplace." *Mortification of Spin*, August 17, 2015. http://www.alliancenet.org/mos/housewife-theologian/john-pipers-advice-for-women-in-the-workforce#.WHRKrvB96Ul.

———. "Sanctified Testosterone?" *Mortification of Spin*, April 21 2016. http://www.alliancenet.org/mos/housewife-theologian/sanctified-testosterone#.WHRMYvB96Ul.

———. "The Silence of Our Friends." *Mortification of Spin*, June 23, 2016. http://www.alliancenet.org/mos/housewife-theologian/the-silence-of-our-friends#.Wk36lkmWaUk.

———. "The Spin of Patriarchy." *Mortification of Spin*, September 24, 2014. http://www.alliancenet.org/mos/housewife-theologian/the-spin-of-patriarchy#.WHRFpPB96Ul.

———. "What's Wrong with Biblical Patriarchy?" *A Daughter of the Reformation,* May 31, 2012. https://adaughterofthereformation.wordpress.com/2012/05/31/whats-wrong-with-biblical-patriarchy/.

Callender, Allen D. "Servants of God(s) and Servants of Kings in Israel and the Ancient Near East." In *Slavery in Text and Interpretation*, edited by Allen D. Callender, 73–77. Semeia 83/84. Atlanta: Society of Biblical Literature, 1998.

Calvin, John. *The Epistle of Paul the Apostle to the Galatians, Ephesians, Philippians and Colossians.* Translated by T. H. L. Parker. Grand Rapids: Eerdmans, 1965.

———. *The Epistle of Paul the Apostle to the Romans and to the Thessalonians.* Translated by Ross Mackenzie. Grand Rapids: Eerdmans, 1973.

———. *Institutes of the Christian Religion.* Translated by Ford L. Battles. Edited by John T. McNeill. London: SCM, 1960.

———. *Paul's Second Epistle to the Corinthians and the Epistles of Timothy, Titus and Philemon.* Translated by Thomas A. Smail. Grand Rapids: Eerdmans, 1964.

Campbell, Alastair, R. *The Elders: Seniority Within Earliest Christianity.* Edinburgh: T&T Clarke, 1994.

Carson, Don. "'Silent in the Churches:' On the Role of Women in 1 Corinthians 14:33b–36." In *Recovering Biblical Manhood and Womanhood: A Response to Biblical Feminism*, edited by Wayne Grudem and John Piper, 140–53. Wheaton, IL: Crossway, 1991.

Carter, Joe. "Debatable: Is Complementarianism Another Word for Patriarchy?" The Gospel Coalition, June 7, 2012. https://www.thegospelcoalition.org/article/debatable-is-complementarianism-another-word-for-patriarchy.

Cartwright, E. N., ed. *Cotton Is King and Pro-Slavery Arguments.* New York: Basic Afro-American Reprints, 1968.

Cassuto, Umberto. *A Commentary on the Book of Genesis*. Vol. 1. Translated by Israel Abrahams. Jerusalem: Magnes, 1961.

Cervin, "On the Significance of *Kephalē* ("Head"): A Study of the Abuse of One Greek Word." *Priscilla Papers* 30.2 (2016) 8–20.

Chirichigo, G. C. *Debt-Slavery in Israel and the Ancient Near-East*. Sheffield: Sheffield Academic, 1993.

Clark, Stephen. *Man and Woman in Christ: An Examination of the Roles of Men and Women in Light of Scripture and the Social Sciences*. Ann Arbor, MI: Servant, 1980.

Clifford R. J., and R. E. M. O'Carm. "Genesis." In *The New Jerome Biblical Commentary*, edited by R. E. Brown, J. A. Fitzmyer, and R. E. Murphy. London: G. Chapman, 1989.

Cohick, Lynn H. *Women in the World of the Earliest Christians: Illuminating Ancient Ways of Life*. Grand Rapids: Baker, 2009.

Collins, John. *Diakonia: A Reinterpretation of Ancient Sources*. Oxford: Oxford University Press, 1990.

Condren, James C. "Toward a Purge of the Battle of the Sexes and 'Return' for the Original Meaning of Genesis 3:16b." *Journal of the Evangelical Theological Society* 60.2 (2017) 227–46.

Conzelmann, Hans. *1 Corinthians, A Commentary on the First Epistle to the Corinthians*. Philadelphia: Fortress, 1975.

Coogan, Donald. *Stewards of the Grace of God*. London: Hodder and Stoughton, 1958.

Corrado, Elizabeth. "The Godliness of Apartheid Planning; The Legitimizing Role of the Dutch Reformed Church." MUP Capstone, University of Illinois, 2013. https://www.ideals.illinois.edu/handle/2142/45241.

Cotter, David W. *Genesis*. Collegeville, MN: Liturgical, 2003.

Cullman, Oscar. *The State in the New Testament*. Revised ed. London: SCM, 1963.

Cundall, Arthur E., and Leon Morris. *Judges and Ruth*. Nottingham: InterVarsity, 2008.

Dabney, Robert L. *Discussions of Robert Lewis Dabney*. London: Banner of Truth, 1981.

D'Angelo, Mary R. "(Re)Presentations of Women in the Gospel of Matthew and Luke-Acts." In *Women in Christian Origins*, edited by Ross S. Kraemer and Mary R. D'Angelo, 174–94. Oxford: Oxford University Press, 1999.

"The Danvers Statement." Council on Biblical Manhood and Womanhood, June 26, 2007. http://cbmw.org/uncategorized/the-danvers-statement/.

Davidson, Robert. *Genesis 1–11*. Cambridge: Cambridge University Press, 1973.

De Vaux, Roland. *Ancient Israel: Its Life and Institutions*. London: Darton, Longman, Todd, 1962.

De Young, Kevin, and Greg Gilbert. *What Is the Mission of the Church? Making Sense of Justice, Shalom, and the Great Commission*. Wheaton, IL: Crossway, 2011.

Dillenberger, John, ed. *Martin Luther: Selections from His Writings*. New York: Anchor, 1962.

"Domestic Violence." The Methodist Church. http://www.methodist.org.uk/about-us/the-methodist-church/views-of-the-church/domestic-abuse/.

Doriani, Daniel. "History of the Interpretation of 1 Timothy 2." In *Women in the Church: A Fresh Analysis of 1 Timothy 2:9–15*, edited by Andreas J. Köstenberger, Thomas R. Schreiner, and H. Scott Baldwin, 213–68. Grand Rapids: Baker, 1995.

Elliott, John H. "Jesus Was Not an Egalitarian: A Critique of an Anachronistic and Idealist Theory." *Biblical Theology Bulletin* 32.2 (2012) 75–91.

Epp, Eldon J. *Junia: The First Woman Apostle*. Minneapolis: Fortress, 2005.

Ezell, Cynthia. "Power, Patriarchy and Abusive Marriages." In *Healing the Hurting: Giving Hope and Help to Abused Women*, edited by Catherine C Kroeger and James R. Beck, 20–43. Grand Rapids: Baker, 1998.

Fee, Gordon D. *The First Epistle to the Corinthians*. Grand Rapids: Eerdmans, 1987.

Fitzmyer, Joseph A. "Another look at *KEPHALĒ* in 1 Corinthians 11:3." *New Testament Studies* 35 (1989) 503–11.

———. *The Gospel According to Luke*. Vol. 1, *I–X*. New York: Doubleday, 1981.

———. "*Kephalē* in 1 Corinthians 11:3." *Interpretation* 47.1 (1993) 52–59.

———. *Romans*. New York: Anchor, 1993.

Flender, Helmut. *St. Luke: Theologian of Redemptive History*. Philadelphia: Fortress, 1967.

Foh, Susan. "What Is Woman's Desire?" *Westminster Theological Journal* 37 (1975) 376–83.

Forbes, Greg W., and Scott D. Harrower. *Raised from Obscurity: A Narratival and Theological Study of the Characterization of Women in Luke-Acts*. Eugene, OR: Pickwick, 2015.

Frame, John. *The Doctrine of the Knowledge of God: A Theology of Lordship*. Phillipsburg, NJ: P&R, 2002.

Fretheim, Terence E. "The Book of Genesis." In *The New Interpreters Bible*, edited by L. E. Keck et al., 17–276. Nashville: Abingdon, 1994.

Friedan, Betty. *The Feminine Mystique*. New York: W. W. Norton, 1962.

Gehring, Roger W. *House Church and Mission: The Importance of Household Structures in Early Christianity*. Peabody, MA: Hendrickson, 2004.

Giles, Kevin. *Better Together: Equality in Christ*. Brunswick East, Australia: Acorn, 2010.

———. "The Biblical Teaching about the Status and Role of Woman: A Select Annotated Bibliography of Some 22 Major Books on the Biblical Teaching on the Role and Status of Woman." *Christian Book Newsletter* 4.4 (1987) 4–10.

———. "Book Review: Grudem and Piper, *Recovering Biblical Manhood and Womanhood: A Response to Biblical Feminism*, Wheaton: Crossway, 1991." *Evangelical Quarterly* 65.3 (1993) 276–81.

———. "Book Review: Wayne Grudem's *Evangelical Feminism*." *Priscilla Papers* 22.3 (2008) 27–30.

———. "Church." In *Dictionary of the Later New Testament Writings and Its Development*, edited by Ralph P. Martin and Peter H. Davids, 194–204. Downers Grove, IL: InterVarsity, 1997.

———. "Church Order, Government." In *Dictionary of the Later New Testament Writings and Its Development*, edited by Ralph P. Martin and Peter H. Davids, 219–26. Downers Grove, IL: InterVarsity, 1997.

———. *Created Woman: A Fresh Study of Biblical Teaching*. Canberra, Australia: Acorn, 1985.

———. "A Critique of the Novel Contemporary Interpretation of 1 Timothy 2:9–15, Given in the Book, *Women in the Church*." Part 1, *Evangelical Quarterly* 72.2 (2000) 151–67; part 2, *Evangelical Quarterly* 72.3 (2000)195–215.

———. "Dear Professor Köstenberger—A Rejoinder to Andreas Köstenberger's *Women in the Church*: A Response by Kevin Giles." *Evangelical Quarterly* 73.2 (2001) 225–45.

———. "Defining the Error Called Subordinationism." *Evangelical Quarterly* 87.3 (2014) 207–24.

———. *The Eternal Generation of the Son: Maintaining Orthodoxy in Trinitarian Theology.* Grand Rapids: Zondervan, 2012.

———. "The Genesis of Confusion: How Complementarians Have Corrupted Communication." *Priscilla Papers* 29.1 (2015) 22–29.

———. "The Genesis of Equality." *Priscilla Papers* 28.4 (2014) 3–9.

———. "House Churches." *Priscilla Papers* 24.1 (2010) 6–8.

———. *Jesus and the Father: Modern Evangelicals Reinvent the Doctrine of the Trinity.* Grand Rapids: Zondervan, 2006.

———. "Jesus and Women." *Interchange* 19 (1976) 131–36.

———. "Jesus and Women." In *Raising Women Leaders,* edited by Shane Clifton and Jacqueline Grey, 89–110. Sydney: Australasian Pentecostal Studies, 2009.

———. *Making Good Churches Better: A Work Book for Church Councils and Church Leaders.* Brunswick East, Australia: Acorn, 2001.

———. *Patterns of Ministry Among the First Christians.* 2nd ed. Eugene, OR: Cascade, 2016.

———. "Prophecy, Prophets, False Prophets." In *Dictionary of the Later New Testament Writings and Its Development,* edited by Ralph P. Martin and Peter H. Davids, 970–77. Downers Grove, IL: InterVarsity, 1997.

———. *The Rise and Fall of the Complementarian Doctrine of the Trinity.* Eugene, OR: Cascade, 2016.

———. *The Trinity and Subordinationism: The Doctrine of God and the Contemporary Gender Debate.* Downers Grove, IL: InterVarsity, 2002.

———. *What On Earth Is the Church: An Exploration in New Testament Theology.* Downers Grove, IL: InterVarsity, 1995.

———. *Women and Their Ministry: A Case for Equal Ministries in the Church Today.* Melbourne: Dove Communications, 1977.

Gleeson, Hayley. "Anglican Diocese of Sydney Makes an Apology to Victims of Domestic Violence." *ABC News,* October 11, 2007. http://www.abc.net.au/news/2017-10-11/anglican-diocese-of-sydney-apologises-to-abuse-victims/9038410.

———. "#ChurchToo: Christian Victims of Abuse Join the Social Media Outpouring." *ABC News,* November 24, 2017. http://www.abc.net.au/news/2017-11-24/church-too-christian-victims-of-abuse-join-social-media-twitter/9188666.

———. "Sydney Anglican Church Confesses to Domestic Violence in Its Ranks." *ABC News,* October 9, 2017. http://www.abc.net.au/news/2017-10-10/sydney-anglican-church-to-unveil-domestic-abuse-policy/9033426.

Glendon, Mary A. "The Pope's New Feminism." *Crisis* 15.3 (March 1997) 28–31. https://www.catholiceducation.org/en/controversy/common-misconceptions/the-pope-s-new-feminism.html.

Goligher, Liam. "Is It Okay to Teach Complementarianism Based on Eternal Subordination?" *Mortification of Spin,* June 3, 2016. http://www.alliancenet.org/mos/housewife-theologian/is-it-okay-to-teach-a-complementarianism-based-on-eternal-subordination#.WGGyLfB96Ul.

Grenz, Stanley J., and Denise M. Kjesbo. *Women in the Church: A Biblical Theology of Women in Ministry.* Grand Rapids: InterVarsity, 1995.

Groothuis, Rebecca Merrill. "Equal in Being Unequal in Role." In *Discovering Biblical Equality; Complementarity without Hierarchy,* edited by Ronald W. Pierce and Rebecca M. Groothuis, 301–54. Downers Grove, IL: InterVarsity, 2005.

Grudem, Wayne. "Appendix 1: The Meaning of *Kephalē* ("Head"): A Response to Recent Studies." In *Recovering Biblical Manhood and Womanhood: A Response to Biblical Feminism*, edited by Wayne Grudem and Joh, 425–68. Wheaton, IL: Crossway, 1991.

———. *Countering the Claims of Evangelical Feminism*. Colorado Springs: Multnomah, 2006.

———. *Evangelical Feminism: A New Path to Liberalism*. Wheaton, IL: Crossway, 2006.

———. *Evangelical Feminism and Biblical Truth: An Analysis of More than One Hundred Disputed Questions*. Sisters, OR: Multnomah, 2004.

———. *Systematic Theology: An Introduction to Biblical Doctrine*. Downers Grove, IL: InterVarsity, 1994.

Grudem, Wayne, and John Piper, eds. *Recovering Biblical Manhood and Womanhood: A Response to Biblical Feminism*. Wheaton, IL: Crossway, 1991.

Guthrie, Donald. *The Pastoral Epistles: An Introduction and Commentary*. Tyndale New Testament Commentaries 14. Grand Rapids: Eerdmans, 1990.

Gutjar, Paul C. *Charles Hodge: Guardian of American Orthodoxy*. Oxford: Oxford University Press, 2011.

Hahn, C. A. *Growing in Authority, Relinquishing Control*. New York: Alban Institute, 1994.

Hartley, John E. *Genesis*. Peabody, MA: Hendrickson, 2000.

Hays, Richard B. *First Corinthians*. Louisville: John Knox, 1997.

Hennecke, E. *New Testament Apocrypha*. Edited by R. M. Wilson. 2 vols. Philadelphia: Westminster, 1965.

Henry, Matthew. *Matthew Henry's Commentary*. Vol. 1. London: Marshall, Morgan and Scott, 1960.

Hess, Richard S. "Equality with Innocence: Genesis 1–3." In *Discovering Biblical Equality: Complementarity without Hierarchy*, edited by Ronald W. Pierce and Rebecca M. Groothuis, 79–95. Downers Grove, IL: InterVarsity, 2005.

Hill, David. *New Testament Prophecy*. London: Marshall, Morgan, and Scott, 1979.

Hill, Edmund, trans. *Augustine: The Trinity*. New York: New City, 1991.

Hodge, Charles. "The Biblical Argument for Slavery." In *Cotton Is King and Pro-Slavery Arguments*, edited by E. N. Cartwright. New York: Basic Afro-American Reprints, 1968.

———. *A Commentary on the Epistle to the Ephesians*. London: Banner of Truth, 1964.

———. *A Commentary on the First Epistle to the Corinthians*. London: Banner of Truth, 1958.

Hubner, Jamin. "Revisiting *authenteō* in 1 Timothy 2:12: What Does the Extant Date Really Show?" *The Journal of Paul and His Letters* 4.1 (2015) 41–70.

———. "Translating *authenteō* in 1 Timothy 2:12." *Priscilla Papers* 29.2 (2015) 16–26.

Ilan, Tal. *Jewish Women in Greco-Roman Palestine*. Peabody, MA: Hendrickson, 1996.

Jensen, Michael. *Sydney Anglicanism: An Apology*. Eugene, OR: Wipf and Stock, 2012.

Jeremias, Joachim. "The Social Position of Women." In *Jerusalem in the Time of Jesus*, by J. Jeremias, 359–76. London: SCM, 1969.

John Paul, Pope, II. *Mulierus Dignitatem: On the Dignity and Vocation of Women*. Homebush, New South Wales: St. Pauls, 1988.

Johnson, Alan F. *How I Changed My Mind About Women in Leadership*. Grand Rapids: Zondervan, 2010.

Kassian, Mary A. *Women in Creation and the Fall: An Examination of the Roles of Men and Women.* Westchester, IL: Servant, 1980.

Keener, Craig S. *Acts: An Exegetical Commentary.* 4 vols. Grand Rapids: Baker, 2012–15.

———. "Luke's Perspective on Women and Gender." In vol. 1 of *Acts: An Exegetical Commentary,* edited by Craig S. Keener, 597–638. Grand Rapids: Baker, 2012.

———. *Paul, Women and Wives: Marriage and Women's Ministry in the Letters of Paul.* Peabody, MA: Hendrickson, 1992.

Keller, Timothy. *Generous Justice: How God's Grace Makes Us Just.* New York: Dutton, 2010.

Kessler, M., and K. Deurloo. *A Commentary on Genesis.* New York: Paulist, 2004.

Kitchen, K. A. "Slavery." In *The New Bible Dictionary,* editd by J. D. Douglas et al., 1121–24. Leicester: InterVarsity, 1992.

Knight, George W. "The Family and the Church." In *Recovering Biblical Manhood and Womanhood: A Response to Evangelical Feminism,* edited by John Piper and Wayne Grudem, 345–57. Wheaton, IL: Crossway, 1991.

———. "Husbands and Wives as Analogues of Christ and the Church, Ephesians 5:21–33, Colossians 3:18–19." In *Recovering Biblical Manhood and Womanhood: A Response to Biblical Feminism,* edited by Wayne Grudem and John Piper, 165–78. Wheaton, IL: Crossway, 1991.

———. *The New Testament Teaching on the Role Relationship of Men and Women.* Grand Rapids: Baker, 1977.

Köstenberger, Andreas J. "A Complex Sentence: The Syntax of 1 Timothy 2:12." In *Women in the Church: An Analysis and Application of 1 Timothy 2:9–15,* edited by Andreas J. Köstenberger and Thomas R. Schreiner, 53–85. Grand Rapids: Baker, 2005.

———. "Women in the Church: A Reply to Kevin Giles." *Evangelical Quarterly* 73 (2001) 205–24.

Köstenberger, Andreas J., and David W. Jones. *God, Marriage, and Family: Rebuilding the Biblical Foundations.* 2nd ed. Wheaton, IL: Crossway, 2010.

Köstenberger, Andreas J., and Margaret E. Köstenberger. *God's Design for Man and Woman: A Biblical-Theological Survey,* Wheaton, IL: Crossway, 2014.

Köstenberger, Andreas J., and Thomas R. Schreiner, eds. *Women in the Church: A Fresh Analysis of 1 Timothy 2:9–15.* 2nd ed. Grand Rapids: Baker, 2005.

Köstenberger, Andreas J., Thomas R. Schreiner, and H. Scott Baldwin, eds. *Women in the Church: A Fresh Analysis of 1 Timothy 2:9–15.* Grand Rapids: Baker, 1995.

Köstenberger, Margaret E. *Jesus and the Feminists: Who Do They Say He Is?* Wheaton, IL: Crossway, 2008.

Kraemer, Ross. "Jewish Women and Christian Origins." In *Women and Christian Origins,* edited by Ross S. Kraemer and Mary R. D'Angelo, 35–49. Oxford: Oxford University Press, 1999.

Kraemer, Ross, and Mary D'Angelo, eds. *Women and Christian Origins.* Oxford: Oxford University Press, 1999.

Kristof, N., and S. WuDunn. *Half the Sky: Turning Oppression into Opportunity for Women Worldwide.* New York: A. Knopf, 2009.

Lim, Anne, "She Left an Abusive Marriage for the Sake of Her Children." *Eternity News,* November 24, 2017. https://www.eternitynews.com.au/in-depth/she-left-an-abusive-marriage-for-the-sake-of-her-children/.

Lincoln, Andrew T. *Ephesians.* Word Biblical Commentary. Dallas: Word, 1990.

Lindgren, Caleb. "Gender and the Trinity: From Proxy War to Civil War." *Christianity Today*, June 16, 2016. http://www.christianitytoday.com/ct/2016/june-web-only/gender-trinity-proxy-war-civil-war-eternal-subordination.html.

Lombard, Peter. *Theological Sentences, Libri Sentenarium.* Liber 1 et 11. 2nd ed. Florentiam: A. D. Claris Aquas, 1916.

Loubser, J. A. *The Apartheid Bible: A Critical Review of Racial Theology in South Africa.* Lewiston, ME: Edwin Mellen, 1987.

Maher, M. *Genesis.* Wilmington, DE: M. Glazier, 1982.

Marshall, I. Howard. "Mutual Love and Submission in Marriage: Colossians 3:18–19 and Ephesians 5:21–33." In *Discovering Biblical Equality: Complementarity without Hierarchy*, edited by Ronald W. Pierce and Rebecca M. Groothuis, 186–204. Downers Grove, IL: InterVarsity, 2005.

———. *The Pastoral Epistles.* International Critical Commentary. Edinburgh: T&T Clark, 1999.

Martin, C. "Slavery." In *Text and Interpretation*, edited by Allen D. Callender, 216–17. Semeia 83/84. Atlanta: Society of Biblical Literature, 1998.

McAlister, Melanie. "How Beth Moore Is Helping to Change the Face of Evangelical Leadership." *Washington Post*, June 22, 2018. https://www.washingtonpost.com/news/post-nation/wp/2018/06/22/beth-moore-is-challenging-and-helping-to-change-the-face-of-evangelical-leadership/?utm_term=.d111d6c948d3.

Miller, Rachel. "Continuing Down This Path, Complementarians Lose." *A Daughter of the Reformation*, May 22, 2015. https://adaughterofthereformation.wordpress.com/2015/05/22/continuing-down-this-path-complementarians-lose/.

———. "Is Complementarian Just Another Name for Patriarchy?" *A Daughter of the Reformation*, September 29, 2014. https://adaughterofthereformation.wordpress.com/2014/09/29/is-complementarian-just-another-word-for-patriarchy/.

Moo, Douglas. *The Epistle to the Romans.* Grand Rapids: Eerdmans, 1996.

Moon, Sarah. "Some Humans Are More Equal than Others; John Piper on Spousal Abuse and Submission." *Patheos*, January 11, 2013. http://www.patheos.com/blogs/sarahoverthemoon/2013/01/some-humans-are-more-equal-than-others-john-piper-abuse-submission/.

Moore, Beth. "A Letter to My Brothers." *The LPM Blog*, May 3, 2018. https://blog.lproof.org/2018/05/a-letter-to-my-brothers.html.

Moore, Russell. "After Patriarchy, What? Why Egalitarians Are Winning the Gender Debate." *Journal of the Evangelical Theological Society* 49 (2006) 569–76.

Moss, Danni. "Paige Patterson's Views on Domestic Violence." Because It Matters: Freedom from Abuse in Christianity (blog), n.d. https://dannimoss.wordpress.com/clergy-abuse-links/abuse-in-the-church/paige-pattersons-views-on-domestic-violence/.

Mowczko, Marg. "TESQUQAH: The Woman's 'Desire' in Genesis 3:16." Marg Mowczko, November 7, 2015. http://margmowczko.com/teshuqah-desire/.

Murphy-O'Connor, Jerome. "Prisca and Aquila." *Bible Review* 8.6 (1992) 40–51.

———. "Sex and Logic in 1 Corinthians 11:2–16." *Catholic Biblical Quarterly* 42 (1980) 482–500.

Myers, Carol. *Discovering Eve: Ancient Israelite Women in Context.* New York: Oxford, 2012.

———. "Was Ancient Israel a Patriarchal Society?" *Journal of Biblical Literature* 133 (2014) 8–27.

Neuer, Werner. *Man and Woman in Christian Perspective.* Translated by Gordon Wenham. London: Hodder and Stoughton, 1981.

Newton, John. *Thoughts on the African Slave Trade.* London: J. Buckland, 1887.

Noll, Mark. *The Civil War as a Theological Crisis.* Chapel Hill: University of North Carolina Press, 2006.

Ortland, Raymond. "Male-Female Equality and Male Headship." In *Recovering Biblical Manhood and Womanhood: A Response to Biblical Feminism,* edited by Wayne Grudem and John Piper, 95–112. Wheaton, IL: Crossway, 1991.

Osiek, Carolyn, and David L. Balch. *Families in the New Testament World: Households and House Churches.* Louisville, KY: Westminster John Knox, 1997.

Osiek, Carolyn, and Margaret Y. McDonald. *A Woman's Place: House Churches in Earliest Christianity.* Minneapolis: Fortress, 2006.

Parkin, Frank. *Max Weber.* Chichester, UK: Ellis Horwood, 1982.

Patterson, Orlando. *Slavery and Social Death: A Comparative Study.* Cambridge, MA: Harvard, 1982.

Pawson, David. *Leadership Is Male.* Crowborough, East Sussex: Highland, 1988.

Payne Philip B. "1 Tim 2.12 and the Use of *Oude* to Combine Two Elements to Express a Single Idea." *New Testament Studies* 54 (2008) 235–53.

———. "Evidence for Meaning 'Source' in Greek Literature and in Paul's Letters." Paper read to the Annual Meeting of the Evangelical Theological Society Pauline Studies session, San Antonio, TX, November 16, 2016.

———. *Man and Woman: One in Christ: An Exegetical and Theological Study of Paul's Letters.* Grand Rapids: Zondervan, 2009.

———. "Vaticanus Distigme-Obelos Symbols Marking Added Text, Including 1 Corinthians 14.34–5." *New Testament Studies* 63.4 (2017) 604–25.

———. "What About Headship? From Hierarchy to Equality." In *Mutual by Design: A Better Model for Christian Marriage,* edited by Elizabeth Beyer, 141–61, 226–32. Minneapolis: Christians for Biblical Equality, 2017.

Pierce, Ronald W. "Deborah: Troublesome Woman or Woman of Valour?" *Priscilla Papers* 32.2 (2018) 3–7.

Pierce, Ronald W., and Rebecca M. Groothius, eds. *Discovering Biblical Equality: Complementarity without Hierarchy.* Downers Grove, IL: InterVarsity, 2005.

Piper, John. "Does a Woman Submit to Abuse?" YouTube, September 1, 2009. www.youtube.com/watch?v=3OkUPc2NLrM.

Plaatjies, Mary-Anne, and Robert Vosloo, eds. *Reformed Churches in South Africa and the Struggle for Justice, Remembering 1960–1990.* South Africa: Sun Press, 2013.

Pulliam Bailey, Sarah. "Southern Baptist Seminary Drops Bombshell: Why Paige Patterson Was Fired." *Washington Post,* June 1, 2018. www.washingtonpost.com/news/acts-of-faith/wp/2018/06/01/southern-baptist-seminary-drops-bombshell-why-paige-patterson-was-fired/?utm_term=.395bb6984ae4.

Ridderbos, Herman N. *Paul: An Outline of His Theology.* Grand Rapids: Eerdmans, 1975.

Saucy, Robert, and Judith TenElshof. *Women and Men in Ministry: A Complementarian Perspective.* Chicago: Moody, 2001.

Scanzoni, Letha D., and Nancy A. Hardesty. *All We're Meant to Be: Biblical Feminism for Today.* Grand Rapids: Eerdmans; 1974.

Schaff, P., and H. Wace, eds. *The Nicene and Post-Nicene Fathers of the Christian Church.* Grand Rapids: Eerdmans, 1971.

Scholer, David. "Women." In *Dictionary of Jesus and the Gospels*, edited by Joel B. Green, Scott McKnight, and I. Howard Marshall, 880–87. Downers Grove, IL: InterVarsity, 1992.

Schreiner, Thomas R. "The Valuable Ministries of Women in the Context of Male Leadership." In *Recovering Biblical Manhood and Womanhood*, edited by Wayne Grudem and John Piper, 209–224. Wheaton, IL: Crossway, 1991.

———. "Women in Ministry." In *Two Views on Women in Ministry*, edited by James Beck and Craig L. Bloomberg, 175–236. Grand Rapids: Zondervan, 2001.

Scullion, John J. *Genesis: A Commentary for Students, Teachers and Preachers*. Atlanta: John Knox, 1982.

Shellnut, Kate. "Divorce After Abuse: How Paige Patterson's Counsel Compares to Other Pastors." *Christianity Today*, April 30, 2018. https://www.christianitytoday.com/news/2018/april/paige-patterson-divorce-domestic-abuse-swbts-cbmw.html.

———. "Paige Patterson Fired by Southwestern, Stripped of Retirement Benefits." *Christianity Today*, May 30, 2018. https://www.christianitytoday.com/news/2018/may/paige-patterson-fired-southwestern-baptist-seminary-sbc.html.

———. "Women Speak Up in #SilenceIsNotSpiritual Campaign." #SilenceIsNotSpiritual, December 20, 2017. http://www.silenceisnotspiritual.org/news/2017/12/20/women-speak-up-in-silenceisnotspiritual-campaign.

Sider, Ron. "Gender and Justice Today." *Priscilla Papers* 21.2 (2007) 1–6.

"silenceisnotspiritual: Breaking the Silence on Violence Against Women and Girls." Silence Is Not Spiritual. https://silenceisnotspiritual.squarespace.com/statement.

Simson, Wolfgang. *Houses that Change the World: The Return of the House Churches*. Carlisle: Paternoster, 2001.

Skinner, J. A. *Critical and Exegetical Commentary on Genesis*. Edinburgh: T&T Clark, 1930.

Speiser, E. A. *Genesis*. New York: Doubleday, 1969.

Spencer, Aida Besancon. *Beyond the Curse: Women called to Ministry*, Peabody, Mass.: Hendrickson, 1985.

———. "Book Review Margaret Köstenberger's *Jesus and the Feminists*." *Priscilla Papers* 23.4 (2009) 26–29.

Storkey, Elaine. *Scars Across Humanity*. London: SPCK, 2015.

Stowe, Harriet Beecher. *Uncle Tom's Cabin: Or, Life Among the Lowly*. Boston: John P. Jewett, 1852.

Strachan, Owen, and Gavin Peacock. *The Grand Design: Male and Female He Made Them*. Ross-shire, UK: Christian Focus, 2016.

Stringfellow, T. "The Biblical Argument; Or, Slavery in the Light of Divine Revelation." In *Cotton is King: And Pro-Slavery Arguments*, edited by David Cristy and Albert T. Bedsloe, 480–81. Google Books, 2014; originally published 1860.

Thielicke, Helmut. *The Ethics of Sex*. Edinburgh: James Clark, 1964.

Thiselton, Anthony C. *The First Epistle to the Corinthians*. Grand Rapids: Eerdmans, 2000.

Thompson, John L. "Was Adam Deceived?" In *Reading the Bible with the Dead*, by John L. Thompson, 161–85. Grand Rapids: Eerdmans, 2007.

Thorley, John. "Junia, A Woman Apostle." *Novum Testamentum* 38 (1996) 18–29.

Thornwell, John H. *The Collected Writings of John Henry Thornwell*. Vol. 4. Edited by D. M. Palmer. London: Banner of Truth, 1986.

Towner, W. S. *Genesis*. Louisville: Westminster John Knox, 2001.

Tracy, Steven R. "Patriarchy and Domestic Violence: Challenging Common Misconceptions." *Journal of the Evangelical Theological Society* 50.3 (2007) 573–94.

———. "What Does 'Submit in Everything' Really Mean? The Nature and Scope of Marital Submission." *Trinity Journal* 29 (2008) 285–312.

Trueman, Carl. "Fahrenheit 381." *Mortification of Spin*, June 7, 2016. http://www.mortificationofspin.org/mos/postcards-from-palookaville/fahrenheit-381.

———. "Motivated by Feminism? A Response to Recent Criticism." *Mortification of Spin*, June 14, 2016. http://www.alliancenet.org/mos/postcards-from-palookaville/motivated-by-feminism-a-response-to-a-recent-criticism#.WFuMRvB96Um.

Turner, Laurence A. *Genesis*. Sheffield: Academic, 2000.

Vagianos, Alanna. "30 Shocking Domestic Violence Statics that Remind Us It's an Epidemic." *Huffington Post*, October 23, 2014. https://www.huffingtonpost.com/2014/10/23/domestic-violence-statistics_n_5959776.html.

Vawter, Bruce. *On Genesis: A New Reading*. London: G. Chapman, 1977;

Verner, David C. *The Household of God: The Social World of the Pastoral Epistles*. Chico, CA: Scholars Press, 1983.

Von Rad, Gerhard. *Genesis: A Commentary*. Translated by John Marks, London: SCM, 1961.

Walton, John H. *Genesis*. The NIV Application Commentary. Grand Rapids: Zondervan, 2001.

Weber, Max. *Economy and Society*. Edited by Guenther Roth and Claus Wittich. Berkeley: University of California, 1978.

Weld, Theodore D. *American Slavery as It Is: Testimony of a Thousand Witnesses*. New York: The African Anti-Slavery Society, 1839.

Westfall, Cynthia Long. "The Meaning of *Authenteō* in 1 Timothy 2:12."*Journal of Greco-Roman Christianity and Judaism* 10 (2014) 138–73.

———. *Paul and Gender: Reclaiming the Apostle's Vision for Men and Women in Christ*. Grand Rapids: Baker, 2016.

Wilson, Andrew. "Complementarianism in Crisis." *Thinking Theology*, July 6, 2016. http://thinktheology.co.uk/blog/article/complementarianism_in_crisis.

Wilson-Heartgrove, Jonathan. *Reconstructing the Gospel: Finding Freedom from Slave-Holding Religion*. Downers Grove, IL: InterVarsity, 2018.

Witherington, Ben. *Women and the Genesis of Christianity*, Cambridge: Cambridge University Press, 1990.

———. *Women in the Earliest Churches*. Cambridge: Cambridge University Press, 1988.

———. *Women in the Ministry of Jesus*. Cambridge: Cambridge University Press, 1984.

Wolters, Albert. "*Authentēs* and Its Cognates in Biblical Greek." *Journal of the Evangelical Theological Society* 52.4 (2009) 719–29.

———. "A Semantic Study of *Authentēs* and Its Derivatives." *Journal for Biblical Manhood and Womanhood* 1.11 (2006) 44–65.

Young, Isabella. "Abuse Inside Christian Marriages—A Personal Story." *Sydney Morning Herald*, March 2, 2015. http://www.smh.com.au/comment/smh-editorial/abuse-inside-christian-marriages--a-personal-story-20150301-13rrvr.html

Youngblood, R. F. *The Book of Genesis*. 2nd ed. Grand Rapids: Baker, 1991.

Subject Index

Author Index

Scripture Index

Made in the USA
Coppell, TX
19 July 2021

59188182R00166